$10.00

This book inaugurates a major series, **ISSUES AND TRENDS IN SOCIOLOGY**, sponsored by the American Sociological Association.

INTERGROUP RELATIONS
Sociological Perspectives

edited by
Pierre van den Berghe

Intergroup Relations represents, in a sense, the voice of American sociology, over the past thirty-five years, on one of the most vital and explosive of human problems. Assuming that the world outside of North America is of "sociological consequence," Professor van den Berghe selected over one-third of his sample to give representation to non–North American materials. Of equal importance, the editor not only chose articles for their theoretical and practical relevance, but also included several "dated" pieces that meet the test of lasting historical significance.

In the introduction, Professor van den Berghe writes:

The great challenge of American sociology in a period of crisis and rapid change is not, I believe, to immerse itself into the revolutionary maelstrom nor even to suggest solutions but to maintain a sufficient degree of detachment from both the established order and the forces of change to enable us to make a credible claim to

lations

ISSUES AND TRENDS
IN SOCIOLOGY

a series of

The American Sociological Association

INTERGROUP RELATIONS

Edited by Pierre van den Berghe

INTERGROUP RELATIONS:

Sociological Perspectives

EDITED BY

Pierre van den Berghe

Basic Books, Inc., Publishers

NEW YORK   LONDON

© 1972 by Basic Books, Inc.
Library of Congress Catalog Card Number: 77–174830
SBN 465–03352–0
Manufactured in the United States of America
DESIGNED BY THE INKWELL STUDIO

Contents

PART III
The African Diaspora and Cultural Survivals: The Frazier-Herskovits Debate

PART IV
Endogamy and Exogamy

PART V
Race and Ethnic Attitudes

Contents

PART VI
The Demography and Ecology of Racism

PART VII
Responses to Oppression

PART VIII
The Culture of Racism

Note

This volume is one of a series on Issues and Trends in Sociology sponsored by the American Sociological Association. Each is the product of a distinguished editor's work. His task has been to assemble from past numbers of the Association's periodical publications the accumulated thought on a selected topic, supplementing those contributions with materials from other sources as needed, and to examine and interpret the state of knowledge represented in the collected papers with reference to its implications for current intellectual and social trends. By this means the association has sought to foster both the advance of scholarship and the understanding of an important issue of the day. We take pleasure in presenting this volume on behalf of the American Sociological Association.

understanding what goes on. Unless we can present a more accurate model of our society than the newspaper columnist, student radical, F.B.I. director, or vice-president of the republic, we have no *raison d'être* as sociologists. The present collection is, if nothing else, a measure of our success or failure in one of the key structural dimensions of our society.

PIERRE VAN DEN BERGHE **is Professor** of Sociology at the University of Washington.

Introduction

The compilation of a "reader" involves, of necessity, a series of arbitrary decisions. Since this particular volume of reprints from the *American Sociological Review* was collected on behalf of the American Sociological Association, it assumes a semi-official character. This casts me, the editor, in the uncongenial role of "the establishment" and constrains me to explain the criteria underlying my choice of articles. The collection represents, in a sense, the voice of American sociology on one of the most vital and explosive of human problems. Yet I am crucially aware that another editor would have made different selections from a universe of 230 relevant pieces (including research notes, brief communications, and rejoinders to articles). The three tables herewith describe some of the important dimensions of this universe from which I selected twenty-seven items, and enable the reader to compare that sample with the universe.

In an endeavor not to overlook any relevant articles, the net was cast rather wide, and perhaps a fourth of the sample of 230 articles had only peripheral relevance to "intergroup relations," defined in terms of both race and ethnicity. Such peripheral articles included, for example demographic pieces that mentioned "race" as one of the variables under study, or ethnographic descriptions of a certain ethnic group which made only passing references to relations to other groups. Another fourth of the articles, while germane, were found unsuitable because of excessive length and verbosity, poor methodology, topical triviality, or the ephemeral nature of their interest and conclusions. This left us with 117 "possibles," slightly over half (50.9 per cent) of the original total. Another round of elimination reduced that number to sixty, and a third round resulted in thirty-seven selections. After having been advised by the publisher that the maximum length of the collection was to be 125,000 words, I went through the most difficult fourth round, boiling down the final choice to the twenty-seven pieces reproduced here.

TABLE 1

Number of ASR Articles on Intergroup Relations by Date, 1936-1969

	Total Universe	In This Volume		Total Universe	In This Volume
1936	5	0	1953	6	0
1937	4	0	1954	9	3
1938	1	0	1955	6	0
1939	3	1	1956	16	2
1940	4	0	1957	7	1
1941	3	0	1958	5	0
1942	7	1	1959	7	1
1943	12	4	1960	5	0
1944	7	0	1961	3	1
1945	10	0	1962	3	0
1946	7	3	1963	10	3
1947	6	1	1964	5	0
1948	10 .	0	1965	7	1
1949	11	1	1966	3	0
1950	13	1	1967	6	0
1951	14	2	1968	3	0
1952	8	1	1969	4	0
			Total	230	27

Let me state explicitly what some of the main criteria of choice were, apart from the ones just mentioned. Table 1 shows that the sample is fairly representative of the universe in terms of date of publication. Nearly four tenths of both the universe (39.1 per cent) and the sample (40.7 per cent) were published before 1950. This is no accident. Unlike many of my colleagues who assume that sociology is a science, and, hence, that its knowledge is cumulative and that scarcely anything published more than ten years ago is worth reading, I believe that these assumptions are so minimally true as to have no significant bearing on the quality of the articles and on their selection. It is true that our quantitative methodology has become more sophisticated and that some of the earlier quantitative pieces would no longer pass muster. But other than that, I found no relationship between quality and date. If anything, I found a greater proportion of the articles published in the 1940's and 1950's more interesting than the more recent ones; however, I recognize that my interest in the older pieces was partly aroused by the fact that I was reading them not primarily as sources of data, but as symptomatic of an epoch, and from the perspective of the sociology of knowledge.

As a matter of conscious choice, I decided that this collection was to be as representative as possible of American sociology throughout the more than three decades of the *Review*. A discipline does not exist in a universalistic, timeless, culture-free *nirvana*. It is a product of its time and place. Hence, I decided that this collection must be temporally representative. To me, this was especially important, since the field of race and ethnic relations has been so thoroughly pervaded by ideological considerations. Unfortunately, the *Review* started publishing well after the Golden Age of American racism; consequently I did not find any examples of the more egregious forms of sociological racism to which Frazier refers in his classic 1947 article reproduced here. The 1930's were an age of extreme social environmentalism and marked the triumphant spread of anti-evolutionary relativism. Racism, though still rampant in American society at large, was no longer *salonfähig* in sociological circles. For most of the history of the *Review*, in fact, the field of race and ethnic relations was dominated by a kind of Candidian optimism. Good American liberals, and sociologists among them, were confident of their society's ability to solve its racial and ethnic problems by gradual meliorism and progressive integration. It took the escalating crisis of the 1960's to shake the academic liberals out of their complacency.

Table 2 is a good measure of the provincialism of American sociology: 81.3 per cent of the articles deal exclusively or predominantly with the continental United States. Like Monsieur Jourdain, who had unwittingly been speaking prose all his life, American sociologists have for the most part been parochial North Americanists deluding themselves that they were developing a science of humanity, a delusion which was of course not unrelated to the very phenomena of racism and ethnocentrism which they were studying. It is interesting to note that several of the best non-United States pieces are also among the older ones, and that there is no discernible trend in this particular group of ASR articles toward a more cosmopolitan approach in later years.

In this respect the present collection is deliberately unrepresentative: non-United States pieces have been given a disproportionate weight on the assumption that the rest of the world is of some sociological consequence. A little over one third (37.0 per cent) of the sample are "comparative" pieces in contrast to less than a fifth (18.7 per cent) of the universe. It is

TABLE 2

Number of ASR Articles on Intergroup Relations by
Region or Country of Subject Matter, 1936-1969

Country	Total Universe	In This Volume
Continental U.S.	187	17
Brazil	6	4
Hawaii	4	1
West Indies	4	1
India	3	0
Panama	2	1
Indonesia	2	0
South Africa	1	0
U.S.S.R.	1	0
Argentina	1	0
Puerto Rico	1	0
Thailand	1	0
New Zealand	1	0
Switzerland	1	1
Surinam	1	0
Britain	1	0
Guatemala	1	0
Africa, General	1	0
General and Comparative	11	2
Total	230	27

noteworthy here that the great Frazier-Herskovits debate on African survivals, which has rebounded of late into renewed relevance, was prompted by a Frazier article on Brazil, and that both Frazier and Herskovits owe in good part their prominence in the field to the fact that they were very much comparativists. I shall leave it to the reader to decide who wins the debate, but, before he reaches his verdict, I should like to point out that, by choosing Brazil as the field of intellectual combat, the cards were stacked in favor of Herskovits. There are many more obvious survivals of African culture in Brazil than in the United States, so that, even if Herskovits "wins" about Brazil, Frazier's structuralist interpretation about U.S. "black culture" is not thereby invalidated.

To have grouped the "comparative" pieces in a special section of the book, as I was first tempted to do, would have given them a kind of "separate and unequal" status which they did not deserve. Therefore I incorporated the "foreign" pieces topically with the North American ones, not only because it made more intellectual sense, but also to dissuade students from believing that the currently fashionable "comparative approach" is a decorative frosting which they can hastily spread over the cake of their sociological education. Sociology, as a nomothetic enterprise, cannot be anything but comparative. Thus, a "comparative" section would have been an implicit recognition of validity to a substantive category which is in fact nothing but a redundancy.

TABLE 3
Number of ASR Articles on Intergroup Relations by Topic, 1936-1969

Topic	Total Universe	In This Volume
Prejudice, Stereotypes, Attitudes	27	5
Culture, Assimilation	25	3
Demography, Migration	21	2
Class, Status, Occupation	20	0
Ethnographic and Descriptive	17	4
Ecology, Segregation Indices	16	0
Family Structure	12	3
Endogamy, Exogamy	12	3
Theory and Methodology	12	3
Genetics, I.Q., Physical	6	1
Urbanization, Industrialization	6	0
Housing, Interracial Contact	6	0
International Relations	5	0
Education, Socialization	5	0
Caste	4	0
Deviance, Crime	4	0
Economics	4	0
Religion	4	0
Ideology, Values, Policies	3	1
Power, Leadership	3	2
Conflict, Violence, Riots	3	0
Personality	2	0
Others	13	0
Total	230	27

As the categories of Table 3 are arbitrary and not mutually exclusive, they are only roughly indicative of the main substantive concerns in the field. Obviously, many of the articles could have been classified under two or more headings, but I resisted the temptation to do so, and forced each piece into the single category which best described its contents. With the exception of the categories of "class, status and occupation" and "ecology, segregation indices," all of the nine headings with twelve or more pieces are represented in the present collection. That, too, was a matter of deliberate choice, as I strove for as wide a substantive coverage as possible. Most noteworthy of all in Table 3 is the relative paucity of literature in the categories of economics, power, and conflict. Of course a number of the pieces not classified as such touch peripherally on these topics; nevertheless, less than 5 per cent of the articles addressed themselves *mainly* to these extremely central aspects of race and ethnic relations. The charge of triviality so profusely leveled at sociology from so many quarters of late is, of course, too much of a blanket indictment, but the fact remains that the key factors of economics and politics which allow one to place the phenomena of race and ethnicity in the total societal structure have received much less attention than they deserve. Nearly all multi-ethnic or multi-racial societies are characterized by a differential distribution of power and wealth between ethnic or racial groups; and these differential relations of power and of production, if they do not exhaust the content of intergroup relations, at least go a long way toward describing the broad structure of these relations and defining their most basic dimensions. Yet it is precisely from these fundamentals that the mainstream of American sociology has let itself be diverted. This phenomenon, of course, begs the question of the place of organized research in the established order. The specialist in knowledge has traditionally been both part of the privileged minority and in an ancillary status *vis à vis* the specialists in power. Thus he has generally shied away from asking the kind of questions that would disturb his patrons.

Similarly, the ability of many sociologists to deal with phenomena of intergroup relations without reference to the notion of conflict and with frequent use of such concepts as "assimilation," "integration," and "accommodation" reveals both a theoretical and a political bias of a staggering degree of magnitude. The convergence of functionalism at the theoretical level with complacent, liberal, and integrationist reformism at the political level has produced the monumental failure of our discipline to forecast, and now to deal with, the escalating racial crisis in the United States since the mid-1960's. The very least this failure should accomplish is to shake sociological claims to "scientific" status.

In addition to the broad criteria of selectivity just described, I have naturally tried to choose pieces on the basis of both the theoretical and the practical relevance of their conclusions. Articles of more ephemeral interest, however competent, have not been included, but I did incorporate several "dated" pieces which met, in my view, the (non-statistical) test of lasting historical significance, both in the intellectual development of sociology and in the empirical evolution of race and ethnic relations. The result is probably a slight overemphasis on non-quantitative pieces as distinguished from quantitative ones. My more statistically inclined colleagues will perhaps ascribe this to my own methodological biases. I am not, of course, arguing that quantification is intrinsically linked with triviality, but, borrowing Sorokin's phraseology, I do believe that, given the scientific pretence of our discipline, intellectual poverty can hide more readily behind a smoke screen of numerology than behind a mask of verbal drivel. Verbal rubbish gets flushed out of journals more readily than quantified rubbish. Hence I often found the non-quantitative pieces more interesting and richer in substance than the quantitative ones.

Another selective factor of which I was consciously aware concerns the length of the articles. Given my aim to present as diverse a sample as possible, shorter pieces had a better probability of inclusion than the lengthier ones (ten or more pages). Presidential addresses, for example, while often satisfying the criteria of relevance and scope, and making for more than averagely palatable reading, have a quality of after-banquet loquacity which militated against their inclusion.

A possible bias which I tried to avoid was the propensity to overrate and to choose pieces by the "big names" in the field. The final table of contents would seem to indicate my failure to control for that bias. "Big names" are indeed much in evidence, several being represented by two or more pieces. While I am aware of the possible circularity of my conclusions, I nevertheless completed the survey of the literature with the conviction that most of the "non-big-names" richly deserved their obscurity, and that most of the "big names" (though far from all) did have an above-average "staying power." Having started with the opposite assumption of nearly total lack of relationship between reputation and merit, I was somewhat surprised at the results.

The only case in which the prominence of the authors was a conscious factor in the choice is that of the Frazier-Herskovits exchange reproduced in Part III. The stature of both authors definitely contributed to the influential nature of the debate, and those pieces were selected as much because of their ideological relevance as because of the intrinsic intellectual merit of their arguments. Sociologically, the extent of African cultural survivals in the Western Hemisphere is of tenuous significance; but the practical import of the question and of the stance taken on the issue in terms of the identity search of Afro-Americans is immense and long-lasting.

"Relevance" has become a battle cry of the "New Left" in America today, and the explosive nature of the subject matter of this book constitutes, I think, sufficient justification for addressing myself briefly to that question. Can we, as sociologists, contribute anything of value to the problems of a society caught in a polarizing dialectic of racism and counter-racism? From our past record, the temptation to answer the question in the negative is strong indeed. Most of us failed to ask the fundamental questions, and thus, as a profession, we dismally failed to understand, much less predict, the social reality in which we were caught. But it was not "irrelevance" or "academism" that was our undoing, as our New Left critics would have us believe. Nor is our contribution likely to increase in quality if we yield to demands that we define "relevance" in terms of the acceptance of new ideological and intellectual credos, such as romantic existentialism, extreme subjectivism, black "nationalism," nihilism, populism, or anarchism.

Diverse and conflicting as these demands are, most of them share an impatience with the intellectual enterprise as such, that is, an impatience with the search for rationality and dispassion. In as deeply anti-intellectual a society as the United States, it is scarcely surprising that the ivory tower is buffeted from both the left and the right by people who deeply mistrust a commitment to reason as distinguished from emotion, and to understanding as distinguished from action.

What so incapacitated us as sociologists in the field of race and ethnic relations was not lack of commitment and relevance, but rather the blatant (though often unrecognized and hence all the more insidious) intrusion of both of these in our intellectual pursuits. Even a casual glance at the evolution of the field shows that most social scientists who worked in it were very committed indeed, and that much of their research was applied and action-oriented to the point of boredom. When racism and social Darwinism dominated Western intellectual life, sociologists, as Frazier has shown, were for the most part orthodox racists. When, starting in the 1920's and 1930's, the ideological winds swung to environmentalism, relativism, and social determinism, sociologists followed suit and developed the now-familiar liberal credo of racism as a social and psychological aberration. With the "bourgeois reformist" political climate of the New Deal, the new anti-racist credo became transformed into integrationist gradualism, ineffective socio-therapy ("racism is a disease of the mind"), and sanguine optimism that things were getting better, however slowly. The trouble with America was not in its basic economic and social structure, but in the fact that it did not live up to its promises. The American Dilemma was born in the minds of well-meaning liberal intellectuals. The stance of the liberal academic establishment on the issue of race (and indeed on many others as well) was not only conservative and politically naive, it was also bad sociology, because it attacked mostly epi-phenomena like attitudes, stereotypes, and discrimination rather than the underlying historical, economic, and political causes of racism. Ask trivial questions and you get trivial answers. And, at the policy level, trivial answers cannot solve fundamental problems (if indeed they were ever meant to).

Jolted out of their complacency by the events of the last few years, and deeply stirred in their feelings of collective racial guilt, academic liberals, including many sociologists, are rallying increasingly to the newly fashion-able orthodoxies of black "nationalism" and racialism. Pandering to black racialism is, of course, a form of neo-paternalism and a new way of extend-ing the ghettoization of the ivory tower and thus of the society at large under the guise of radicalism. Far from transcending the dialectic of racism, many intellectuals are inextricably caught up in it. What is needed is neither more commitment, nor of course a retreat to naive positivism, but a sophisticated understanding of the structure of inequality in American society and of the place of the scholar within his society. This requires a certain amount of dispassion and moral courage. Empirically, it also dic-tates a comparative research strategy. The tendency, for example, of some American sociologists to reify "race" as something inherent in phenotypical differences could not long be sustained in a non-racist society. The great challenge of American sociology in a period of crisis and rapid change is not, I believe, to immerse itself into the revolutionary maelstrom nor even to suggest solutions but to maintain a sufficient degree of detach-ment from both the established order and the forces of change to enable us to make a credible claim to understanding what goes on. Unless we can present a more accurate model of our society than the newspaper columnist, student radical, F.B.I. director, or vice-president of the republic, we have no *raison d'être* as sociologists. The present collection is, if noth-ing else, a measure of our success or failure in one of the key structural dimensions of our society.

PART I

Theory

Editor's Introduction

Of all the disciplines with a pretense to status as a generalizing science, sociology stands near the bottom in the scale of theoretical achievements. Political science does perhaps a little worse, but other social sciences with a less encompassing subject matter, such as linguistics and economics, have done notably better. E. Franklin Frazier's article is a classic case study of the racist heritage of sociology. While it is true that "scientific" racism, which became the ruling orthodoxy of early American sociology, grew out of the biological theory of evolution, the ready acceptance of biological evolution in sociology and its uncritical extension to human societies constituted a distinct regression over the theories of society prevailing in eighteenth-century Europe. But racism, of course, once it was given the accolade of science, served the status quo well in racist and colonial societies. Other sociological theories have done equally well in later times, as illustrated by Marxism in the "people's democracies" and functionalism in the "bourgeois democracies."

Sociologists are far from unique in their responsiveness to the interests of those who pay them, but since their subject is the nature of the social order itself, the link between sociological theory and political ideology is particularly intimate. What is true of sociology as a whole is doubly so in the specialty of race and ethnic relations. Since this subject deals in good part with one of man's nastiest forms of snobbery, it excites passions, and a history of the specialty reveals that "theories" have closely followed every shift in the ideological weather vane. It is to the credit of sociologists, however, that race and ethnic relations have enjoyed a deservedly low status. Even by sociological standards, the field has been characterized by a greater than average amount of provincialism, being overwhelmingly based, until the 1960's, on North American data.

Theories of race and ethnic relations can be broadly divided into the social psychology of prejudice and the sociology of discrimination. The former has been dominated by psychoanalytically oriented scholars and has given rise to the "frustration-aggression" and the "authoritarian personality" theories, as well as to an abundant literature on miscegenation and sexual phobias in the racial field. That body of theory was scarcely represented at all in the *American Sociological Review*. Sociological theories, on the other hand, have been much more diverse in their orientation. They have included the Marxist interpretation of racism as a superstructural rationalization for colonialism, slavery, and other forms of economic exploitation; sequential theories of phases of intergroup contact; typologies based on one or more variables (as in the Lieberson piece herewith); empirical generalizations based on one or more case studies (Walker); the testing of hypotheses through the use of demographic data about population ratios, segregation indices, and so on; and semi-experimental and observational studies on the effect of intergroup contact. No sociological theory of intergroup relations has achieved the near-hegemony that the psychoanalytically oriented social psychologists did in their field in the 1950's. Only in the last few years have sufficient data about non-Western or even Western-dominated colonial or formerly colonial societies become available to enable scholars to lay the groundwork for empirical generalizations on a world-wide scale. This is clearly a prerequisite to any kind of general theory. Much of what has hitherto been passed off as theory in sociology textbooks has in fact been North American ethnography overlaid with a thick crust of functionalist jargon. Now that a generation of non-Western social scientists is coming of age, the situation will, hopefully, improve.

SOCIOLOGICAL THEORY
AND RACE RELATIONS

The first sociological treatises to be published in the United States were concerned with race relations. In 1854 there appeared Henry Hughes' *Treatise on Sociology, Theoretical and Practical* which undertook to demonstrate that the slave system was "morally and civilly good" and that "its great and well-known essentials" should "be unchanged and perpetual."[1] During the same year there appeared George Fitzhugh's *Sociology for the South: or the Failure of Free Society*, which possessed more significance because of the political philosophy upon which it was based.[2] As indicated in the title, this book was not only a justification of Negro slavery, but was opposed to the democratic theory of social organization. Fitzhugh declared that the Declaration of Independence was opposed to "all government, all subordination, all order."[3] In his attack upon laissez-faire and a competitive society, he stated that a society did not exist in the free countries where each man acted for himself.[4] Expressing a philosophy closely resembling Fascist doctrines, he declared that liberty, equality and freedom had brought crime and pauperism to Europe and that socialism and the struggle of women for equality with men were the results of the failure of a free society. Only in a society built upon slavery and Christianity as the South was built, could morality and discipline be maintained.

The sociological theories of Hughes and Fitzhugh undertook to provide a philosophical justification of slavery. Although their sociological theories cannot be ignored in the history of sociological theories of race relations

From E. Franklin Frazier, "Sociological Theory and Race Relations," in *American Sociological Review*, 12 (1947), 265–271.

in the United States, they have scarcely any relation to the later development of sociological thought in this field. Therefore, we shall turn to the so-called fathers of sociology—Ward, Sumner, Giddings, Cooley, Small, and Ross—who established sociology as an academic discipline.

Although Lester Ward did not make any specific contribution to the theory of race relations in the United States, his sociological theories contain implications concerning the racial problem. Ward accepted the position of Gumplowicz and Ratzenhofer that the state and other phases of social organization such as caste and class had grown out of group conflict, especially the struggle of races.[5] But in accepting the theory of race struggle Ward did not accept the theory of fundamental racial differences. He rejected the theories of Galton concerning superior races and superior classes. In fact, he took the position that the dominant position of the superior races in the world was due to "the longest uninterrupted inheritance and transmission of human achievement."[6] Through what he termed "sociocracy" or the scientific control of the social forces by the collective mind, equal opportunities for all races and classes would remove the differences in achievement in civilization. Finally, he looked forward to the "period in which the races of men shall have all become assimilated, and when there shall be but one race—the human race."[7]

Sumner's sociological theories have had an influence upon the study of race relations that is still reflected in studies of race relations at the present time. I refer especially to his concept of the mores. First, it should be pointed out that Sumner took the position that "modern scholars have made the mistake of attributing to race much which belongs to the ethos" of a people.[8] Therefore, the most important factor that separated the various races were their mores. In the South, before the Civil War the two races had learned to live together and mores had developed regulating their relations. The Civil War had destroyed the legal basis of race relations and the resulting conflict and confusion had prevented the emergence of new mores. However, new mores were developing along lines different from those advocated by reformers and legislators who could exercise no influence on the character of the developing racial patterns. Myrdal in his *An American Dilemma* has pointed out the fatalism contained in this conception of the problem of race relations and in fact the inapplicability of the concept of mores to a modern urban industrial society.[9]

Giddings did not offer any broad and systematic theory of race relations although he thought his concept of the "consciousness of kind" explained racial exclusiveness. In regard to the racial mixture, he accepted current notions concerning the instability of mixed races.[10] He was of the opinion, however, that the mental plasticity of mixed races was an important contribution to the development of nations. The social disabilities suffered by the Negro and Indian were an indication of the extent to which the social constitution had not become differentiated from the social composition of the nation.[11]

Cooley's position in regard to the native endowment of different races is set forth in a criticism of Galton's theories in an essay which appeared in *The Annals* in 1897. In that essay, he pointed out that even Galton admitted that Negroes and whites could not be compared because they do not mingle and compete in the same social order under the same conditions.[12] However, Cooley's sociological theory regarding race relations was set forth in his *Social Organization.* He stated: "Two races of different temperament and capacity, distinct to the eye and living side by side in the same community, tended strongly to become castes, no matter how equal the social system may otherwise be."[13] In a chapter devoted to caste, Cooley presented a clear analysis of the caste character of race relations in the South. In his *Social Process* which was published nine years later in 1919, he continued his analysis of Negro-white relations in a chapter on "Class and Race." In this chapter he pointed out the lack of positive knowledge of racial differences but felt it reasonable to assume that during the process of biological differentiation of races, mental differences had developed.[14] His conclusion was that race should not be dealt with as a separate factor. He recognized that caste and democracy could not be reconciled and hoped for some form of cooperation and good-will between the races. He concluded, however, that Orientals should be excluded from the United States and whites from Oriental countries in order not to create racial problems.

The remaining two "fathers" of American sociology, Ward and Ross, did not make any contributions to sociological theory in regard to race relations. Ross was of the opinion that there was a "Celtic temperament" and that there was no doubt that races differed in regard to intellectual ability.[15] Moreover, he felt that the more intelligent white race had an obligation to civilization to prevent Negroes from overwhelming it by mere numbers. He did not believe, however, that the superior race should exploit or maltreat the inferior race.

In discussing the development of sociological theory and race relations, one cannot overlook a book by one of Giddings' students which had considerable influence on thinking in regard to the Negro. In 1910 Odum published his *Social and Mental Traits of the Negro*, which became for many students a source of information on the mental and social condition of the Negro. When one views today the opinions expressed in the book, it is clear that they reflect not only outmoded conceptions concerning primitive people but all the current popular prejudices concerning the Negro.

The point of view of Odum's book was that the Negro was primarily a social problem and would remain a social problem because he could not be assimilated. It is not strange, therefore, that in the treatment of the Negro as a social problem there is an implicit sociological theory concerning race relations. We might take as typical of the first two decades of the present century two books. In his *Sociology and Modern Social Problems*, first published in 1910, Ellwood devoted a chapter to the Negro problem. In this chapter it is assumed that the Negro has a "racial" temperament and that his "shiftlessness and sensuality" are partly due to heredity and that he is inferior in his adaptiveness to a complex civilization. The infiltration of white blood is responsible for ambition and superiority on the one hand and vice and immorality on the other. It is not strange that since "industrial education" was one of the shibboleths at the time, industrial training is regarded as one of the means of solving the problem. The problem of the Negro is recognized to be a moral problem— not in the sense that Myrdal said that it was a moral problem; namely, the moral obligation of whites to live up to the American creed of human equality. According to Ellwood, it is a moral problem in the sense that the socially superior race should have good will and assist the socially inferior race on the other side of the fence.

The second book on social problems, first published in 1920, by Dow, not only regards the Negro as an unassimilable element in the population but proposes his gradual segregation in a single area or state.[16] Dow accepts as true many of the stereotypes concerning the racial traits of the Negro but states that he believes selection and environment are stronger. While Ellwood thinks that more white teachers should be employed to help the inferior Negro race, Dow thinks that white teachers should not be employed because of the possible tendency toward social equality. White teachers from the North did more harm than good, and the Fifteenth Amendment to the Constitution was the worst political blunder in the history of the American people. Northern people do not understand Negro nature. Mulattoes are addicted to crime because, as Dow states, they have the degenerate blood of good white families. Industrial education is a partial solution and caste is the solution for the present, though ultimate segregation is necessary.

In considering these books, one should not overlook an article by

Weatherly which appeared in the *Journal* in 1910 on "Race and Marriage."[17] The author took the position that there was a natural aversion to intermarriage which was designed to preserve race purity as a necessary condition for social development. Another article along similar lines, entitled "The Philosophy of the Color Line" by Mecklin appeared in the *Journal* in 1913.[18] This writer found justification for "white supremacy" in the necessity to preserve purity.

The sociological theory in regard to race relations which was current during the first two decades of the present century was doubtless not unrelated to public opinion and the dominant racial attitudes of the American people. The racial conflict in the South had subsided and the North had accepted the thesis that the South should solve the racial problem. The southern solution had been the disfranchisement of the Negro and the establishment of a quasi-caste system in which the Negro was segregated and received only a pittance of public funds for education and social services. The famous formula of Booker T. Washington, involving the social separation of the races and industrial education, had become the accepted guide to future race relations. The sociological theories which were implicit in the writings on the Negro problem were merely rationalizations of the existing racial situation.

During this period there began to emerge a sociological theory of race relations that was formulated independent of existing public opinion and current attitudes. As early as 1904, W. I. Thomas presented in an article entitled "The Psychology of Race Prejudice," in the *Journal*, a systematic theory of race relations.[19] Thomas undertook first to determine the biological basis for the phenomenon of race prejudice. He thought that he discovered this in certain reflex and instinctive reactions of the lower animals to strange elements in their environment. But in the case of human beings, he held that the development of sympathetic relations was the important factor. Sympathetic relations were most highly developed within the family group and only gradually included larger social groupings. Although race prejudice had an organic basis and could not be reasoned with, it could be dissipated through human association. Thus Thomas assumed that race prejudice could be destroyed and he did not assume that people of divergent racial stocks must inevitably remain apart or could only live together in the community where a caste system existed. The relation between caste and race prejudice is summed up by him in the following statement:

Psychologically speaking, race-prejudice and caste-feeling are at bottom the same thing, both being phases of the instinct of hate, but a status of caste is reached as the result of competitive activities. The lower caste has either been conquered and captured, or gradually outstripped on account of the mental and economic inferiority. Under these conditions, it is psychologically important to the higher caste to maintain the feeling and show of superiority, on account of the suggestive effect of this on both the inferior caste and on itself; and signs of superiority and inferiority, being thus aids to the manipulation of one class by another, acquire a new significance and become ineradicable. Of the relation of black to white in this country it is perhaps true that the antipathy of the southerner for the Negro is rather caste-feeling than race-prejudice, while the feeling of the northerner is race-prejudice proper. In the North, where there has been no contact with the Negro and no activity connections; there is no caste-feeling, but there exists a sort of *skin*-prejudice—a horror of the external aspect of the Negro—and many northerners report that they have a feeling against eating from a dish handled by a Negro. The association of master and slave in the South was, however, close, even if not intimate, and much of the feeling of physical repulsion for a black skin disappeared.[20]

Thus as early as 1904 Thomas had shown the caste character of race relations in the South and had shown how race relations there differed from race relations in the North. Moreover, Thomas in another article had undertaken to show how social and mental isolation had been responsible for the failure of the Negro to make outstanding achievements in civilization.[21]

The sociological theories of Park in regard to race relations were developed originally in close association with Thomas. Park, who was observing race relations in the South, was in constant communication with Thomas. Park's theories which represent the most comprehensive and systematic sociological theories of race relations developed by American sociologists and have had the greatest influence on American sociology began to appear at a time when the Negro problem was assuming a new character in American life. The migration of Negroes to the metropolitan areas of the North had destroyed the accommodation that had been achieved to some extent following the racial conflict during and following Reconstruction. The publication of *Introduction to the Science of Sociology* by Park and Burgess coincided with the study of the race riot in Chicago in 1919. The new impact of the Negro problem on American life undoubtedly helped Park as much as his experience in the South in the formulation of a sociological theory.

For Park the phenomenon of race relations is to be studied within his general sociological frame of reference—competition, conflict, accommodation, and assimilation. "Nowhere do social contacts so readily provoke conflicts as in the relations between the races, particularly when racial differences are re-enforced; not merely by differences of culture, but of color."[22] Concerning the nature of race prejudice he wrote:

Race prejudice, as we call the sentiments that support the racial taboos, is not, in America at least, an obscure phenomenon. But no one has yet succeeded in making it wholly intelligible. It is evident that there is in race prejudice, as distinguished from class and caste prejudice, an instinctive factor based on the fear of the unfamiliar and the uncomprehended. Color, or any other racial mark that emphasizes physical differences, becomes the symbol of moral divergences which perhaps do not exist. We at once fear and are fascinated by the stranger, and an individual of a different race always seems more of a stranger to us than one of our own. This naïve prejudice, unless it is re-enforced by other factors, is easily modified, as the intimate relations of the Negro and white man in slavery show.[23]

Although Park held that there was an instinctive element in race prejudice, he nevertheless stated that the conflict of culture was a more positive factor in race prejudice. The central fact in the conflict of culture was, he wrote, "the unwillingness of one race to enter into personal competition with a race of a different or inferior culture." In a later article he made the factor of status the most important element in race prejudices.[24] In making status the most important factor in race prejudice, Park took the position that race prejudice was based upon essentially the same attitudes as those at the basis of class and caste. A prejudiced reaction to members of another race is the normal tendency of the mind to react to individuals as members of categories. The categories into which people are placed generally involve status. Since the Negro is constantly rising in America, he arouses prejudices and animosities. Race prejudice is "merely an elementary expression of conservatism."[25]

Up to about 1930, Park's sociological theory in regard to race relations in the United States did not go beyond the theory of a biracial organization in which vertical social distance between the two races would become a matter of horizontal social distance. A biracial organization would preserve race distinctions but it would change its content in that there would be a change in attitudes. The races would no longer look up and down but across.[26] The development of the biracial organization marked a fundamental change in status since the Negro was acquiring the status of a racial or cultural minority. In an article published in 1939, Park presented the case of the American Negro in the general frame of reference which he had developed for the study of race relations in the modern world.[27] In that article he showed how the migration of the Negro to northern cities had changed the character of race relations and he pointed out that caste was being undermined and that the social distance between the races at the different class levels was being undermined. Moreover, he regarded race relations in the United States as part of a world process in which culture and occupation was coming to play a more important role than inheritance and race. Thus for Park, the "racial frontiers" that were developing in various parts of the world were the seed-beds of new cultures.

In Park's development of a sociological theory in regard to race relations, there are several important features which are significant for the future of sociological theory in this field. The original emphasis of his theory was upon the social psychological aspects of race contacts. It was concerned primarily with providing an explanation of behavior in terms of attitudes. This was not only peculiar to Park's theory but it was characteristic of the theories of other scholars. In this connection one might cite Faris' penetrating analysis of race prejudice in an essay entitled, "Race Attitudes and Sentiments."[28] In the social psychological approach there was a tendency to ignore or pay little attention to the structural and organizational aspects of race relations on the one hand and the dynamic aspects of the problem on the other. The so-called "caste and class" school of students of race relations that has challenged the position of the sociologist has focused attention upon this phase of the problem. However, it should be pointed out that while the "caste and class" school has focused attention upon the structural aspects of race relations, they have only documented the concept of caste. They have not provided any new insights concerning the attitudes and behavior of whites and Negroes. Since the concept of caste has been an essentially static concept, it has failed to provide an orientation for the dynamic aspects of race relations. This brings us to another phase of the sociological theories of Park in regard to race relations.

Park's sociological theory was originally a static theory of race relations. His theory not only contained the fatalism inherent in Sumner's concept of the mores. His theory was originally based upon the assumption that the races could not mix or mingle freely. This is apparent even in his concept of the biracial organization. But as Park saw the changes which were occurring in the United States and other parts of the world, he modified his theory to take into account these changes. His latest theory of race relations in the modern world took into account the dynamic elements in the situation. It remains for his students and other scholars to make a more precise formulation of these theories through research and reflection.

This last statement seems appropriate, since Park's last formulation of his theory of race relations indicates a trend in research, only a brief reference to which can be made here. Current sociological research has not only discarded the older assumptions about racial characteristics but it is approaching the problem of "race relations" from a different standpoint. For the sociologist the problem of "race relations" has become a problem of intergroup relations. This change in viewpoint, it might be pointed out, is evident even in the programs of so-called "intercultural education" which are gradually becoming programs of "intergroup" relations. Sociological theory has had some influence on this new orientation.

In summary, the development of sociological theory in regard to race relations may be stated as follows:

1. The sociological theories of the founders of American sociology as an academic discipline were only implicitly related to the concrete problems of race relations. Their theories concerning race relations were derived from European scholars who were concerned with the universal phenomenon of race contact. Cooley was an exception in that he offered an analysis of race relations in the South based upon his theories of the origin and nature of caste and its relation to class.

2. Sociological theories relating to the concrete problems of race relations in the United States were implicit in the sociological analysis of the Negro problem as a social problem. The analysis of the Negro problem was based upon several fairly clear assumptions: that the Negro is an inferior race because of either biological or social heredity or both; that the Negro because of his physical character cannot be assimilated; and that physical amalgamation is bad and undesirable.

3. The sociological theories implicit in the studies of the Negro problem were developed during the period when the nation held that the attempt to make the Negro a citizen was a mistake, and a new accommodation of the races was being achieved in the South under a system of segregation. Therefore, these theories were rationalizations of American public opinion and the dominant attitudes of the American people.

4. Sociological theory in regard to race relations began to assume a more systematic formulation following the first World War. Park was the chief figure in the formulation of this sociological theory which provided the orientation for empirical studies of race relations. These studies were based upon the theory that race was a sociological concept and utilized such social psychological tools as attitudes and social distance and Sumner's concept of the mores. As the relation of the Negro to American life changed and the problems of race relations throughout the world became more insistent Park developed a more dynamic theory of race relations.

5. A so-called new school of thought, utilizing the concept of caste and

class, has undertaken new studies of race relations. Whereas this new school has focused attention upon the neglected phase of race relations—the structural aspects—it has documented the concept of caste rather than provided new insights.

6. What is needed is the further development of a dynamic sociological theory of race relations, which will discard all the rationalizations of race prejudice and provide orientation for the study of the constantly changing patterns of race relations in American life.

NOTES

1. Henry Hughes, *Treatise on Sociology, Theoretical and Practical* (Philadelphia, 1854).

2. George Fitzhugh, *Sociology for the South: or the Failure of the Society* (Richmond, 1854). See Harvey Wish, *George Wish, Propagandist of the Old South* (Baton Rouge, La., 1943).

3. *Ibid.*, p. 175.

4. *Ibid.*, p. 33.

5. Lester F. Ward, *Pure Sociology* (New York, 1921), pp. 203–220.

6. *Ibid.*, p. 238.

7. *Ibid.*, p. 220.

8. William G. Sumner, *Folkways* (New York, 1906), p. 74.

9. Gunnar Myrdal, *An American Dilemma* (New York, 1944), Vol. 2, pp. 1031–1032.

10. Franklin H. Giddings, *The Principles of Sociology* (New York, 1908), pp. 324–335.

11. *Ibid.*, pp. 316–317.

12. Charles H. Cooley, "Genius, Fame and Comparison of Races," which appeared in the *Annals of the American Academy of Political and Social Science*, 9 (May 1897), pp. 1–42, in Charles H. Cooley, *Sociological Theory and Social Research* (New York, 1930), pp. 121–159.

13. Charles H. Cooley, *Social Organization* (New York, 1923), p. 218.

14. Charles H. Cooley, *Social Process* (New York, 1915), pp. 274 ff.

15. Edward A. Ross, *Principles of Sociology* (New York, 1921), pp. 59 ff. In his autobiography *Seventy Years of It* (New York, 1936), pp 276 ff., Ross repudiated his former notions concerning racial differences.

16. Grove S. Dow, *Society and Its Problems* (New York, 1920), pp. 157 ff.

17. Ulysses G. Weatherly, "Race and Marriage," *American Journal of Sociology*, 15 (1910), pp. 433–453.

18. John M. Mecklin, "The Philosophy of the Color-Line," *American Journal of Sociology*, 19 (1913), pp. 343–357.

19. William I. Thomas, "The Psychology of Race Prejudice," *American Journal of Sociology*, 9 (1944), pp. 593–611.

20. Thomas, *op. cit.*, pp. 609–610.

21. W. I. Thomas, "Race Psychology: Standpoint and Questionnaire," *The American Journal of Sociology*, 17 (1952), pp. 745 ff.

E. Franklin Frazier

22. Robert E. Park, *Introduction to the Science of Sociology* (Chicago, 1924), p. 578.

23. *Ibid.*, p. 578.

24. Robert E. Park, "The Basis of Race Prejudice," *The American Negro. The Annals*, 140 (1928), pp. 11–20.

25. Park, *op. cit.*, p. 13.

26. *Ibid.*, p. 20.

27. Robert E. Park, "The Nature of Race Relations," in Edgar T. Thompson (Ed.), *Race Relations and the Race Problem* (Durham, N.C., 1939).

28. Ellsworth Faris, *The Nature of Human Nature* (New York, 1937), pp. 317–328.

CHANGES IN THE STRUCTURE
OF RACE RELATIONS
IN THE SOUTH

This paper deals with an analysis of the changes occurring in the social structure of bi-racial communities.[1] It is concerned with the social system which is manifested in the formal and informal social relations existing between the members of two groups by virtue of the fact that they are defined as being racially different. It is in this sense that we can refer to this social system as the structure of race relations.

The available evidence indicates that the structure of race relations has been undergoing considerable modification since the abolition of the slave system. Following the elimination of the legal basis of the institution of slavery, a new form of accommodation between the white and Negro groups emerged, which, like all changes in the social order, incorporated many elements of the old order. This new form of accommodation was established on the basis of habits and customs which had grown up during the period of slavery.

In rural areas of the South after the Civil War and Reconstruction, the accommodation of the races tended to reach an equilibrium in a relatively stable social organization. Even in these areas, however, recent developments, such as technological innovations in agriculture, the extension of federal services, the pervasive influence of urban centers, and the shifting of population, have brought about a gradual modification of the traditional system of race relations. In industrial centers the structure of race relations has undergone even greater and more significant changes.

From Harry J. Walker, "Changes in the Structure of Race Relations in the South," in *American Sociological Review*, 14 (1949), 377–383.

Harry J. Walker

An examination of both the formal and informal relations between whites and Negroes suggests three stages in the development of the structure of race relations. These stages can be characterized as follows: (1) the stage following the Civil War, in which personal contacts between whites and Negroes constituted the mechanism of racial understanding and adjustment; (2) a second stage in which, as a result of the evolution of a Negro social world based upon the growth of segregated Negro communities, Negro-white relationships have tended to become more formalized, and in which the Negro community is represented by a type of leadership which performs a liaison function with leaders of the white community; and (3) the third stage in which integration, in the sense of a more or less equal participation of Negroes with whites in community activities, is taking place.

Like all such social developments, these stages can be identified only in a general way with particular geographical areas and historical periods. This is to say that these stages of development are not occurring uniformly throughout the country or even within a single community. In this paper an attempt is made only to conceptualize and identify the changes which are taking place in race relations, though some aspects of all stages of development may be apparent in any given community.

Personal Relationships as the Basis of Race Adjustment

The social order of the South which emerged out of the ruins of the slave system was characterized by the persistence of intimate and personal relationships between whites and the former slaves.

The persistence of these intimate Negro-white relationships has been observed in the post-Civil War period by several writers.[2] As will be shown later, this type of relationship is gradually disappearing in urban centers of the South; however, it still exists in rural communities. The fact that Negroes and whites following the Reconstruction Period were able to establish a relatively orderly community life without prolonged racial friction is a result of an adjustment which was achieved on the basis of the personal relationships which existed between members of the two groups.

It has been noted that these personal relationships between whites and Negroes were characteristic of the slave society. "When it is remembered," says Thompson, "that the ante-bellum plantation was usually a small and

27

closely knit community in which individuals, both white and black, were brought up with a prospect of lifelong association with each other, then it is realized how the plantation offered very much the same sort of human experience that the family represents."[3]

The kind of relationship which grew up between slave and master in the process of accommodation was marked by submissive behavior on the part of the slave and paternalism on the part of the master. In those instances where slaves did not accept their subordinate status, their behavior often exhibited sullen rebellion and in a few instances resulted in open revolt. But over the years as the slave group became more and more accommodated, many of them sought status inside the slave system and in the eyes of their masters by a kind of adaptation marked by submissiveness in expectation of preferential, and even affectionate, treatment.

In the period following the abolition of slavery as a legal institution, the personal relations which existed between Negroes and their former masters provided the basis for the development of a *modus vivendi* for the two groups. This was inevitable in a social system in which whites had reestablished their dominant position during Reconstruction. Thus the former slaves found it necessary to rely upon personal influence with whites as a means of protection, acquiring assistance in time of distress, securing favors, and in developing a sense of security.

Johnson has noted that these relationships not only have a protective function in rural communities of today, but afford Negroes a sense of security in a society dominated by whites. In a report of a study of a rural county in Alabama in 1934, he observed that it is the "unfailing rule of life" that Negroes "should get for themselves a protecting white family."[4] Raper, after examining a number of cases, has shown that in the effort of Negro farmers to purchase land the friendship of a white landowner is a factor of utmost importance.[5] It is well known that when a Negro becomes enmeshed in the toils of the law, evidence as to his innocence may not be as important in securing justice or leniency as the active interest of a "white friend."[6]

Dollard also has commented on the affection shown for Negroes by upper-class whites and planters who reflect the tradition of the ante-bellum South. He has noted also that this group showed less antagonism to Negroes than did lower-class whites, who view Negroes as a competitive group.[7] It is because of the traditional antagonism of the poor whites to Negroes that the existence of personal and intimate relationships between Negroes and whites constituted a significant factor in racial adjustment.

It should be noted, however, that the expression of friendliness and intimacy on the part of Negroes and whites toward each other is governed by what Doyle has called the "etiquette of race relations."[8] This racial ritual, as observed in such forms of behavior as salutations, greetings, casual and formal meetings involving members of the two groups, served in a way to permit expressions of intimacy while maintaining social distance between the two groups. Moreover, as Doyle has indicated, it constituted a means of social control which functioned to maintain the dominant position of whites while effectively impressing upon Negroes their subordinate status in the society. The fact that this type of intimate relationship was carried over from slavery made it possible for the two groups to work out an adjustment which minimized the possibility of conflict.

It should be understood that in the open rural communities and towns of the South such social institutions among Negroes as the church and family formed the basis for a simple type of separate social organization. But in the area of race relations a member of each Negro family maintained a friendly relationship with some white persons, or stood in such a relationship to some other Negro who could represent him in his dealings with whites. What is important here is that in the southern rural society there is no necessity for the representation of the entire group, since race relations developed within the framework of personal relationships which characterize a folk culture.

Inevitably, however, economic and social changes incident to industrialization and urbanization in the South have tended to effect a tremendous change in the character of race relations. The most significant development in this connection has been the increase in the segregation of the Negro urban population.

Growth of a Negro Social World and the Rise of a Negro Leadership

One of the consequences of the urban process has been the growth of segregated Negro communities within the larger urban communities. Along with the growing physical segregation of the Negro population there have developed separate Negro social institutions and associations. The development of a segregated school system and the creation of a pattern of separation in the use of public facilities, such as transportation, eating places, and places of public assembly, have formed the basis for the development of the segregated Negro community. This segregated community comprises a Negro social world which effectively insulates many Negroes from contact with whites. In fact, many Negroes have only impersonal contacts with whites—the whites whom they meet in such capacities as salesclerks, laundrymen, and collectors. This growing impersonality of contacts in the urban community has tended to destroy the basis for racial adjustment which existed in the intimate personal relations between individual whites and Negroes.

Even in domestic service pursuits, where relationships between Negro servants and their employers would be expected to retain some of the traditional intimacy, marked changes have occurred. Whereas, formerly, servants of the older generation were identified, both in their own conception and in that of their employers, with the white families for which they worked, the younger generation of Negroes, farther removed from the plantation tradition, do not form such intimate bonds. Moreover, this new generation of servants now lives in a Negro world where they acquire new values and new conceptions of themselves.

An important feature of this Negro world is its developing class structure. While many aspects of the traditional system of race relations remain, including personal relations between whites and Negroes as a mechanism of adjustment, the development of a Negro class structure and social world is resulting in a new orientation of Negroes in the social order.

The development of a class structure within the Negro group has placed a severe strain on a social system which has maintained a subordinate status for the entire Negro group. The emergence of a Negro world has enabled many Negroes to achieve a higher status in business, academic, and other professional pursuits. In accordance with this new status in the Negro community new social roles emerge which result not only in new social horizons but also in new attitudes and sentiments regarding the Negro's status in the larger community.

Members of the lower class have not been unaffected by this development. The possibility of rising in status within the Negro world gives all Negroes a different evaluation of themselves. They acquire feelings of importance and power. This is reflected in the emphasis upon social ritual in professional and business pursuits; it, in effect, forms a resistance to the sense of inferiority and feelings of repression arising out of subordination in the general society. Not only is there the possibility of rising in status within the Negro world, but there exist among Negroes admiration and pride in the achievements of members of their group. Status values are no longer associated only with the white group.

The growth of a Negro world has resulted in a decrease in the traditional, intimate relationships between whites and Negroes. This has been due not only to increased segregation but also to the mobility and impersonal character of social contacts in the urban world. Members of the Negro group now live predominantly in a Negro world which is to a great extent both physically and psychologically isolated from the white world. Yet these two groups must carry on a common existence in many areas of social life.

A new *modus vivendi* for the two groups has been established through the rise of a Negro leadership whose representatives act as spokesmen for the Negro in matters of common interest to the two racial groups. These spokesmen perform an essential liaison function with representatives of the white world. They maintain contact with white leaders in order to make possible harmonious race relations; they fulfill the need for adjusting conflicting interests and disputes involving members of the two racial groups; they participate in working out solutions to common community problems.

In southern communities, where aspects of the traditional form of race relations exist, Negro leaders are of a conservative type, characterized by attitudes of dependence and deferential behavior toward whites as a counterpart of attitudes of paternalism on the part of the politically dominant whites with whom they must deal. This conservative leadership is an expression of the traditional system of race relations based upon the existence of personal understandings between whites and Negroes.

With the emergence of the somewhat isolated Negro world, Negroes who had been closest to leading white people, as a matter of course, became the spokesmen for the Negro group. In some instances these were persons who had served in the capacity of servants for white people. It can fairly be said that this type of leadership is selected by white people and is recruited from those whose backgrounds of relationships with whites have been such as to fit them for a more or less subservient role in dealing with whites. It should be recognized, however, that some Negroes, who apparently are not directly influenced by southern tradition, assume the role of conservative leaders of their group because they have vested interests in the segregated Negro world. In this role are found such persons as ministers, educators, and businessmen.

Over against this type of leadership is that composed of persons farther removed from the plantation tradition. The developing organization of the Negro community, which is a product of the increased isolation of the individual Negro from whites, has resulted in a growing race consciousness and an increasing racial solidarity. A result of this process has been

31

the rise of a new leadership which can be characterized in its extreme manifestation as militant. It is recruited largely from persons who have not had the experience of being servants to white people, persons who have been subjected (insofar as southern racial mores are concerned) to the disruptive influence of isolation from the plantation tradition. Many of these are persons whose background of experience includes white-collar jobs of middle-class respectability; many of them have received training in northern institutions of higher education; still others are products of the American labor movement.

Representatives of this latter type of leadership are leaders in the sense that they represent the aims and aspirations of the Negro community or segments of it, such as political, labor, and religious groups within the Negro world. Whereas the conservative leader depends upon personal influence with whites in order to achieve some end, the militant leader has bargaining power by virtue of the fact that he has a following. His relationship to members of the white community can be characterized as a political relationship in which his influence is based on social pressure or a kind of political power.

What should be evident, now, is that we are considering two social structures, the larger world of the white man, and the somewhat isolated world of the black man. Since these two social worlds are functionally related in the common economic and social life of American society, it is essential that there be some mechanism for race adjustment. This is found in the liaison role performed by Negro and white leaders.

The conservative leader, or what Myrdal has called the accommodating leader, is more likely to emphasize the necessity for maintaining racial harmony and to oppose attempts at radical changes in the status of the Negro. He usually has vested interests in the business, religious, or other institutions of the Negro community. In the South, as a result of his conservative role as spokesman for the Negro community, he has a favored position in the white community, and to the extent that his influence is used in the interest of Negroes, he has prestige in the Negro community.

Integration of Negroes in Community Activities

The growth of a separate Negro world has resulted in an increase in race consciousness and racial solidarity. The more militant Negro leadership which has its roots in the Negro community is seeking, through various institutions and associations, to organize and give direction to this race consciousness in a struggle for more equal participation in the larger society. At the same time the growing recognition by whites of the common social interests of the two groups has meant increased cooperation and participation on the part of members of the two groups in certain community activities.

Among succeeding generations of whites there are also those who are farther removed from the plantation tradition. They are also being subjected to new ideologies and contacts with the wider world. This, together with the changes in the roles of Negroes in the Negro world, has formed the basis for the development of a counter-process—a process which in certain areas of life of the general community is breaking down the isolation of the two racial groups.

It is characteristic of urban life that people develop numerous associations based on common interests. These interests often cut across racial lines, necessitating organization of groups which include Negroes. Thus Negroes are drawn into such groups as labor organizations, political parties, and community welfare and educational associations. It is in these activities that we see the emergence of the third stage in the development of race relations—the gradual integration of Negroes in community activities. This process is not as far advanced in southern communities as in northern communities.

It is necessary here to suggest only a few examples of this process. In the community studied by the author of this paper, Negroes participate with whites in many civic and welfare programs. In the organization of the Community Chest movement, for example, Negro workers meet with whites to plan the drive. While members of the two groups do not eat together as in the larger urban centers of the North, they do, nevertheless, meet together to discuss their common problems. In urban centers of the North, such as Chicago and New York, Negroes and whites not only meet at dinner, but Negroes serve on important committees which evaluate the programs of social agencies and allocate funds. In Washington, D.C., a border city, Negroes and whites attend dinner meetings held by the Community Chest.

There are numerous instances of cooperation by whites and Negroes in recreational activities in the southern community studied by the author. For example, both Negro and white civic leaders participated in the planning of a new city park and recreational center for Negroes. On the occasion of the dedication of the park, Negroes and white leaders took part in the program.

Race contact in industry in this community has not led to as extensive integration of Negroes as is found in some other southern cities and in northern urban centers. For example, in a city like Chicago, Negroes are not only included in the membership of unions on an equal basis with whites, but in many instances have been elected as officers of both local and regional labor organizations. Although Negro workers are organized in separate locals in this community, there is cooperation among white and Negro labor leaders to plan strategy and the operation of the union's program. In many instances the relationships between white and Negro union officials are of the traditional type, with whites playing a paternalistic and Negroes a dependent role. However, this represents an initial step in integration which has possibilities of followng the pattern developed in Birmingham, in which Negroes in the steel industry eventually were organized on a non-segregated basis in locals.

Further evidence of integration of whites and Negroes is also apparent in business activities of this community. Here Negroes own and operate a banking and insurance enterprise—the latter being the largest Negro insurance company in the country. The Negro bank is strategically located in the central business section. While at the time of this study the bank was not admitted to membership in the local clearing-house association, the services of the latter were available to the bank, and officials of the bank were permitted to attend meetings of the association. The bank also had a considerable number of white depositors because of its strategic location and perhaps because of the anonymity it afforded its white patrons.

The necessity for the cooperation of Negroes in educational and health programs has also drawn together Negro and white professional persons having these interests in common. In this community and other cities Negro and white physicians have cooperated in meeting problems of health education and hospitalization. In the field of education the inclusion of Negro teachers in the state teachers association of Missouri is another example of the process. Many other examples are found in the mixed professional and scientific societies organized on a regional and national basis.

It is in the political life of the community that integration has occurred most extensively. This is an area which is of crucial importance to race relations because it has direct bearing on the status of the Negro group in the social system.

Since 1920 when the poll-tax restriction was removed, Negro political leaders have developed a strong political organization. The first Negroes to enter politics were servants who could be trusted by whites to get out a "safe" Negro vote. It is significant that when Negroes first began voting in the community, conservative Negro leaders remained aloof from political activity and actually opposed Negro participation. However, those Negroes who were close to white political leaders and who could be counted on to see that a limited number of Negroes "voted right" were responsible for making Negro voting respectable in the community.

Now that voting on the part of Negroes is accepted by the white community and especially by the conservative Negro leadership, the younger, more aggressive Negro leaders have been making a somewhat successful effort to organize Negro voters to secure greater political power. A measure of their influence is indicated in the fact that they meet informally with white candidates seeking support in elections; they participate in the local party meetings held by whites; and more recently they have been represented on the local Democratic committee. In recent years, Negro political leaders have also placed Negro candidates on the ballot for such local offices as city councilman and membership on the Board of Education. While these efforts were unsuccessful, it is significant that Negro candidacy did not arouse any serious opposition from whites.

The development of a political organization has given Negroes influence which carries over into other areas of community activity. For example, favorable consideration is often secured in arrests, cases of police brutality, and court trials involving Negroes. It is also an important factor in acquiring more adequate public services, such as schools, recreational facilities, and street paving. This means that Negroes are consulted or represented on committees which plan and execute programs involving their interests.

The relationships established by representatives of the militant Negro leadership with white leaders are based on political power as contrasted with the personal influence of conservative Negro leaders with whites. Even where a militant Negro leader has established a personal relationship with white political leaders, it is of a different character from that which exists between conservative Negro leaders and whites. The former is a political relationship, while the latter is based on the traditional, servile role of the Negro in relation to a paternalistic master.

Finally, it should be recognized that many Negroes develop personal ties with whites of influence as a means of acquiring positions of leadership with all the economic and political advantages which this implies. The more militant Negroes, on the other hand, often resort to attempts at organizing the Negro, thereby defining and expressing the aims and aspirations of the group as a means of achieving leadership. There is no doubt that all of these factors are to be found in the current situation involving the effort to break down segregation in higher education in the South, and the counter-effort at compromise in segregated regional schools.

Conclusions

The three stages in the development of race relations described above also comprise a sociological frame of reference for the study of many problems in this field. This frame of reference conceivably might be used in the following ways: (1) the three kinds of structures of race relations may be regarded as ideal types for making comparative studies of the racial situation, or some phase of it, in various areas in which each kind of structure is most closely approximated, and (2) such problems may be studied in a single area where two or more of these patterns exist concurrently but in which one type is dominant. Both approaches, especially the first, might possibly contribute to a clearer analysis and understanding of the natural history of race relations. Moreover, this point of view has the advantage of emphasizing the dynamic character of race relations, whereas such a frame of reference as that of caste and class tends, at least as it has been developed and used, to present these relations as being more static in nature.

It is proposed that, in utilizing the frame of reference presented here, a more complete understanding might be gained concerning certain specific problems in the field of race relations. Among these problems are racial tension and overt conflict; the function of white and Negro leadership in a changing system of race relations; problems of racial movements, including the Negro's struggle for equal rights and a new status; problems involving the resistance of whites to changes in the status of the Negro group; analysis of the use of political power to effect status changes of the Negro in the social system; and an analysis of the areas of social life in which integration of Negroes is taking place, which, among other things, conceivably would lead to a determination of those areas in which the greatest resistance to integration would be encountered.

Harry J. Walker

NOTES

1. The main observations in this paper are based upon a detailed study of changes in race accommodation in a southern community.

2. Booker T. Washington, *The Story of the Negro; The Rise of the Race from Slavery* (Garden City, New York: Doubleday, Page and Company, 1909), I, p. 189. Robert E. Park, "Racial Assimilation in Secondary Groups," *Publication of the American Sociological Society*, 8 (1913), 75–82.

3. Edgar T. Thompson, "The Physical Basis of Traditional Race Relations," in Edgar T. Thompson (Ed.), *Race Relations and the Race Problem* (Durham, N.C.: Duke University Press, 1939), p. 205.

4. Charles S. Johnson, *The Shadow of the Plantation* (Chicago: The University of Chicago Press, 1934), p. 27.

5. Arthur Raper, *Preface to Peasantry* (Chapel Hill: The University of North Carolina Press, 1936), p. 122.

6. *Ibid.*, p. 293.

7. John Dollard, *Caste and Class in A Southern Town* (New Haven: Yale University Press, 1937), pp. 82–83.

8. Bertram W. Doyle, *The Etiquette of Race Relations in the South* (Chicago: University of Chicago Press), p. 193.

A SOCIETAL THEORY OF
RACE AND ETHNIC RELATIONS

"In the relations of races there is a cycle of events which tends everywhere to repeat itself."[1] Park's assertion served as a prologue to the now classical cycle of competition, conflict, accommodation, and assimilation. A number of other attempts have been made to formulate phases or stages ensuing from the initial contacts between racial and ethnic groups.[2] However, the sharp contrasts between relatively harmonious race relations in Brazil and Hawaii and the current racial turmoil in South Africa and Indonesia serve to illustrate the difficulty in stating—to say nothing of interpreting—an inevitable "natural history" of race and ethnic relations.

Many earlier race and ethnic cycles were, in fact, narrowly confined to a rather specific set of groups or contact situations. Bogardus, for example, explicitly limited his synthesis to Mexican and Oriental immigrant groups on the west coast of the United States and suggested that this is but one of many different cycles of relations between immigrants and native Americans.[3] Similarly, the Australian anthropologist Price developed three phases that appear to account for the relationships between white English-speaking migrants and the aborigines of Australia, Maoris in New Zealand, and Indians of the United States and Canada.[4]

This paper seeks to present a rudimentary theory of the development of race and ethnic relations that systematically accounts for differences between societies in such divergent consequences of contact as racial nationalism and warfare, assimilation and fusion, and extinction. It postulates that the critical problem on a societal level in racial or ethnic contact is initially each population's maintenance and development of a social order com-

From Stanley Lieberson, "A Societal Theory of Race and Ethnic Relations," in *American Sociological Review*, 26 (1961), pp. 902–910.

patible with its ways of life prior to contact. The crux of any cycle must, therefore, deal with political, social, and economic institutions. The emphasis given in earlier cycles to one group's dominance of another in these areas is therefore hardly surprising.[5]

Although we accept this institutional approach, the thesis presented here is that knowledge of the nature of one group's domination over another in the political, social, and economic spheres is a necessary but insufficient prerequisite for predicting or interpreting the final and intermediate stages of racial and ethnic contact. Rather, institutional factors are considered in terms of a distinction between two major types of contact situations: contacts involving subordination of an indigenous population by a migrant group, for example, Negro-white relations in South Africa; and contacts involving subordination of a migrant population by an indigenous racial or ethnic group, for example, Japanese migrants to the United States.

After considering the societal issues inherent in racial and ethnic contact, the distinction developed between migrant and indigenous superordination will be utilized in examining each of the followng dimensions of race relations: political and economic control, multiple ethnic contacts, conflict and assimilation. The terms "race" and "ethnic" are used interchangeably.

Differences Inherent in Contact

Most situations of ethnic contact involve at least one indigenous group and at least one group migrating to the area. The only exception at the initial point in contact would be the settlement of an uninhabited area by two or more groups. By "indigenous" is meant not necessarily the aborigines, but rather a population sufficiently established in an area so as to possess the institutions and demographic capacity for maintaining some minimal form of social order through generations. Thus a given spatial area may have different indigenous groups through time. For example, the indigenous population of Australia is presently largely white and primarily of British origin, although the Tasmanoids and Australoids were once in possession of the area.[6] A similar racial shift may be observed in the populations indigenous to the United States.

Restricting discussion to the simplest of contact situations, i.e., involving one migrant and one established population, we can generally observe sharp differences in their social organization at the time of contact. The indigenous population has an established and presumably stable organization prior to the arrival of migrants, i.e., government, economic activities adapted to the environment and the existing techniques of resource utilization, kinship, stratification, and religious systems.[7] On the basis of a long series of migration studies, we may be reasonably certain that the social order of a migrant population's homeland is not wholly transferred to their new settlement.[8] Migrants are required to make at least some institutional adaptations and innovations in view of the presence of an indigenous population, the demographic selectivity of migration, and differences in habitat.

For example, recent post-war migrations from Italy and the Netherlands indicate considerable selectivity in age and sex from the total populations of these countries. Nearly half of 30,000 males leaving the Netherlands in 1955 were between 20 and 39 years of age whereas only one quarter of the male population was of these ages.[9] Similarly, over 40,000 males in this age range accounted for somewhat more than half of Italy's male emigrants in 1951, although they comprise roughly 30 per cent of the male population of Italy.[10] In both countries, male emigrants exceed females in absolute numbers as well as in comparison with the sex ratios of their nation. That these cases are far from extreme can be illustrated with Oriental migration data. In 1920, for example, there were 38,000 foreign-born Chinese adult males in the United States, but only 2,000 females of the same group.[11]

In addition to these demographic shifts, the new physical and biological conditions of existence require the revision and creation of social institutions if the social order known in the old country is to be approximated and if the migrants are to survive. The migration of eastern and southern European peasants around the turn of the century to urban industrial centers of the United States provides a well-documented case of radical changes in occupational pursuits as well as the creation of a number of institutions in response to the new conditions of urban life, e.g., mutual-aid societies, national churches, and financial institutions.

In short, when two populations begin to occupy the same habitat but do not share a single order, each group endeavors to maintain the political and economic conditions that are at least compatible with the institutions existing before contact. These conditions for the maintenance of institutions can not only differ for the two groups in contact, but are often conflicting. European contacts with the American Indian, for example, led to the decimation of the latter's sources of sustenance and disrupted religious and tribal forms of organization. With respect to a population's efforts to maintain its social institutions, we may therefore assume that the presence of another ethnic group is an important part of the environment. Further, if groups in contact differ in their capacity to impose changes on the other group, then we may expect to find one group "superordinate" and the other population "subordinate" in maintaining or developing a suitable environment.

It is here that efforts at a single cycle of race and ethnic relations must fail. For it is necessary to introduce a distinction in the nature or form of subordination before attempting to predict whether conflict or relatively harmonious assimilation will develop. As we shall shortly show, the race relations cycle in areas where the migrant group is superordinate and indigenous group subordinate differs sharply from the stages in societies composed of a superordinate indigenous group and subordinate migrants.[12]

Political and Economic Control

Emphasis is placed herein on economic and political dominance since it is assumed that control of these institutions will be instrumental in establishing a suitable milieu for at least the population's own social institutions, e.g., educational, religious, and kinship, as well as control of such major cultural artifacts as language.

MIGRANT SUPERORDINATION

When the population migrating to a new contact situation is superior in technology (particularly weapons) and more tightly organized than the indigenous group, the necessary conditions for maintaining the migrants' political and economic institutions are usually imposed on the indigenous population. Warfare, under such circumstances, often occurs early in the contacts between the two groups as the migrants begin to interfere with the natives' established order. There is frequently conflict even if the initial contact was friendly. Price, for example, has observed the following consequences of white invasion and subordination of the indigenous populations of Australia, Canada, New Zealand, and the United States:

> During an opening period of pioneer invasion on moving frontiers the whites decimated the natives with their diseases; occupied their lands by seizure or by pseudo-purchase; slaughtered those who resisted; intensified tribal warfare by supplying white weapons; ridiculed and disrupted native religions, society and culture, and generally reduced the unhappy peoples to a state of despondency under which they neither desired to live, nor to have children to undergo similar conditions.[13]

The numerical decline of indigenous populations after their initial subordination to a migrant group, whether caused by warfare, introduction of venereal and other diseases, or disruption of sustenance activities, has been documented for a number of contact situations in addition to those discussed by Price.[14]

In addition to bringing about these demographic and economic upheavals, the superordinate migrants frequently create political entities that are not at all coterminous with the boundaries existing during the indigenous populations' supremacy prior to contact. For example, the British and Boers in southern Africa carved out political states that included areas previously under the control of separate and often warring groups.[15] Indeed, European alliances with feuding tribes were often used as a fulcrum for the territorial expansion of whites into southern Africa.[16] The bifurcation of tribes into two nations and the migrations of groups across newly created national boundaries are both consequences of the somewhat arbitrary nature of the political entities created in regions of migrant superordination.[17] This incorporation of diverse indigenous populations into a single territorial unit under the dominance of a migrant group has considerable importance for later developments in this type of racial and ethnic contact.

INDIGENOUS SUPERORDINATION

When a population migrates to a subordinate position considerably less conflict occurs in the early stages. The movements of many European and Oriental populations to political, economic, and social subordination in the United States were not converted into warfare, nationalism, or long-term conflict. Clearly, the occasional labor and racial strife marking the history of immigration of the United States is not on the same level as the efforts to expel or revolutionize the social order. American Negroes, one of the most persistently subordinated migrant groups in the country, never responded in significant numbers to the encouragement of migration to Liberia. The single important large-scale nationalistic effort, Marcus Garvey's Universal Negro Improvement Association, never actually led to mass emigration of Negroes.[18] By contrast, the indigenous American Indians fought long and hard to preserve control over their habitat.

In interpreting differences in the effects of migrant and indigenous subordination, the migrants must be considered in the context of the options available to the group. Irish migrants to the United States in the 1840's, for example, although clearly subordinate to native whites of other origins, fared better economically than if they had remained in their mother country.[19] Further, the option of returning to the homeland often exists for populations migrating to subordinate situations. Jerome reports that net migration to the United States between the midyears of 1907 and 1923 equaled roughly 65 per cent of gross immigration.[20] This indicates that immigrant dissatisfaction with subordination or other conditions of contact can often be resolved by withdrawal from the area. Recently subordinated indigenous groups, by contrast, are perhaps less apt to leave their habitat so readily.

Finally, when contacts between racial and ethnic groups are under the control of the indigenous population, threats of demographic and institutional imbalance are reduced since the superordinate populations can limit the numbers and groups entering. For example, when Oriental migration to the United States threatened whites, sharp cuts were executed in the quotas.[21] Similar events may be noted with respect to the decline of immigration from the so-called "new" sources of eastern and southern Europe. Whether a group exercises its control over immigration far before it is actually under threat is, of course, not germane to the point that immigrant restriction provides a mechanism whereby potential conflict is prevented.

In summary, groups differ in the conditions necessary for maintaining their respective social orders. In areas where the migrant group is dominant, frequently the indigenous population suffers sharp numerical declines and their economic and political institutions are seriously undermined. Conflict often accompanies the establishment of migrant superordination. Subordinate indigenous populations generally have no alternative location and do not control the numbers of new ethnic populations admitted into their area. By contrast, when the indigenous population dominates the political and economic conditions, the migrant group is introduced into the economy of the indigenous population. Although subordinate in their new habitat, the migrants may fare better than if they remained in their homeland. Hence their subordination occurs without great conflict. In addition, the migrants usually have the option of returning to their homeland and the indigenous population controls the number of new immigrants in the area.

Multiple Ethnic Contacts

Although the introduction of a third major ethnic or racial group frequently occurs in both types of societies distinguished here, there are significant differences between conditions in habitats under indigenous domination and areas where a migrant population is superordinate. Chinese and Indian migrants, for example, were often welcomed by whites in areas where large indigenous populations were suppressed, but these migrants were restricted in the white mother country. Consideration of the causes and consequences of multi-ethnic contacts is therefore made in terms of the two types of racial and ethnic contact.

MIGRANT SUPERORDINATION

In societies where the migrant population is superordinate, it is often necessary to introduce new immigrant groups to fill the niches created in the revised economy of the area. The subordinate indigenous population frequently fails, at first, to participate in the new economic and political order introduced by migrants. For example, because of the numerical decline of Fijians after contact with whites and their unsatisfactory work habits, approximately 60,000 persons migrated from India to the sugar plantations of Fiji under the indenture system between 1879 and 1916.[22] For similar reasons, as well as the demise of slavery, large numbers of Indians were also introduced to such areas of indigenous subordination as Mauritius, British Guiana, Trinidad, and Natal.[23] The descendents of these migrants comprise the largest single ethnic group in several of these areas.

McKenzie, after observing the negligible participation of the subordinated indigenous populations of Alaska, Hawaii, and Malaya in contrast to the large numbers of Chinese, Indian, and other Oriental immigrants, offers the following interpretation:

The indigenous peoples of many of the frontier zones of modern industrialism are surrounded by their own web of culture and their own economic structure. Consequently they are slow to take part in the new economy especially as unskilled laborers. It is the individual who is widely removed from his native habitat that is most adaptable to the conditions imposed by capitalism in frontier regions. Imported labor cannot so easily escape to its home village when conditions are distasteful as can the local population.[24]

Similarly, the Indians of the United States played a minor role in the new economic activities introduced by white settlers and, further, were not used successfully as slaves.[25] Frazier reports that Negro slaves were utilized in the West Indies and Brazil after unsuccessful efforts to enslave the indigenous Indian populations.[26] Large numbers of Asiatic Indians were brought to South Africa as indentured laborers to work in the railways, mines, and plantations introduced by whites.[27]

This migration of workers into areas where the indigenous population was either unable or insufficient to work in the newly created economic activities was also marked by a considerable flow back to the home country.

For example, nearly 3.5 million Indians left the Madras Presidency for overseas between 1903 and 1912, but close to 3 million returned during this same period.[28] However, as we observed earlier, large numbers remained overseas and formed major ethnic populations in a number of countries. Current difficulties of the ten million Chinese in Southeast Asia are in large part due to their settlement in societies where the indigenous populations were subordinate.

INDIGENOUS SUPERORDINATION

We have observed that in situations of indigenous superordination the call for new immigrants from other ethnic and racial populations is limited in a manner that prevents the indigenous group's loss of political and economic control. Under such conditions, no single different ethnic or racial population is sufficiently large in number or strength to challenge the supremacy of the indigenous population.

After whites attained dominance in Hawaii, that land provided a classic case of the substitution of one ethnic group after another during a period when large numbers of immigrants were needed for the newly created and expanding plantation economy. According to Lind, the shifts from Chinese to Japanese and Portuguese immigrants and the later shifts to Puerto Rican, Korean, Spanish, Russian, and Philippine sources for the plantation laborers were due to conscious efforts to prevent any single group from obtaining too much power.[29] Similarly, the exclusion of Chinese from the United States mainland stimulated the migration of the Japanese and, in turn, the later exclusion of Japanese led to increased migration from Mexico.[30]

In brief, groups migrating to situations of multiple ethnic contact are thus subordinate in both types of contact situations. However, in societies where whites are superordinate but do not settle as an indigenous population, other racial and ethnic groups are admitted in large numbers and largely in accordance with economic needs of the revised economy of the habitat. By contrast, when a dominant migrant group later becomes indigenous, in the sense that the area becomes one of permanent settlement through generations for the group, migrant populations from new racial and ethnic stocks are restricted in number and source.

Conflict and Assimilation

From a comparison of the surge of racial nationalism and open warfare in parts of Africa and Asia or the retreat of superordinate migrants from the former Dutch East Indies and French Indo-China, on the one hand, with the fusion of populations in many nations of western Europe or the "cultural pluralism" of the United States and Switzerland, on the other, one must conclude that neither conflict nor assimilation is an inevitable outcome of racial and ethnic contact. Our distinction, however, between two classes of race and ethnic relations is directly relevant to consideration of which of these alternatives different populations in contact will take. In societies where the indigenous population at the initial contact is subordinate, warfare and nationalism often—although not always—develops later in the cycle of relations. By contrast, relations between migrants and indigenous populations that are subordinate and superordinate, respectively, are generally without long-term conflict.

MIGRANT SUPERORDINATION

Through time, the subordinated indigenous population begins to participate in the economy introduced by the migrant group and, frequently, a concomitant disruption of previous forms of social and economic organization takes place. This, in turn, has significant implications for the development of both nationalism and a greater sense of racial unity. In many African states, where Negroes were subdivided into ethnic groups prior to contact with whites, the racial unity of the African was created by the occupation of their habitat by white invaders.[31] The categorical subordination of Africans by whites as well as the dissolution and decay of previous tribal and ethnic forms of organization are responsible for the creation of racial consciousness among the indigenous populations.[32] As the indigenous group becomes increasingly incorporated within the larger system, both the saliency of their subordinate position and its significance increase. No alternative exists for the bulk of the native population other than the destruction or revision of the institutions of political, economic, and social subordination.

Further, it appears that considerable conflict occurs in those areas where the migrants are not simply superordinate, but where they themselves have also become, in a sense, indigenous by maintaining an established population through generations. In Table 3–1, for example, one can observe how

TABLE 3-1
Nativity of the White Populations
of Selected African Countries, Circa 1950

Country	Per Cent of Whites Born in Country
Algeria	79.8
Basutoland	37.4
Bechuanaland	39.5
Morocco[a]	37.1[c]
Northern Rhodesia	17.7
Southern Rhodesia	31.5
South West Africa[b]	45.1
Swaziland	41.2
Tanganyika	47.6
Uganda	43.8
Union of South Africa	89.7

Source: United Nations, *Demographic Year-book*, 1956, Table 5.

Note: Other non-indigenous groups included when necessary breakdown by race is not given.

[a]Former French zone.

[b]Excluding Walvis Bay.

[c]Persons born in former Spanish zone or in Tangier are included as native.

sharply the white populations of Algeria and the Union of South Africa differ from those in nine other African countries with respect to the per cent born in the country of settlement. Thus, two among the eleven African countries for which such data were available[33] are outstanding with respect to both racial turmoil and the high proportion of whites born in the country. To be sure, other factors operate to influence the nature of racial and ethnic relations. However these data strongly support our suggestions with respect to the significance of differences between indigenous and migrant forms of contact. Thus where the migrant population becomes established in the new area, it is all the more difficult for the indigenous subordinate group to change the social order.

Additionally, where the formerly subordinate indigenous population has become dominant through the expulsion of the superordinate group, the situation faced by nationalities introduced to the area under earlier conditions of migrant superordination changes radically. For example, as we noted earlier, Chinese were welcomed in many parts of Southeast Asia where the newly subordinated indigenous populations were unable or unwilling to fill the economic niches created by the white invaders. However, after whites were expelled and the indigenous populations obtained political mastery, the gates to further Chinese immigration were fairly well closed and there has been increasing interference with the Chinese already present. In Indonesia, where Chinese immigration had been encouraged under Dutch domain, the newly created indigenous government allows only token immigration and has formulated a series of laws and measures designed to interfere with and reduce Chinese commercial activities.[34] Thompson and Adloff observe that,

Since the war, the Chinese have been subjected to increasingly restrictive measures throughout Southeast Asia, but the severity and effectiveness of these has varied with the degree to which the native nationalists are in control of their countries and feel their national existence threatened by the Chinese.[35]

INDIGENOUS SUPERORDINATION

By contrast, difficulties between subordinate migrants and an already dominant indigenous population occur within the context of a consensual form of government, economy, and social institutions. However confused and uncertain may be the concept of assimilation and its application in operational terms,[36] it is important to note that assimilation is essentially a very different phenomenon in the two types of societies distinguished here.

Where populations migrate to situations of subordination, the issue has generally been with respect to the migrants' capacity and willingness to become an integral part of the on-going social order. For example, this has largely been the case in the United States where the issue of "new" vs. "old" immigrant groups hinged on the alleged inferiorities of the former.[37] The occasional flurries of violence under this form of contact have been generally initiated by the dominant indigenous group and with respect to such threats against the social order as the cheap labor competition of Orientals in the west coast,[38] the nativist fears of Irish Catholic political domination of Boston in the nineteenth century,[39] or the desecration of sacred principles by Mexican "zoot-suiters" in Los Angeles.[40]

The conditions faced by subordinate migrants in Australia and Canada after the creation of indigenous white societies in these areas are similar to that of the United States; that is, limited and sporadic conflict, and great emphasis on the assimilation of migrants. Striking and significant contrasts to the general pattern of subordinant immigrant assimilation in these societies, however, are provided by the differences between the assimilation of Italian and German immigrants in Australia as well as the position of French Canadians in eastern Canada.

French Canadians have maintained their language and other major cultural and social attributes whereas nineteenth and twentieth century immigrants are in process of merging into the predominantly English-speaking Canadian society. Although broader problems of territorial segregation are involved,[41] the critical difference between French Canadians and later groups is that the former had an established society in the new habitat prior to the British conquest of Canada and were thus largely able to maintain their social and cultural unity without significant additional migration from France.[42]

Similarly, in finding twentieth-century Italian immigrants in Australia more prone to cultural assimilation than were German migrants to that nation in the 1800's, Borrie emphasized the fact that Italian migration occurred after Australia had become an independent nation-state. By contrast, Germans settled in what was a pioneer colony without an established general social order and institutions. Thus, for example, Italian children were required to attend Australian schools and learn English, whereas the German immigrants were forced to establish their own educational program.[43]

Thus the consequences of racial and ethnic contact may also be examined in terms of the two types of superordinate-subordinate contact situations considered. For the most part, subordinate migrants appear to be more rapidly assimilated than are subordinate indigenous populations. Further, the subordinate migrant group is generally under greater pressure to assimilate, at least in the gross sense of "assimilation" such as language, than are subordinate indigenous populations. In addition, warfare or racial nationalism—when it does occur—tends to be in societies where the indigenous population is subordinate. If the indigenous movement succeeds, the economic and political position of racial and ethnic populations introduced to the area under migrant dominance may become tenuous.

A Final Note

It is suggested that interest be revived in the conditions accounting for societal variations in the process of relations between racial and ethnic groups. A societal theory of race relations, based on the migrant-indigenous and superordinate-subordinate distinctions developed above, has been found to offer an orderly interpretation of differences in the nature of race and ethnic relations in the contact situations considered. Since, however, systematic empirical investigaton provides a far more rigorous test of the theory's merits and limitations, comparative cross-societal studies are needed.

NOTES

1. Robert E. Park, *Race and Culture* (Glencoe, Ill.: The Free Press), 1950, p. 150.

2. For example, Emory S. Bogardus, "A Race-Relations Cycle," *American Journal of Sociology*, 35 (January, 1930), pp. 612–617; W. O. Brown, "Culture Contact and Race Conflict" in E. B. Reuter, editor, *Race and Culture Contacts* (New York: McGraw-Hill, 1934), pp. 34–47; E. Franklin Frazier, *Race and Culture Contacts in the Modern World* (New York: Alfred A. Knopf, 1957), pp. 32 ff.; Clarence E. Glick, "Social Roles and Types in Race Relations" in Andrew W. Lind, editor, *Race Relations in World Perspective* (Honolulu: University of Hawaii Press), 1955, pp. 243–262; Edward Nelson Palmer, "Culture Contacts and Population Growth" in Joseph J. Spengler and Otis Dudley Duncan, editors, *Population Theory and Policy* (Glencoe, Ill.: The Free Press), 1956, pp. 410–415; A. Grenfell Price, *White Settlers and Native Peoples*, Melbourne: Georgian House, 1950. For summaries of several of these cycles, see Brewton Bern, *Race and Ethnic Relations* (Boston: Houghton Mifflin, 1958), Chapter 6.

3. Bogardus, *op. cit.*, p. 612.

4. Price, *op. cit.*

5. Intra-urban stages of contact are not considered here.

6. Price, *op. cit.*, chaps. 6 and 7.

7. Glick, *op. cit.*, p. 244.

8. See, for example, Brinley Thomas, "International Migration" in Philip M. Hauser and Otis Dudley Duncan, editors, *The Study of Population* (Chicago: University of Chicago Press, 1959), pp. 523–526.

9. United Nations, *Demographic Yearbook* (1957), pp. 147, 645.

10. United Nations, *Demographic Yearbook* (1954), pp. 131, 669.

11. R. D. McKenzie, *Oriental Exclusion* (Chicago: University of Chicago Press, 1928), p. 83.

12. See, for example, Reuter's distinction between two types of direct contact in E. B. Reuter, editor, *op. cit.*, pp. 4–7.

13. Price, *op. cit.*, p. 1.

14. Stephen Roberts, *Population Problems of the Pacific* (London: George Routledge & Sons, 1927).

15. John A. Barnes, "Race Relations in the Development of Southern Africa" in Lind, editor, *op. cit.*

16. *Ibid.*

17. Witness the current controversies between tribes in the newly created Congo Republic. Also, for a list of tribes living on both sides of the border of the Republic of Sudan, see Karol Józef Krótki, "Demographic Survey of Sudan" in *The Population of Sudan*, report on the sixth annual conference (Khartoum: Philosophical Society of Sudan, 1958), p. 35.

18. John Hope Franklin, *From Slavery to Freedom*, second edition (New York: Alfred Knopf, 1956), pp. 234–238, 481–483.

19. Oscar Handlin, *Boston's Immigrants*, revised edition (Cambridge, Mass.: The Belknap Press of Harvard University Press, 1959), Chap. 2.

20. Harry Jerome, *Migration and Business Cycles* (New York: National Bureau of Economic Research, 1926), pp. 43–44.

21. See, George Eaton Simpson and J. Milton Yinger, *Racial and Cultural Minorities*, revised edition (New York: Harper & Brothers, 1958), pp. 126–132.

22. K. L. Gillion, "The Sources of Indian Emigration to Fiji," *Population Studies*, 10 (November 1956), p. 139; I. M. Cumpston, "A Survey of Indian Immigration to British Tropical Colonies to 1910," *ibid.*, pp. 158–159.

23. Cumpston, *op. cit.*, pp. 158–165.

24. R. D. McKenzie, "Cultural and Racial Differences as Bases of Human Symbiosis" in Kimball Young, editor, *Social Attitudes* (New York: Henry Holt, 1931), p. 157.

25. Franklin, *op. cit.*, p. 47.

26. Frazier, *op. cit.*, pp. 107–108.

27. Leo Kuper, Hilstan Watts, and Ronald Davies, *Durban: A Study in Racial Ecology* (London: Jonathan Cape, 1958), p. 25.

28. Gillion, *op. cit.*, p. 149.

29. Andrew W. Lind, *An Island Community* (Chicago: University of Chicago Press, 1938), pp. 218–229.

30. McKenzie, *Oriental Exclusion*, *op. cit.*, p. 181.

31. For a discussion of territorial and tribal movements, see James S. Coleman, "Current Political Movements in Africa," *The Annals of the American Academy of Political and Social Science*, 298 (March 1955), pp. 95–108.

32. For a broader discussion of emergent nationalism, see, Thomas Hodgkin, *Nationalism in Colonial Africa* (New York: New York University Press, 1957); Everett C. Hughes, "New Peoples" in Lind, editor, *op. cit.*, pp. 95–115.

33. United Nations, *Demographic Yearbook*, 1956, Table 5.

34. B. H. M. Vlekke, *Indonesia in 1956* (The Hague: Netherlands Institute of International Affairs, 1957), p. 88.

35. Virginia Thompson and Richard Adloff, *Minority Problems in Southeast Asia* (Stanford, Calif.: Stanford University Press, 1955), p. 3.

36. See, for example, International Union for the Scientific Study of Population, "Cultural Assimilation of Immigrants," *Population Studies*, supplement, March 1950.

37. Oscar Handlin, *Race and Nationality in American Life*, Garden City (New York: Doubleday Anchor Books, 1957), Chap. 5.

38. Simpson and Yinger, *op. cit.*

39. Oscar Handlin, *Boston's Immigrants*, *op. cit.*, Chap. 7.

40. Ralph Turner and Samuel J. Surace, "Zoot-Suiters and Mexicans: Symbols in Crowd Behavior," *American Journal of Sociology*, 62 (July 1956), pp. 14–20.

41. It is, however, suggestive to consider whether the isolated settlement of an area by a racial, religious, or ethnic group would be permitted in other than frontier conditions. Consider, for example, the difficulties faced by Mormons until they reached Utah.

42. See Everett C. Hughes, *French Canada in Transition* (Chicago: University of Chicago Press, 1943).

43. W. D. Borrie assisted by D. R. G. Packer, *Italians and Germans in Australia* (Melbourne: F. W. Cheshire, 1954), *passim*.

PART II

The Ethnography of Race and Ethnic Relations

Editor's Introduction

It is fashionable in sociology to dismiss ethnographic-type studies (of which the four pieces reproduced here are fine examples) as "merely" descriptive. In view of the paucity of good holistic accounts of actual systems of intergroup relations on which to base theory, this kind of snobbery is deleterious to the very development of theory that is regarded as the aim and acme of sociological inquiry. The pieces by Mayer and by Broom are at the "macro" level, i.e. they deal with entire societies; the Francis and Johnson articles, on the other hand, have a narrower regional focus.

Switzerland and Jamaica are especially interesting cases as they stand at opposite extremes of the consensus-coercion continuum. Switzerland represents the most successful and long-lasting case of a multi-national state held together not through the political domination of one ethnic group over the other as is so frequently the case, but through a mutually agreeable *modus vivendi* between four groups of greatly unequal size. Jamaica, along with the other island societies of the Caribbean, has developed out of a slave society and indeed out of one of the most thoroughly enslaved societies that the world has ever seen. By comparison, slavery in the United States accounted for only one of the main economic sectors (plantation agriculture) and for only one fifth of the population.

53

The two pieces on the United States, while much narrower in focus, give the kind of detailed account of intergroup relations and of group definition that one needs to understand race and ethnicity at any depth. The Johnson article, by documenting a case where the sharp white-black dichotomy does not obtain, reveals that the color line in the United States is in fact far more complex and problematic than most of us generally assume. Nor will it do to dismiss such case studies as "exceptions" because most of our theories are in fact based on conglomerates of "special cases" in which we find it convenient to stress the common elements and underplay the idiosyncracies. Such is the price of generalizing; but if generalizations are not to become ludicrous caricatures of reality, they must be grounded on extensive familiarty with as wide a range of empirical data as possible. Sound ethnography is the underpinning of good theory.

The Francis piece on a multi-ethnic situation in the southwestern United States should serve as a corrective to the politically motivated but academically provincial "ethnic studies programs" that are lately mushrooming on American campuses. Since racial and ethnic discrimination are, by definition, the product of relations between unequally placed groups, nothing can be more academically sterile and politically stultifying for the groups concerned than to focus on the position, history, and characteristics of a single group. Nothing short of a study of discrimination or racism as holistic systems of *interrelations* can yield any understanding of the situation, and hence result in politically effective action programs. Black studies, Chicano studies, Asian studies, women's studies, and the like, by endeavoring to isolate an oppressed group from both the dominant group and from other oppressed groups, necessarily result in parochialism and escapism. Francis' article is a good example of how to avoid this currently fashionable blind alley.

　　　　　　　　　　　　　　　　　　Guy B. Johnson

PERSONALITY IN A WHITE-INDIAN-NEGRO COMMUNITY

Scattered throughout the South, there are over a hundred groups of people who are classified by the Census Bureau as "Indians." Some of these groups, like the Catawba and the Eastern Cherokee of North Carolina, the Seminoles of Florida, and the Choctaws of Mississippi, are of relatively pure Indian stock and are recognized as such by the government, but the majority are "Indians" by courtesy. They represent varying mixtures of white, Negro, and Indian blood, but as a rule the white strain predominates, and Indian culture is either very weak or extinct.

Most of these groups are small, but there were at least thirty which had 100 or more members in 1930, and there was one, the so-called Croatan Indian group centering in Robeson County, North Carolina, which totaled nearly 15,000 members.

Although these mixed-blood communities differ in numerous minor ways, there is one thing they all have in common: they have a social status which is intermediate between that of whites and Negroes. This results from two factors: their own determination not to be classed as Negroes, and the white people's determination not to accept them as white. Thus, suspended as they are between the white man's world and the Negro's world, they must live in a social world of their own, and it is this fact which brings them to our attention for sociological study.

To delimit the scope of this paper, I use this tentative classification: (1) those groups which are disintegrating and are being absorbed primarily

From Guy B. Johnson, "Personality in a White-Indian-Negro Community," in *American Sociological Review*, 4 (1939), pp. 516–523.

into the Negro group, (2) those which are being assimilated chiefly into the white group, (3) those which have established some degree of accommodation to the larger white and Negro worlds and are, for the present at least, functioning as intermediate groups. All of these groups have certain things in common, but those of the third type are more unique and more interesting because they are exceptions to the rigid biracial system in the South. Maintaining such groups involves a great deal of strain and it should be of some interest to observe problems of personal adjustment to which this gives rise. This paper is based upon field work among the largest and most significant of these groups, the so-called Croatan Indians of Robeson County, North Carolina.

A glimpse at the history of the Robeson County Indians is essential to an understanding of their present situation. Their early history is uncertain. Their origin goes back to early colonial days. In fact, they have been connected by some historians with America's greatest historical mystery, namely, the fate of Sir Walter Raleigh's Lost Colony of Roanoke Island (1587). The name, Croatan, which they once proudly claimed but which has fallen into disrepute among them (for reasons which I shall explain later) was derived from the Croatoan Indians, an Algonkin tribe which lived on the North Carolina coast in the sixteenth century and which befriended the Roanoke Island colonists. According to legend, the survivors of the colony mixed with the Croatoan Indians and moved inland to the swamps of Robeson County where the family names of some of the Roanoke colonists survive to this day.

Whether this story is true or not, it cannot account for the heterogeneous group now known as Indians in Robeson County. Much could have happened in the 140 years between the disappearance of Raleigh's colony and the settlement of Robeson County by Scotch and English. When the white people entered the area in the 1730's, they found a mixed-blood people inhabiting the swamps, living by fishing, hunting, and small farming, speaking an English dialect, and having an English type of culture. Mention of these people in colonial records was scarce, but when they were mentioned, they were referred to as "a roving band of mulattoes," or "a mixed and motley crew." They were listed in the early federal Censuses as "free colored." It seems safe to say that during the period of slavery the original nucleus, which may have been white-and-Indian, was augmented by runaway slaves, free Negroes, remnants of Indian tribes, and by all sorts of white adventurers. Only thus can we account for the heterogeneity of the present-day Robeson Indians.

These mixed, despised, and nameless people were classed as colored by the white people, but they cherished an intense desire to escape this stigma and be recognized as white. When the state constitution was revised in 1835, they were deprived of the suffrage, along with the free Negroes, and they were told that they could not attend the public schools for whites. Resentful, some of them built little one-room schools of their own, or kept their children out of school, rather than send them to school with Negroes.

The Civil War brought about a crisis which has much to do with the subsequent fortunes of these people. The white people tried to draft the Indians into the service of the Confederacy, assigning them to heavy duty along with Negroes. The Indians would express their resentment by going home. Bad feeling increased. One day in 1864, a group of Home Guards decided to make an example out of some of the Indians. They arrested three men of the Lowry family for desertion, took them into the woods, made them dig their own graves, and shot them down in cold blood. A younger member of the family, Henry Berry Lowry, is said to have witnessed the shooting from his hiding place. He organized a band of kinsmen and friends to avenge the killing of the Lowrys and history records that he was unusually successful. It was not until nearly eight years had passed and Robeson County had become the laughing stock of the nation that Henry Berry Lowry and his outlaw gang were killed. The truth was that Lowry was something of a Robin Hood; he had many friends among the whites.

In a sense, Henry Berry Lowry was the making of the Indians. He was their martyr and hero, and he focused attention upon their grievances in a dramatic way. A prominent white man took up their cause, discovered their legend of descent from the Lost Colony, and proposed a legislative solution to their problem. The legislature of 1885 passed an act which read in part as follows:

Whereas the Indians now living in Robeson County claim to be descendants of a friendly tribe who once resided in eastern North Carolina on the Roanoke River, known as the Croatan Indians; therefore,

The General Assembly of North Carolina do enact:

Section 1. That the said Indians and their descendants shall hereafter be designated and known as the Croatan Indians.

Section 2. That said Indians and their descendants shall have separate schools for their children, school committees of their own race and color, and shall be allowed to select teachers of their own choice, . . .

Thus the Croatans were set apart as a separate people, were given "a local habitation and a name." Their little social world developed remarkably. Schools, churches, and lodges prospered. The state even provided a special teachers' college for them. Their enumerated population grew by leaps and bounds, from 174 in 1890 to 3877 in 1900, and to 12,404 in 1930.

Today, Robeson County is a unique triracial laboratory. Its 66,000 population is distributed as follows: white, 47 per cent; Negro, 34 per cent; Indian, 19 per cent. If these Indians were *bona fide* Indians, the situation would not be unique, but since they have no trace of Indian culture and have a very small proportion of Indian blood, they constitute a glaring exception to the southern white man's dictum that a drop of Negro blood makes a man a Negro. The very existence of such a group is something of an anachronism.

We are now ready to enquire into the problem of the personality of the mixed bloods who form the middle caste in this triracial society. What are the points of strain and what personal adjustments are made?

The keystone in this problem is, of course, the white man's determination not to accept the Indian as his equal and, as far as possible, to put him into the same category as the Negro. In all of his relations with white people, this principle is either expressed or implied. The Indian is restricted to his own schools, and he is forbidden to marry a white person. He is supposed not to enter a white man's front door. He is not addressed as "mister" by white people and if he attends a theatre, he has to choose between one which provides a three-way segregation and one which seats him with Negroes. There is not an eating place in the county which permits him to enter the front door and eat with the white people. In numerous subtle ways, by glances, gestures, and intonations, he is reminded by whites and Negroes of the unmentionable stigma which attaches to him.

The Indian, then, is forever on the defensive. He feels that there is always a question mark hanging over him. His wish to escape the stigma of Negro kinship, and thus to be identified with the white man, is uppermost in his mind. It is this wish which dominates his behavior and determines his modes of personal adjustment to the other races.

One of the chief sources of mental conflict in the Indian arises from his Negroid physical traits. In 1885, when the Indians were legally declared a separate race and were named Croatan, they faced the problem of deciding just who was Indian and who was not. They wanted to weed out those who were considered "undesirables," but it was difficult for them to draw the line. They evidently fell back on a sort of pragmatic definition, viz.: an Indian is a person called an Indian by other Indians. It was as if they had said, "All right, everyone who is already in can stay in, but woe unto anybody with Negro blood who tries to get in hereafter." At their request, the legislature passed two laws which strengthened their position. One of these provided "that all marriages between a Croatan Indian and a Negro, or between an Indian and a person of Negro descent to the third generation, inclusive, shall be utterly void." Another provided "that there shall be excluded from such separate schools for the said Croatan Indians all children of the Negro race to the fourth generation." The Indians themselves were to be final judges on matters of genealogy.

It is certain that very little new Negro blood has found its way into the group in recent times. However, the Croatans today are undoubtedly one of the most heterogeneous groups ever brought together under one name. They range from pink skin, blue eyes, and flaxen hair to unmistakably Negroid color, hair, and other features. Many could pass for white anywhere else, and many would be taken for Negroes anywhere else. Even in the same family, the children often have a wide range of color and hair types. Every growing child notices these things and ponders over them. He learns that it is taboo to discuss such things. He learns that the ultimate insult that anyone can give an Indian is to intimate that he has Negro blood. He stands ready to defend his personal honor and the honor of his whole group from such intimations from any source. So intense is the feeling on this subject that one can only conclude that there is present in many persons a certain "sense of guilt" which arises from the observed reality and which calls for constant denial of the reality.

As might be expected, the strength of this color prejudice varies with the physical types. The whiter Indians seem to worry less over this matter. While they resent any attacks on the "purity" of the Indians as a group, they feel less than the darker people the necessity for personal justification. They travel about a good deal and find that they are taken for white or for Indian-white mixtures. Their very appearance is a badge of security. Indeed, they feel that if all of the Indians were like them there would be no problem. They blame the dark Indians for the stigma attached to the group and they hate them for it, but their hatred must be kept below the surface.

The darker Indians, on the other hand, are apt to be more sensitive on the matter of physical features. Their chances for unpleasant experiences are, of course, greater, and they feel more keenly the impulse to "whiten" their ancestry. Furthermore, they are jealous of the whiter Indians. Thus there is an incipient but never openly admitted cleavage between the darker Indians and the lighter ones.

The hypersensitiveness of the Croatans has led them on several occasions to drive out people who were offshoots from the main body and who came in from adjoining counties to take advantage of the Indian schools. The excuse was always, "We can't be sure about these people. We think they have Negro blood." Incidentally, some of these rejected people petitioned for a special set of schools for their benefit, but school officials threw up their hands and declared that three school systems were enough.

Another aspect of the Croatans' struggle for a status of respectability is their concern over their history and their group name. When the legislature of 1885 gave them the name "Croatan" and, by implication, recognized their Lost Colony legend, it was trying to present them with a proud past and a good name, but the name "Croatan" soon went sour. For the first time, the whites and Negroes had a term which they could apply to these hitherto nameless people. They pronounced it with a sort of sneer or they shortened it to "Cro"—with the all too obvious implication. It soon became a fighting term, and for many years it has been virtually taboo in the presence of Indians.

Now the Indians were divided for a time over the merits and demerits of "Croatan," but the majority of them finally embraced a theory that there was really nothing to the Lost Colony legend and that "Croatan" was not their true name. Accordingly, they got the legislature in 1911 to strike out the word "Croatan," leaving their name simply "Indians of Robeson County." Thus, they were willing to give up their Lost Colony legend for the removal of the curse of "Croatan."

The vagueness of the word "Indian" was a challenge to them, because it was in a way an admission that they did not know what they were. So a new theory of history came to the front: they were really Cherokee. They again asked the legislature for help, and in 1913, over the protest of the Eastern Cherokee of the Great Smoky Mountains, they were legally named "Cherokee Indians of Robeson County." The law bore the flattering title, "An act to restore to the Indians of Robeson and adjoining counties their rightful and ancient name." But no one ever calls them Cherokee, and the problem of the name keeps gnawing at their consciousness. Lately, there has been a shift in tactics. Some of their more literate men have searched history and ethnology and have concluded that the group originated from the remnants of the Siouan tribes which once lived in central North Carolina. For several years now they have been begging Uncle Sam to name them "Siouan Tribes of Lumber River" and to take them under his wing as wards of the federal government. This, according to one young Indian, would settle the problem once and for all.

In various other ways, the Indians are striving to construct a history which will do them justice. Most significant is their attitude toward Henry Berry Lowry and the outlaw years. They reject the picture of Lowry as murderer and outlaw and substitute a picture of a warm-hearted, courageous man who chose to fight in order that his people might not forever be oppressed, and what is more striking, some of the Indians have refused to let Lowry die. They contend that he escaped from Robeson County in 1872 and that he still lives in some faraway secret place. Others admit that he was killed in 1872, but they insist that he killed himself accidentally with his own gun.

The situations which I have discussed thus far are largely situations which can be met by subjective adjustments. The Indian can deny or affirm this or that, can invent theories to fit the exigencies of the situation, but what does he do when the realities of the caste structure call for more overt behavior? Apparently, he takes some of the sting out of the realities of caste by avoiding as far as possible those situations which are most heavily charged with caste meaning. Here, again, the answer seems to be that he "corrects" the reality in accordance with his wish. In so far as possible, he conducts himself in such a way that the unpleasant reality is negated. He avoids theatres where his only choice is to sit with Negroes. If he must eat in town, he either takes along a lunch or patronizes an open-air "hot-dog" stand rather than sit with Negroes in the back room of a cafe.

In his work, the Indian's aim is to have as little to do with white people as possible. He thereby reduces his chances of being insulted. His economic outlook is greatly restricted because he will not engage in various menial tasks which Negroes engage in. His ideal is to own a farm and be his own master. With the exception of a handful of teachers, preachers, and small shopkeepers, the Indians are all farmers. They are especially expert in tobacco culture. When they are tenants for white farmers they advertise their difference from the Negro by refusing to take the subservient role of the Negro. I asked an Indian tenant how he got along with his landlord. "Oh, all right," he replied, "I don't have any more to do with him than I have to. I never go to his house, because I don't want to have any trouble with him." By this, he meant that if he went to the white man's house the white man would expect him to go to the back door—then there might be trouble. The white farmers, for their part, recognize this independence of the Indian when they say, "If you want a tenant to take care of your land and make money, get an Indian. *But don't try to boss him.* He wears his pride like a sore thumb."

Thus, the Indian avoids some caste situations and brings about some degree of modification in others by sheer pride and belligerence; but he cannot avoid or negate everything. He knows well enough that the restrictions and prohibitions are there, whether he tests them out or not, and he carries a constant sense of frustration and tension.

In civic and political affairs the Indian meets with further frustration. He sees his vote count for almost nothing because of the wiles of the County Democratic Machine. He sees his one little town, Pembroke, his social center and seat of his normal school, taken over largely by white merchants. He sees the selection of town officers removed from his own control and placed in the hands of the legislature so that white people can be appointed. He has been, from Reconstruction days until the past year, without representation on any jury in Robeson County. He sees instances of brutality on the part of officers of the law. He sees many things which make his blood boil, and he feels utterly powerless to do anything about them. He feels that his little world is carefully guarded, controlled, and exploited by the white man. He is blocked at every point, yet he cannot give up the struggle, for to do so would be to admit that he is no better than the Negro. So he lives in this continuing state of compromise between the world of the white man and the world of the black man.

It might be expected that a group which has to meet the situations which the Croatans face would produce a great many bitter, aggressive, and desperate persons who would strike back at the white man in various ways, but this is not the case—at least, up to the present. Minor altercations occur occasionally, but assaults and homicides against white persons are rare. The Indian is noted for his restraint in this respect. It has long been said in Robeson County that whatever else may be said about the Indian, he never molests a white woman. In November 1938, when an Indian was convicted of rape on a white woman, the judge of the county court delivered a dramatic denunciation of the prisoner for having broken this long and enviable record. If the situation of the Indian produces bitterness toward the white man, it also produces caution and a sense of the futility of violence except as a last resort.

In the Indian's own world, there seems to be some evidences of the disorganizing effect of his anomalous social position. There are certain families and certain neighborhoods which are known as "tough," and these produce an unusual amount of drunkenness, assault, and homicide. Whether this represents a primary result of caste status is difficult to say, but I am inclined to believe that it is in some measure correlated with the frustration experiences of the Indian and with certain cleavages in the Indian community.

These cleavages are probably of major importance for the understanding of interpersonal relations within the Indian community. They are roughly correlated with physical traits, and yet it is probable that the latter have no genetic significance. At the bottom of the social scale are the darker Indians. They are on the whole poorer than the others, they are conscious of what others think of their appearance, and they are jealous of the lighter Indians. They are credited with a good deal of what is sometimes called "hell-raising." Next come the intermediate Indians. They are a little too dark to pass as white and they are especially sensitive to physical appearance. They envy the lighter ones and resent the darker ones, and they incline to be the militant, agitating type. Finally, there are the "white" Indians. They could pass for white almost anywhere. On the whole, they have a better economic status, a better education, and higher prestige. These color cleavages are a tabooed subject with the Indians, and yet they permeate the whole society. They are no doubt at the bottom of much of the violent crime of Indian against Indian. They also have something to do with the lack of strong group solidarity, the presence of factions, and the timidity of leaders.

I should not leave the impression, however, that the Indians are typically disorganized and unstable. On the contrary, most of them lead relatively calm, moderate, and industrious lives. They have a strong sentimental attachment to their native soil, and in spite of all their troubles, relatively few of them seek escape through permanent migration. They are perhaps one more example of the well-known adaptability of the human personality. Apparently, when people have work to do, have strong community institutions and a few things to be proud of, they can adjust their thought-ways and behavior so as to absorb a great deal of emotional strain.

This situation, however, is by no means static. It is difficult to conceive of a community like the Croatan community surviving indefinitely. It seems likely that the Indian will rebel more and more against his caste status. Education, wider travel, and reading, are already beginning to have their effects. The changing situation will produce personalities who no longer see virtue in patience and compromise. The Indians are becoming more group conscious. They have recently demanded the right to serve on juries, they are talking of running for political office, and they are saying among themselves that "if things don't get better we may have to start killing." The future holds interesting and unpleasant possibilities.

E. K. Francis

MULTIPLE INTERGROUP RELATIONS IN THE UPPER RIO GRANDE REGION

The term "intergroup relations" somehow conjures up the mental image of several organisms interacting with each other on the same plane, and struggling for the pre-eminence or at least preservation of their particular ways of life. Actually, an ethnic group is a segmental social system operating within a large society which has precisely the function of organizing a great variety of groups, including ethnic groups, into a complex unit.[1] Thus, the dominant is not at all of the same order as the ethnic group, and their relationship cannot be explained by differences in culture, power or size alone.[2] Moreover, what is sometimes conceived as one particular ethnic or culture group may in reality consist of several different sections which are differently related to the large society and occupy different positions in its structure. By analyzing a particular case, this paper draws attention to some factors which must be taken into account in any attempt to describe adequately the relationship of an ethnic group to the large society. The dynamic nature of such relations makes a rapid, even crude, summary of the ethnic history of the Upper Rio Grande Region the most appropriate approach to our problem.

As is well known, the area had been inhabited by several communities of Pueblo Indians before it was conquered and colonized by the Spaniards. Consequently, the originally separate native societies were integrated into a social system which was an extension of the large society of colonial Spain. The intergroup relations were based upon force and domination,

From E. K. Francis, "Multiple Intergroup Relations in the Upper Rio Grande Region," in *American Sociological Review*, 21 (1956), pp. 84–87.

but involved also more intimate interactions. First, there was the common need of defense against an external enemy, the Plains Indians. Second, the economy favored exchange and a certain division of labor. Still more crucial was the fact that the Spaniards imposed upon the native folk groups an heteronomous institutional framework which nevertheless, left them considerable freedom to manage their internal affairs. This institutional framework extended primarily to the political, military, and economic sphere. The Spaniards also occupied all the strategic positions in the emerging regional society in which a total social system of Spanish design, the large society, was combined with several localized folk societies or ethnic groups. Finally, the Christianization of the Indians made them equal members of a religious system which formed an integral part of Spanish society. It implied a sharing of important values and co-operation in very decisive activities such as religious ceremonies. Still more significant, intermarriage was not only made possible but actually enforced by the church where sexual contact could not be avoided.[3]

On the eve of the American conquest the social structure consisted of a thin layer of upper-class Spaniards, a broad peasant substratum of Spanish colonial culture and mixed racial origin, and several semi-autonomous communities of Pueblo Indians, while the Plains Indians remained outside the pale. There had also existed since the 1820's a little colony of foreigners who mingled freely with the natives. The position of these *Americanos*,[4] soon to be strengthened through further immigration, was changed radically when the army of occupation entrusted them with the key positions of civil administration. Yet the new situation was not really characterized by either culture conflict or the coexistence of two separate and distinctive social bodies. For the Americanos continued to participate directly in the indigenous Hispano society, although, because of their newly won influence and prestige, they now associated primarily with the native upper class with whom they intermarried to a considerable degree. The new upper class was, if anything, more Spanish-American than Anglo-American. The decisive shift occurred rather on the institutional level. It was above all a question of who had the power to interpret and enforce the rules of the game, mainly in the economic, political and legal sphere, and who selected and controlled the personnel for all strategic positions in the territory. The number of *Anglos* was small, their inner coherence vague and their cultural contributions indifferent, but their direct and indirect power was real. Moreover, they functioned as representatives of the large society upon which the *Hispanos* now depended, and which had the final word in all controversial matters. It was this relationship which transformed New

Mexico's native people into an ethnic group or minority. In passing we might mention that the Pueblo Indians at first continued to identify themselves with the old order, but that they gradually drifted away from the Hispano-dominated society into Anglo-American tutelage.

Almost a full generation later, intergroup relations changed again when a mighty stream of immigrants from all walks of life entered the Territory. While united administratively, the country was thereby divided sociologically into two sections, the Old Spanish Core and the New Settlement.[5] In the former the Hispano society remained largely intact, and so did the relations to the large society and to its local representatives which had developed in the early days of the occupation. The other section, however, was first effectively occupied by Americans and became indistinguishable from the rest of America. It was largely dominated by the *Texanos* who to the Hispanos appeared almost as another race; they were enemies and intruders while the Anglos in their own midst constituted a component of the indigenous society. Of course, the case is oversimplified to stress a real difference. The Hispanos, on the other hand, who migrated from the Old Core into the New Settlement found themselves in quite a different position which resembled much more that which was, for instance, typical of the French Canadians crossing the border to New England. In order to distinguish between these two types of intergroup relations the term "primary" and "derivative" minority groups are used.[6] The former applies to situations like the one found in New Mexico's Old Core; the latter describes conditions as they prevail in most other parts of the United States. At one time, this cleavage was clearly reflected in the economy of New Mexico. The small farms in the irrigated valleys and on the more humid mountain slopes were occupied by Hispanos who also held a monopoly over sheep grazing. Cattle ranching and dry farming, however, were the domain of Texans and other "Americans," who included many readily assimilated foreigners from overseas. Less complete yet clearly perceptible was the separation in other branches of the regional economy where the upper ranks were heavily weighted in favor of the Anglos, while Hispanos were found, often in large numbers, among the lower ranks and unskilled labor.

Today the division between Old Core and New Settlement has become blurred inasmuch as the Hispano society itself is being transformed from a primary into a derivative ethnic group, to a large extent because migratory labor, military service, mass communications and education[7] have tended to increase interaction with the dominant. Because education followed the pattern of the large society, its area of institutional dominance was vastly increased and affected a more sensitive sphere of the minority culture than could be reached by politics, economy or law. While mere accommodation sufficed before, the dominant now aimed at cultural homogeneity which involved the remodelling of the minority after its own image. Political and economic domination was replaced by cultural imperialism.

Under its impact the social structure has changed again. The old upper class has been reduced to near insignificance. Superior wealth, power, and prestige now reside outside the region. Simultaneously, the regional class structure has become a replica of the American class structure. The center of gravity and group conflict is now in the middle class which includes a far greater proportion of Anglos. Middle-class occupations offer much fewer opportunities to Hispanos, whose principal social elevators are confined to politics and education. American middle class standards of cultural uniformity are fully operative. They find their familiar expression in racial prejudice and discrimination. But there are also real cultural differences which handicap the Hispanos: they simply do not possess the qualifications recognized as conditions for social acceptance and advancement. The broad substratum of society is composed mainly of Hispano, and in part Indian peasants and laborers. Locally, the old Hispano social system still functions, but it has been deprived of its natural élite and economic base without which it cannot maintain its closure and independence.[8] Hispanos strive now as individuals to improve their lot within the framework of American society. They resent the blocks which prevent them from equal participation and from rising in social status, but they accept as valid the conditions under which social advancement is possible in this country.

The acceptance of American social definitions is also demonstrated by the effort of the Hispanos to differentiate themselves from the Mexicans, that is, more recent immigrants from Mexico, in order to escape the treatment accorded to foreigners and "colored" races. There is also much less co-operation between Hispanos and Indians than before. The sense of a common destiny has disappeared which once had united Pueblo Indians and Hispano peasants under the leadership of the Hispano upper class and the native clergy[9] against the American aggressors. The two groups keep well apart from each other. The Indians, who have come under the influence of American schools and other means of cultural diffusion, now deal directly with the large society and its agents. There is some advantage in being classified as an Indian rather than a Spanish-American or Mexican. The Hispanos, on the other hand, have accepted the American color scheme and find a sense of superiority and a certain protection against discrimination in their European cultural and racial heritage. The distinction between Texanos and Anglos can still be recognized. The former are apt to define their relations with the Hispanos in the racial terms of the South. This is felt as an embarrassment by the Anglos who are more ready to look upon the Hispanos as just another Old World culture group to be integrated into the American melting pot. The complexity of intergroup relations in the Upper Rio Grande Region is further increased through the presence of smaller yet locally important Old World ethnic groups such as the Jews and Syrians. Because of their greater linguistic, religious and cultural affinity to the Hispanos, the Italians, French, and French Canadians appear ethnically ambivalent. Another complication is introduced by the great variety of Indian folk societies which had to be neglected in this short paper.[10]

The foregoing sketch seems to indicate that in the analysis of intergroup relations it is not sufficient to treat the dominant and the ethnic groups as social systems functioning separately on the same level, or to stress differences in their cultural heritage. This relationship is more significantly determined by the institutional framework within which all the components of an ethnically mixed society must operate. It is heteronomous to the minority but not to the dominant. Attention must be paid not only to the degrees of heteronomy and cultural differences. It is equally important to know which spheres of ethnic group life are, partially or wholly, regulated by the large society and its organs. Other significant factors include the control of strategic positions in a regional society as well as the class position of the representatives of the large society with whom ethnics interact most frequently and directly.

In conclusion it should be pointed out that in a complex society the conditions and problems of different parts of one and the same ethnic group may vary greatly according to their position in the total social structure, both vertically and horizontally. Among the factors which favor disorganization of so-called primary ethnic groups are shifts in size and power as well as increasing communication and interaction. But above all the dislocation is due to the extension of the institutional framework, which the large society imposes upon the ethnic group, to ever wider and more sensitive spheres of social and personal life. Once disorganized, a primary ethnic group need not disappear through the successful assimilation of its members. It may persist in the modified form of a derivative ethnic group which is characterized by quite different behavior patterns. No longer does such a group possess an inner coherence and a group solidarity which is able to resist the cultural and social pressures of the large society and which is often strong enough to absorb its local representatives. A derivative ethnic group is rather determined by social categorizations and definitions adopted from the large society, and by the qualifications required from individuals for direct participation in its various strata.

NOTES

1. As a rule, the term "ethnic group" is used in a very narrow sense which also colors the current sociological meaning of "intergroup relations." Both refer to politically and socially dependent groups and tend to exclude from sociological consideration the relations between independent ethnic groups or people studied more commonly by historians, political scientists, and ethnologists. It would be good sociological theory if both kinds of intergroup relations were viewed systematically as two species of the same genus rather than as separate compartments to be dealt with by different learned disciplines.

Sociologists have vaguely applied the term "large society" to the "obvious" but undefined residue of a modern nation after it has been divested of all those particular institutions, associations, subgroups, classes, minorities, and so on, with which contemporary members of the profession are mostly concerned. Despite its shortcomings, the term is accepted because it does not imply a commitment to any particular type of total society.

2. The term "dominant," instead of the conventional but misleading phrase "dominant group," has been adopted from Charles F. Marden, *Minorities in American Society* (New York: American Book Company, 1952), p. 29.

Sociologically speaking a "minority" may actually be larger than the "majority."

3. For the sake of brevity the very interesting case of the *Genizaros* must be disregarded. These Christianized and Hispanized descendants of captives from among the various tribes of Plains Indians have been completely absorbed by the Hispano ethnic group. To them several Spanish places in New Mexico owe their origin, e.g. Abiquiu, Belen or San Miguel. The Mexican interlude (1821–1846) is also passed over. But this changed little if anything in the intergroup relations of New Mexico itself except that during these years a local variety of Spanish colonial society was developed which, due to political animosity and lack of communication, became more and more distinct from the parent society.

4. The Spanish words have been retained because they seem less ambiguous than their often cumbersome English equivalents. The more recent word for "Americanos" is "Anglos" to signify that New Mexico's Hispanos, too, are Americans.

5. The Old Core includes the Rio Grande valley between Socorro and Taos with later contiguous expansions into the Chama, Pecos, Mora, and Puerco valleys as well as the original sections of several towns now predominantly Anglo-Saxon like Albuquerque or Las Vegas. The Doña Ana area near El Paso, Texas, has been omitted from these considerations because of its peculiar history. What has been called here the New Settlement includes the rest of New Mexico and all the more recent towns and cities. Some of it appears more as an extension of Texas than a part of the Upper Rio Grande Region with which it is united administratively in the State of New Mexico; it is, in fact, locally referred to as "Little Texas."

6. Cf. E. K. Francis, "Variables in the Formation of So-Called 'Minority Groups,' " *American Journal of Sociology*, 59 (July 1954), pp. 6–14.

7. The term "education," as used here, refers not only to the public school, always a powerful agent of assimilation, but also to many activities of churches and voluntary associations.

8. Today most Hispanos do not see any particular value in the preservation of their own society and culture; at any rate they do not see any realistic hope for it.

9. The role of the Mexican clergy in this struggle and their displacement through foreign, primarily French, missionaries is treated by the author in an as yet unpublished essay, "Padre Martinez: A New-Mexican Myth."

10. A book-length presentation is now being prepared in order to do justice to the actual multiplicity of ethnic relations in the Upper Rio Grande Region, under the tentative title: "Die spanischen Bergbauern im neumexikanischen Oberland: Das Schicksal einer amerikanischen Minderheit."

CULTURAL PLURALISM AND LINGUISTIC EQUILIBRIUM IN SWITZERLAND

Next to its scenic beauty, what fascinates the whole world most about Switzerland is the amazing spectacle of its cultural pluralism which is nevertheless integrated into a stable and harmonious unity. Switzerland is the famous and oft-quoted exception to the rule in contemporary Europe that marks of cultural diversity generally serve as rallying points for hate and conflict. No wonder that "the concept of Switzerland as a microcosm, an orderly little world of its own, reflecting the reconciled components of the greater, but disorderly, world around it, has caught the fancy of not a few dispensers of good advice,"[1] and has been held up as a shining example for a sick world to follow.

The phenomenon of Swiss harmony, however, is often only imperfectly understood. Historically the Swiss nation has originated from the desire of a group of heterogeneous communities to preserve their local independence through a system of mutual defense alliances. As a result of this long and often very stormy historical process, the Swiss have finally learned to blend their cultural differences into a national equilibrium. Today they no longer regard their cultural heterogeneity as an obstacle to the perpetuation of national unity and political stability. To a large extent this national equilibrium rests on an underlying balance of demographic factors which is not always perceived. Even the Swiss themselves do not commonly realize how fortunate it is for Swiss harmony that the basic

From Kurt Mayer, "Cultural Pluralism and Linguistic Equilibrium," in *American Sociological Review*, 16 (1951), pp. 157–163.

demographic equilibrium has remained practically undisturbed for more than a century. The two most important ingredients of Swiss cultural pluralism are the ethnic-linguistic and the religious structure of the Swiss population. This paper will be concerned only with the former.

Data on the linguistic composition of the Swiss population have been collected since the Census of 1850, but the methods of enumeration have varied somewhat. In 1850 it was attempted to ascertain the linguistic distribution of the population on the basis of the official language spoken in each community, while in the censuses of 1860 and 1870 the language spoken in each household was recorded. Only since the Census of 1880 has each individual been enumerated by the language spoken. The Swiss Census asks for the "usual" or customary language of the individual; only in the case of children who cannot talk is the "mother" tongue recorded. No questions are asked about knowledge of other languages.

TABLE 6-1

Percentage Distribution of the Swiss
Population by Language, 1850-1941

Years	German	French	Italian	Romansh	Other
1850	70.2	22.6	5.4	1.8	—
1880	71.3	21.4	5.7	1.4	0.2
1888	71.4	21.8	5.3	1.3	0.2
1900	69.8 ·	22.0	6.7	1.2	0.3
1910	69.1	21.1	8.1	1.1	0.6
1920	70.9	21.2	6.2	1.1	0.6
1930	71.9	20.4	6.0	1.1	0.6
1941	72.6	20.7	5.2	1.1	0.4

Source: *Statistisches Jahrbuch der Schweiz. 1948.*

The national languages of Switzerland are German, French, Italian, and Romansh, all of which are expressly recognized as equal in the Federal Constitution. They are, however quite unequal in importance: the French-, Italian-, and Romansh-speaking Swiss are outnumbered by the German-speaking Swiss almost three to one. As Table 6-1 shows, no changes have occurred in the relative position of each of the four national languages since 1850; in fact, the linguistic composition of the population has remained remarkably stable on the whole. From 1850 to 1941 roughly 70 per cent of the Swiss population have always been German-speaking and a little above 20 per cent have been French-speaking. Indeed, the same relation between these two most important languages seems to have obtained even earlier; according to an estimate approximately 22 per cent of the population spoke French, and at least 70 per cent spoke German in 1798.[2]

From 1850 to 1880 only very minor shifts occurred between the language groups; moreover, due to the different methods of enumeration the figures of 1850 and 1880 are not strictly comparable. From 1880 to 1910 somewhat greater changes took place; the proportion of both the German-speaking and the French-speaking decreased somewhat while the Italian-speaking rose from 5.7 to 8.1 per cent. The explanation lies in a strong wave of Italian immigration: whereas only 42,000 Italian citizens resided in Switzerland in 1880, their number had increased to 203,000 by 1910. After the outbreak of the first World War, however, a large proportion of the Italians returned home, and consequently the percentage of Italian-speakers in Switzerland was again reduced. Since 1910 the language distribution has been enumerated separately for Swiss citizens and for alien residents. Table 6–2 shows that the proportion of Italian-

TABLE 6-2

Percentage Distribution of Swiss Citizens and of Alien Residents by Language, 1910-1941

Years	German	French	Italian	Romansh	Other
Swiss Citizens					
1910	72.7	22.1	3.9	1.2	0.1
1920	73.0	21.7	4.0	1.2	0.1
1930	73.7	21.0	4.0	1.2	0.1
1941	73.9	20.9	3.9	1.1	0.2
Alien Residents					
1910	48.6	15.3	32.1	0.2	3.8
1920	52.3	17.6	25.0	0.2	4.9
1930	53.2	14.7	26.3	0.2	5.6
1941	49.1	18.1	27.7	0.4	4.7

Source: *Statistisches Jahrbuch der Schweiz, 1948.*

speaking Swiss has remained practically stable since 1910; the fluctuations of the Italian language are therefore entirely attributable to the migrations of Italian citizens.

Not all the shifts in the linguistic structure are due to international migrations, however. Apart from the fluctuations of Italian, it is evident from tables 6–1 and 6–2 that in recent decades the German language has been gaining slightly on the French, not only in the population as a

TABLE 6-3

The Birth Rates of the Swiss Cantons,
1901-1910 and 1941-1948

Cantons	Live Births per 1,000 Population	
	1901-1910	1941-1948
German-Speaking:		
Zurich	24.4	17.4
Berne[a]	29.0	20.6
Lucerne	27.7	21.9
Uri	32.7	25.3
Schwyz	28.6	22.2
Obwalden	28.5	24.6
Nidwalden	29.7	27.0
Glarus	22.6	19.2
Zug	25.8	21.3
Solothurn	30.8	21.2
Basel-Stadt	25.1	15.0
Basel-Land	25.7	18.3
Schaffhausen	24.8	19.8
Appenzell Ausser-Rhoden	26.7	17.2
Appenzell Inner-Rhoden	32.2	19.8
St. Gall	28.0	20.5
Grisons[b]	24.7	21.3
Aargau	27.5	21.0
Thurgau	25.4	19.8
French-Speaking:		
Vaud	24.7	16.5
Neuchatel	24.5	15.2
Geneva	17.9	12.6
Preponderantly French-Speaking:		
Fribourg[c]	33.4	23.2
Valais[d]	30.0	24.7
Italian-Speaking:		
Ticino	29.0	15.9
Switzerland Total	26.9	19.2

Source: *Statistiches Jahrbuch der Schweiz, 1948.*

[a]In 1941, 83.6 per cent of the population spoke German, while 15.4 per cent spoke French.

[b]In 1941, 54.9 per cent of the population spoke German, 31.3 per cent spoke Romansh, and 12.8 per cent spoke Italian.

[c]In 1941, 66.8 per cent of the population spoke French, 32.4 per cent spoke German.

[d]In 1941, 65.5 per cent of the population spoke French, 33.2 per cent spoke German.

whole, but also among the Swiss citizens themselves. The explanation must be sought in the considerable fertility differentials which exist between the French- and the German-speaking areas of the country. As Table 6–3 shows, the three wholly French-speaking cantons—Geneva, Neuchatel, and Vaud—have had considerably lower birth rates than most of the German-speaking cantons. This difference, which has widened since the turn of the century, has been only partly offset by the relatively high fertility rates of the preponderantly French-speaking but less populous cantons Fribourg and Valais.

These differences in fertility, which are not offset by differential mortality[3] would undoubtedly lead to a greater ascendancy of the German language and to serious threats to the traditional linguistic equilibrium, were it not for the effects of internal migrations. French is spoken in a compact territorial area which comprises the western part of the country, while German is the language of the central and eastern regions, and Italian is spoken only south of the Alps. (See tne accompanying language map, figure 6–1.) However, ever since the Constitution of 1848 guaranteed freedom of migration and settlement within the whole country, increasing numbers of persons have moved across the language boundaries. As Table 6–4 shows, the Census of 1930 enumerated 114,000 German-speaking persons living in French language territory, but only 53,000 French-speaking individuals living in the German language areas. Thus, the French regions of the country have proved much more attractive to German-speaking migrants than the German regions have to the French-speaking Swiss. Now, the migrants tend to become rapidly assimilated to the new language. This is especially the case with their children who can use only the official language of the region in school. As a matter of empirical fact, therefore, migration regularly involves an eventual change of language: the second generation no longer uses the tongue of its parents but the official language of the area as its customary language. The 114,-000 German-speaking persons who lived in French-language territory in 1930 must therefore be considered as a reservoir for the French language.

Assimilation takes place, of course, among the migrants to all the four language zones, but it is especially rapid in French Switzerland where German is taught only quite perfunctorily in the schools, while French is given much more emphasis as a second language in the schools of both German and Italian Switzerland. Although there are unfortunately no statistics available on the subject, it is a well-known fact that French is the second language of a very large number of German-Swiss, especially those connected with commerce and business, while the reverse is not nearly

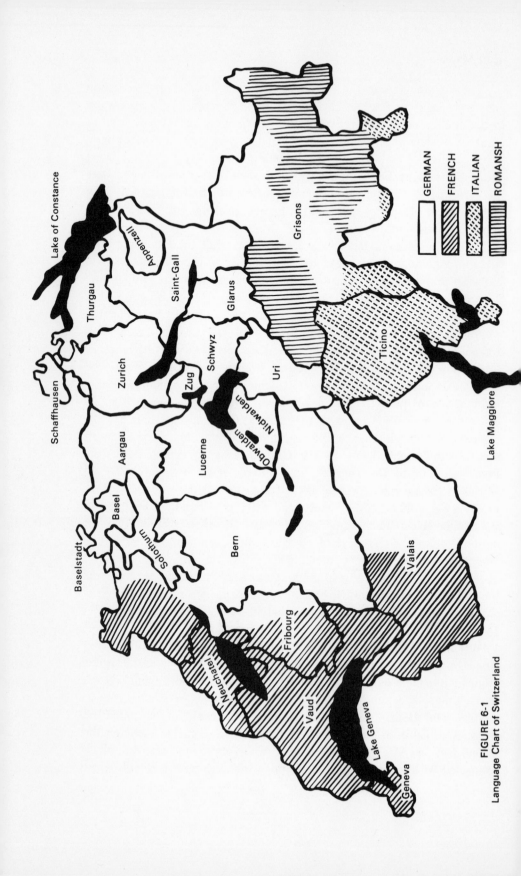

FIGURE 6-1
Language Chart of Switzerland

GERMAN
FRENCH
ITALIAN
ROMANSH

Lake of Constance

Schaffhausen

Thurgau

Appenzell

Saint-Gall

Glarus

Grisons

Zurich

Schwyz

Zug

Uri

Aargau

Basel

Lucerne

Obwalden

Nidwalden

Solothurn

Bern

Valais

Ticino

Lake Maggiore

Neuchâtel

Fribourg

Vaud

Lake Geneva

Geneva

TABLE 6-4

Population of Switzerland by Language
Area and Language Spoken, 1930

Language Spoken	Language Areas Numbers in 000's				
	German	French	Italian	Romansh	Total
German	2,791	114	12	6	2,924
French	53	776	1	—	830
Italian	56	28	157	2	243
Romansh	10	1	—	33	44
Other	10	14	1	—	25
Total	2,921	933	171	41	4,066

Source: W. Ott, "Sprache," in *Die Bevoelkerung der Schweiz* (1939), p. 20.

as true.[4] This difference is, of course, a factor in migration: knowing French fairly well, many German-Swiss find it easy to live in French Switzerland, while the French-Swiss find the language difference to be a barrier.[5]

In general, there is a widespread misconception abroad that every Swiss speaks all the national languages and possibly English as well. In fact, most Swiss know only one language well, although it is true that the proportion of those who have a more or less extensive command of other languages than their own is much greater in Switzerland than in most other countries of the world. A knowledge of several languages is essential in a country so dependent on foreign trade and on foreign tourists, and it is therefore not surprising that a working knowledge of foreign languages is a prerequisite for many jobs in the fields of commerce and finance, transport and communications, and, above all, in the hotel industry.

The facts, then, are that although Switzerland maintains more than one official language, the four national languages are spoken in clearly defined territorial areas. There is no extensive mixture of divergent tongues; the linguistic boundaries are generally clear (even though the French-German line splits some communities right down the middle); and the individual Swiss are no more bilingual or multilingual than are people in other countries, although it is true that a good many of them have a good working knowledge of several languages in addition to their own.

High mountains mark off the boundaries between the Italian-speaking zone and the rest of Switzerland, thus preserving the Italian language area intact; but the dividing line between the French- and German-speaking zones is not marked by any natural boundaries. This is a purely historical line created at the end of the fifth century A.D. by the influx of German-speaking Alemanni into the territory previously occupied by another Germanic tribe, the Burgundians, who had, however, become Latinized. The line dividing the settlements of the Latin-speaking Burgundians and those of the Germanic-speaking Alemanni eventually evolved into the language boundary between the French- and the German-speaking zones of Switzerland. In an age where ethnic diversity has become the focal point of raving nationalism, it is rather amusing to note that the ethnic origin of the French- and the German-speaking Swiss seems to have been the same; but it is true, of course, that the linguistic differences maintained over 1,500 years have led to fundamental cultural divergences between the French- and the German-Swiss.

The dividing line between these two major language areas has remained remarkably stable throughout the centuries although numerous minor changes have occurred in time. The line recognizes no cantonal boundaries: the northwest portion of Berne speaks French while the rest of the canton speaks German (84 per cent); the canton Fribourg is split into a larger French-speaking (67 per cent) and a smaller German-speaking section, and the same is true of the Valais where 66 per cent speak French. (See Figure 6–1.) Such minor changes as have occurred in the nineteenth and twentieth centuries have been in favor of the French zone which has expanded slightly in the canton of Berne and especially in the Valais where a couple of formerly German-speaking communities have acquired French-speaking majorities as the result of migrations and have accordingly switched their official language.[6]

In the fourteen cantons entirely within the German-speaking area, German is the only official language for all legal relations with cantonal authorities; in the three cantons which are completely inside the French zone, French is the only official language, as is Italian in the canton Ticino; but three of the cantons are officially bilingual, and one is trilingual. In Berne, Fribourg, and Valais, German and French are both official, although in Berne, German, and in Fribourg, French enjoy the privilege of being the original language in which the cantonal Constitution and the laws are drafted, and according to which they are, in case of doubt, to be construed. In the Grisons, German, Italian, and Romansh are all three declared to be official languages, but German, spoken by 55 per cent, is given preference over the other two.[7]

Romansh, a peculiar tongue of Latin origin, has been maintained by the descendants of the native Rhaetii in the Grisons canton without interruption from Roman times to the present day. Spoken by only 46,000 people in Switzerland, it is a branch of the Rhaeto-Romanic tongue which is also spoken in parts of the Italian Tyrol and Friuli, and it has an old and extensive literature. The Romansh language area is entirely located in the Grisons canton. It is the only one of the Swiss language areas which has been shrinking as a result of encroachment by the German language. This has been largely due to the tourist trade which has brought German-speakers into some originally Romansh communities that have become internationally famous tourist centers, such as St. Moritz, for example. Partly as an effort to stem this adverse tide, Romansh was elevated to the dignity of a fourth national language in 1938 through an amendment to the constitution adopted by a popular vote. Whether this can stop the shrinkage of its language area remains to be seen.

The linguistic equilibrium manifest in the multilingual principle is of fairly recent historical origin. Up to 1798 German was the only official language of the Swiss Confederation, in which all official documents were drafted.[8] The present French-, Italian- and Romansh-speaking cantons were not equal members of the Confederation politically; they were either semi-independent allies or subject provinces of the German-speaking cantons. Only as a result of the influences of the French revolution were these areas admitted to the Confederation as fully equal partners; German, French and Italian were declared to be the national languages of Switzerland in the Constitution of 1848, and Romansh was added 90 years later.

As a legal consequence of the multilingual principle it has been recognized that in all official relations with federal authorities, German-, French-, Italian- and Romansh-speaking Swiss have the right to use their own language. However, in order to save the expense of having to translate all laws and official documents, Romansh was not made an official language of the Confederation; and Italian, although an official language of the Confederation, has not claimed an absolute parity of position. Though all federal laws are published in the three official languages—German, French, and Italian—which are all equally authoritative, most of the official documents appear only in German and French. Even Italian-Swiss representatives usually speak French in the Federal Parliament, as do Italian-Swiss lawyers appearing before the Federal Supreme Court, while the Romansh-speaking Swiss use German on those occasions.

On the other hand, no effort whatsoever is made by the German-Swiss, who are in the overwhelming majority numerically, to assert any linguistic dominance. There are no linguistic minorities in Switzerland either in a legal or in an informal sense. On the contrary, since the multilingual principle is considered an integral element of national unity, great care is taken to preserve the integrity of all the national languages and to keep the linguistic equilibrium intact. Thus, by unwritten law, at least two, and often three, of the seven places on the Federal Council, which is the Swiss cabinet, have always been reserved for French- and Italian-speaking confederates, and only four or five members of the Federal Council can be citizens of German-speaking cantons. Similar informal arrangements also prevail in the selection of justices for the Federal Tribunal.

In summary, the linguistic equilibrium which represents one of the foremost stabilizing and integrating influences in the modern Swiss democracy and which is the envy of a strife-torn world, originated at a time before language was made a symbol of rampant nationalism and has been kept on an even keel for more than a century mainly because of a fortunate balancing of demographic factors. It is quite true, however, that this demographic equilibrium has also been consciously reinforced through wise and statesmanlike political measures designed to prevent any upsets and disturbances throughout an era when other countries have permitted language to become a focus of conflict and division.

NOTES

1. Christopher Herold, *The Swiss Without Halos* (New York: Columbia University Press 1948), p. 3.

2. Wilhelm Bickel, *Bevoelkerungsgeschichte und Bevoelkerungspolitik der Schweiz* (Zurich: Buechergilde, Gutenberg, 1947), p. 140.

3. The death rate in 1941, corrected for age, was 10.91 for the nineteen German-speaking cantons and 11.53 for the French-speaking cantons, a differential of only 0.62 per 1,000.

4. Herold, *op. cit.*, p. 16.

5. In justification of the French-speaking Swiss it should be noted here that they face a much greater linguistic handicap when they migrate to the German area than do the German-speaking Swiss when they move into French territory. The reason is that German is a written, but not a spoken language in German Switzerland. Official documents, newspapers, and most literary works are written in standard German, but the spoken tongue is a Germanic dialect, or rather, as every canton has its own, a variety of dialects. These dialects are sufficiently alike to be universally understood in all cantons, but sufficiently different from the standard German spoken in Germany to form a real obstacle in familiar intercourse and to act as a protective device against too much German influence. The Swiss dialects, moreover, are more than a mere vernacular, since they are spoken by all Swiss Germans regardless of class or level of education, while dialects are usually only the tongue of the uneducated. In fact, therefore, the German-Swiss write standard German but usually speak a dialect so different from it that it is not understood in Germany and their children have to learn to write and speak standard German in school as if it were a foreign language. The French-speaking Swiss, therefore,

who wishes to settle in German Switzerland must learn practically two difficult languages, a written and a spoken one, which does not make things any easier.

6. W. Ott, "Sprache," in *Die Bevoelkerung der Schweiz* (Herausgegeben vom Eidgenoessischen Statistischen Amt, Berne, 1939), p. 20.

7. William E. Rappard, *The Government of Switzerland* (New York: Van Nostrand, 1936), p. 9.

8. Cf. Rappard, *op. cit.*, pp. 6–8.

THE SOCIAL DIFFERENTIATION
OF JAMAICA

This paper will outline the development and present character of the system of social differentiation[1] in Jamaica with special reference to ethnicity and color. Although a large part of the phenomena discussed are ordinarily treated under the heading of stratification, they are here considered under the more inclusive designation of differentiation.

The differentiated elements of the population are examined according to their discrete functions, which need not have hierarchical significance, and the function-canalizing effects of ethnicity, which do not directly pertain to stratification.

Jamaica has long attracted the interest of American sociologists. Here a British colony, close to our shores, experienced color slavery and arrived at a kind of "race relations" different from that developed in the United States. Jamaica, passing through a brief stage termed "Apprenticeship," achieved emancipation of her slaves a third of a century earlier than did the United States, and without civil war. Her whites constitute a small minority.

The Historical Setting

The basic racial pattern of Jamaica was laid down in the eighteenth century. At the end of the seventeenth century there were an estimated ten thousand whites and forty thousand slaves, principally blacks. Less

From Leonard Broom, "The Social Differentiation of Jamaica," in *American Sociological Review*, 19 (April 1954), pp. 115–125.

than a century later the whites numbered about eighteen thousand, but there were a quarter of a million slaves—an increase of over two hundred thousand. An additional increment of whites in the first quarter of the nineteenth century was followed by a decline after the Apprenticeship period. By 1844 there were less than sixteen thousand whites in the Island, and their number has since fluctuated little. The census of 1943 reported 13,400, hardly more than the white population of 1775. Meanwhile the colored (mixed bloods) increased from 68,500 in 1844 to 216,000 in 1943, and the black population increased from 293,000 in 1844 to nearly a million in 1943. The whites, barely maintaining their numbers, have steadily declined in proportion from about 4 per cent of the population in 1844 to 1 per cent a century later. Table 7–1 summarizes the changing racial composition of Jamaica.

Historians of the British Caribbean have amply documented the drain of white population out of the area.[2] The high sugar prices in the latter half of the eighteenth century accelerated the movement, for the planters could live luxuriously in England on the returns from their holdings. According to Ragatz,[3] "When the permanent decline in revenues from tropical American holdings . . . set in, overseas owners as a class failed to return, take personal possession and salvage what they might, but instead, after exhausting credit, they transferred their estates to holders of their paper, while planters actually in the West Indies, becoming hopelessly entangled in debt . . . forsook the colonies." The practice of sending the planters' children to England for their education, whence they often failed to return or returned miseducated for colonial life, reinforced this tendency. The consequence was a heavy drain of the trained talent out of the Island and an abdication of insular responsibilities to multiple office holders, agents, and mortgagees. In their turn the agents often departed. "Social stability was . . . far to seek; how far must be clear to anyone who cares to search among the names of the chief men in Jamaica in the eighteen-thirties . . . for the names of men who held . . . offices a hundred years before."[4] The reasons for this discontinuity are to be found in vital as well as migratory causes. The sex ratio was heavily masculine, the life expectancy of the poorer immigrants, the clerks and overseers was exceedingly low, and the practice of concubinage reduced legitimate fertility.

Throughout Jamaican history the whites were thus drained off as fast as they arrived, and a vacuum was created in positions of intermediate responsibility. One segment of the population, the manumitted or freeborn colored, was always present to enter the vacuum. Many of these were children of the planters and their concubines. Some had European

83

TABLE 7-1

The Racial Composition of Jamaica, 1673-1943 *

Year		Source[1]	Black	Colored	White	Chinese	East Indian	Total
1673	N	a	9.5		7.7			17.2
	per cent		55		45			100
1696	N	b	40.0		10.0			(47.4)[2]
	per cent		84		21			
1736	N	a	80.0		8.0			(94.2)
	per cent		85		8			
1775	N	a	200.0		12.7			(209.6)
	per cent		95		6			
1788	N	b	256.0		18.3			(291.4)
	per cent		88		6			
1793	N	c	261.4[3]		30.0			291.4
	per cent		90		10			100
1844	N	a	293.0	68.5	15.8			377.4
	per cent		78	18	4			100
1861	N	a	346.4	81.1	13.8			441.3
	per cent		79	18	3			100
1871	N	a	392.7	100.1	13.1			506.1
	per cent		78	20	2			100
1881	N	d	444.2	109.9	14.4	.1	11.0	580.8
	per cent		76	19	3	...	2	100
1891	N	d	488.6	121.9	14.7	.5	10.1	639.5
	per cent		76	19	2	...	2	100
1911	N	d	630.2	163.2	15.6	2.1	17.4	831.4
	per cent		76	20	2	...	2	100
1921	N	d	660.4	157.2	14.5	3.7	18.6	858.1
	per cent		77	18	2	...	2	100
1943	N	d	965.9	216.2	13.4	12.4	26.5	1237.1[4]
	per cent		78	18	1	1	2	100

*Frequencies are given in thousands; percentages are given to the nearest per cent; . . . signifies less than 1 per cent.

[1] The sources follow. Full references will be found in the text. (a) Gardner, *passim*. (b) Burn, *passim*. (c) Edwards, Vol. I, p. 230. (d) *Eighth Census of Jamaica* (1943), p. 93.

[2] Numbers in parentheses are census estimates which do not equal the sum of the racial components.

[3] This figure includes 1,400 Maroons, 250,000 Negro slaves, and 10,000 "freed Negroes and people of colour." Edwards, *loc. cit.*

[4] Includes "Not otherwise specified."

education, and even those less trained compared favorably enough with the impoverished, forgotten men of the plantation, the English clerks and indentured whites. *The precondition for the differentiation of the black and colored populations was then established,* just as it was in South Africa, Brazil, and the United States. But in Jamaica the lack of an adequate population of qualified whites, or indeed of unqualified whites, afforded the colored a greater opportunity to differentiate themselves from the blacks.

Spanish definitions of color long persisted in Jamaica, and in the eighteenth century the recognized gradations were black, mulatto, terceroon, quadroon, mustee, musteefino, and white. The child of a white and a musteefina (or mustee, or quadroon, according to various writers) was called "English, free of taint."[5] Thus Edwards at the end of the eighteenth century wrote: "The children of a White and Quinteron consider themselves as free from all taint of the Negro race. Every person is so jealous of the order of their tribe or caste, that if, thru inadvertence, you call them by a degree lower than what they actually are, they are highly offended."[6]

Lightness, valued as a promise of higher status, became valued for itself, and status became equated with lightness. The early literature often refers to colored free men but black slaves. Certainly the differential statuses, which are all too apparent in the 1943 census, are reinforced by the selective perception of census takers. For example, a phenotypically black civil servant of the upper categories is most likely to be classified as colored. A dark-colored peasant is most likely to be classified black.

Differential manumission operated so that, according to Gardner,[7] "the greatest portion of those fairer than the mulattoes were free" at the beginning of the nineteenth century, and the "creole distinction of brown lady, black woman was . . . strictly observed; and except in the smaller towns, different shades of color did not readily mingle."[8] John Stewart reported in 1823 that 95 per cent of the white males had colored mistresses and that into the hands of their male children "much of the property of the country (was) fast falling," certainly an overstatement of the case. Polite society ruled by white women might admit a few highly educated and well-to-do colored men, but colored women were much more rigidly excluded.[9] The distinction between the society of men and of women presumably was a by-product of concubinage, and its effects persist to this day.

If colored persons had little or no entrée to high society, some were accumulating the necessary equipment for substantial middle class status as early as the eighteenth century. An Assembly inquiry in 1763 showed that property valued at 250,000 pounds sterling had been left to colored children. The list included four sugar estates and thirteen cattle pens. The legislature then passed a statute invalidating bequests by whites to non-whites in excess of 1,200 pounds. Subsequently by individual acts the Assembly from time to time permitted what it had expressly forbidden. Inheritance of property by colored persons from colored persons was unrestricted, so that the accumulation of wealth in the hands of the colored was only retarded.[10]

The colored population made most general progress in the urban areas where they entered the professions, administrative jobs and trades. Even before Apprenticeship they comprised the majority of the voters in Kingston and in three of the parishes. Had they voted *en bloc*, they could have elected at least nine of the forty-five members of the Assembly, but prior to 1837, there were only three colored members. In 1837 eight were elected.[11]

Here is a rough approximation of the status ladder as it appeared in the Island in the first quarter of the nineteenth century, before Apprenticeship and Emancipation:

1. The invisible man, the absentee landlord; the executive; the resident creole planters and the top representatives of overseas companies—all whites.
2. Estate attorneys and agents and well-to-do Scottish and Jewish merchants; some professionals—all whites.
3. Other merchants and urban specialists, including some colored; a few colored planters and professionals.
4. Colored artisans, tradesmen and semi-professionals.
5. Brown slaves not in field labor.
6. Black slaves working in the fields

The first two categories were, of course, very small in numbers. The indicated correlation of color and status was not perfect. For example, blacks could be found in the levels immediately above field slavery, and there were some colored at the very bottom. An additional, I trust unnecessary, caution should be kept in mind: no interval values can be assigned to the several positions.

The avenues of vertical mobility and their categorical limitations have been indicated in the foregoing discussion. Colored slaves were manumitted more often than blacks; colored slaves were more often than blacks employed in domestic, urban, and entrepreneurial activities (e.g. as peddlers) where they could acquire the prerequisite skills for further mobility. For the first few steps up the ladder some training was more important than some land. At higher levels, although literacy and training in themselves had status value, the validation of high status rested on land ownership or, at least, its control.

After "the fall of the planter class" the merchants increased in relative importance and, as urban influences grew, the roles of Jews (see below) and the colored expanded. Some of those, e.g. Scots and Jews, who had achieved higher status in urban functions penetrated the planter group or emigrated to England, but the colored elements consolidated and developed their intermediate positions. This was done by further education, the acquisition of real estate especially in urban areas, intermarriage, and an expansion in trades and professions. All of these processes were retarded by the persistently low level of the Jamaican economy. Planter interests maintained their strong representation in the Assembly, and colored men who never comprised more than a third of its membership up to its dissolution in 1865, generally opposed the Country party, dominated by the English planters. The black and colored peasantry increased, and overseas companies tended to replace individual absentee landlords.

The varieties of colored employment are worth detailing. John Bigelow, proprietor and editor of the *New York Evening Post,* who visited Jamaica in 1850, reported that the pilot in Kingston harbor was a mulatto, that the revenue officers were mostly colored, that most of the eight-hundred-men police force were colored. In a visit to court he found two lawyers, all but one of the officers of the court, and most of the jurors colored.[12] At this time Edward Jordan, a colored man, was public printer, editor of the *Kingston Morning Journal,* and leader of the Administration party. His is said to be the first portrait of a colored man to appear in the history gallery of the Institute of Jamaica.[13]

Americans have been impressed with the permissiveness of Jamaican race relations for more than a century. Bigelow summarized the case as well as we could ask: ". . . one accustomed to the proscribed condition of the free black in the United States will constantly be startled at the diminished importance attached here to the matter of complexion. Intermarriages are constantly occurring between the white and colored people, their families associate together within the ranks to which by wealth and color they respectively belong, and public opinion does not recognize any social distinctions based exclusively on color. Of course, cultivated or fashionable people will not receive colored persons of inferior culture and worldly resources, but the rule of discrimination is scarcely more rigorous against those than against whites. They are received at the 'Kings House' . . . and they are invited to (the governor's) table with fastidious courtesy.

The wife of the present mayor of Kingston is a 'brown' woman . . . so also is the wife of the Receiver General himself, an English gentleman, and one of the most exalted public functionaries upon the island. . . . One unacquainted with the extent to which the amalgamation of races has gone here, is constantly liable to drop remarks in the presence of white persons, which, in consequence of the mixture of blood that may take place in some branch of their families, are likely to be very offensive. I was only protected from frequent *contretemps* of this kind, by the timely caution of a lady, who in explaining its propriety, said that unless one knows the whole collateral kindred of a family in Jamaica, he is not safe in assuming that they have not some colored connections."[14]

The Status Cleavage

Social stratification in Jamaica cannot be understood as an uninterrupted continuum of status positions. No matter what empirical criteria are employed, gross discontinuities are to be found. Given the historical forces briefly reviewed, this fact should cause no surprise, but the extreme character of this status cleavage affects all facets of Jamaican society.

As elsewhere in the Western world, literacy and education are preconditions to vertical mobility. In Table 7–2 are summarized the relevant sta-

TABLE 7-2

Literacy and Education by Color and Ethnic Identity, Jamaica, 1943

	Black	Colored	White	Chinese and Chinese Colored	East Indian and E.I. Colored	Syrian and Syrian Colored	Total[1]
Total population 7 yrs. & older	794,574	179,532	12,477	9,234	21,378	857	1,018,955
Per cent illiterate	28.1	13.8	3.8	13.9	48.6	5.6	25.6
Per cent literate (schooling)	71.9	86.2	96.2	86.1	51.4	94.4	74.4
Pre-prof. and professional	.3	1.3	13.1	.4	.2	1.9	.6
Secondary or practical	1.1	9.8	48.1	12.0	2.1	46.4	3.4
Elementary	70.5	75.1	35.0	73.6	49.1	46.1	70.4

*Computed from *Eighth Census of Jamaica* (1943), Table 54, p. 108.
[1]Includes "Not otherwise specified."

tistics. A little over one per cent of the blacks have more than an elementary schooling and fully 28 per cent are illiterate. Only the East Indians show a higher rate of illiteracy. The colored and Chinese groups occupy an intermediate position, but both have substantial populations with more than elementary schooling. The whites and Syrians[15] are far better off. Stated crudely, 96 per cent of the Jamaican population is an undifferentiated mass in regard to education, with elementary schooling or none. Combining illiterates with those having only elementary schooling, we find the groups have the following percentages of illiteracy: Blacks, 98.6; East Indians, 97.7; Colored, 88.9; Chinese, 87.5; Syrians, 51.7; Whites, 38.8. These figures are for the population seven years of age and older. The residual population of illiterates and those with limited education is subject to reduction for all groups, but disproportionately so for Syrians and whites.

The same relationships exist in the distribution of secondary schooling. The whites are five times better off than the colored, the colored ten times better off than the blacks. In this respect the Syrians approximate the other whites, the Chinese resemble the colored, and the East Indians again resemble the blacks. One qualification must be made to the statistical generalization about the educationally depressed characteristics of the Chinese. Their limited formal schooling is ameliorated by extensive *informal* practical training in small commercial enterprises, which is not revealed in Table 7–2. Effectively they are better educated than the Census records suggest.

The data on professional and pre-professional schooling are presented in the next section. Suffice it to say that the educational prerequisites for even modest vertical mobility are available for only a small part of the colored and for a very small proportion of blacks and East Indians.

Table 7–3 approaches the phenomenon of status cleavage with different data. About half the black and East Indian and about a third of the colored wage earners got ten shillings a week or less, an exchange value in 1943 of about two dollars in U.S. currency. This does not take into account a high rate of unemployment, which operates selectively against the low wage earners and reduces their mean earnings disproportionately. The heavy concentration of blacks and East Indians in agricultural labor largely contributes to their disadvantageous position. The better wage status of the colored is, on the other hand, probably related to their higher incidence of urban employment. The other color and ethnic groups had very small numbers in the lowest wage category.

Jamaica has a predominantly agricultural economy. The size of farms

TABLE 7-3

Wage Earnings by Color and Ethnic Identity, Jamaica, 1943*

	Black	Colored	White	Chinese and Chinese Colored	East Indian and E.I. Colored	Syrian and Syrian Colored	Jewish	Total
Total wage earners	151,101	33,630	2,990	1,526	4,770	163	233	194,458[1]
Per cent earning:								
More than 100s/wk.[2]	.3	5.6	41.5	5.0	.5	17.8	33.5	1.9
Less than 10s/wk.	58.4	32.1	2.1	6.1	49.8	2.5	1.7	52.2

*Computed from *Eighth Census of Jamaica* (1943), Table 125, p. 220.
[1]Includes "Not otherwise specified."
[2]The shilling was then valued at about 20 cents U.S.

operated may, therefore, be taken as another measure of the degree of differentiation of the several elements of its population. Table 7–4 shows that once again the blacks, East Indians, and colored are found in an inferior position. In this case the Chinese and Syrians resemble the undifferentiated groups, but their involvement in agriculture is small, and their poor agricultural status is, therefore, of little importance. The Census

TABLE 7-4

Farm Land Tenure by Color and Ethnic Identity, Jamaica, 1943*

	Black	Colored	White	Chinese and Chinese Colored	East Indian and E.I. Colored	Syrian and Syrian Colored	Jewish	Total
Total farm operators	51,763	12,398	950	81	922	18	19	66,173[1]
Per cent operating:								
More than 100 acres	.7	4.9	43.3	3.7	2.2	5.5	52.6	2.1
Less than 10 acres	78.4	61.6	23.8	65.4	72.2	77.8	10.5	74.3

*Computed from *Eighth Census of Jamaica* (1943), Table 200, p. 306.
[1]Includes "Not otherwise specified."

data do not permit us to treat separately the colored segments of the Chinese and Syrians, but we may guess that these elements constitute most of the small operators, grouped in their respective ethnic categories.

Three sets of data have thus been used to suggest the gross characteristics of Jamaican stratification. Each criterion—education, wage earnings, and farm land tenure—showed the blacks and the East Indians in a very disadvantageous position and the colored population only somewhat better off.

Further comment on the depressed elements of these populations should bear on the channels of mobility open to them rather than on additional stratification details. The available data will permit us only to suggest the broad outlines of such an analysis. Very large proportions of blacks and East Indians, and to a lesser extent the colored, are agricultural laborers or small peasants who lack the minimal educational skills. An expansion of the agricultural economy might incidentally improve their status by providing steadier employment at somewhat higher rates of pay or, in the case of peasants, by yielding better returns on crops. In other words, assuming continued agricultural functions, changes in their life chances lie in changes in the whole economy (except, of course, in the cases of the movement of unusually lucky or able individuals). In any event, the relative position of these groups in the economy would not be significantly altered. Given their lack of education and experience, urban employment can only offer unskilled work or the opportunity to acquire limited skills in such jobs as domestic service.

The depressed urban workers move in a more fluid and differentiated labor market in which some opportunities for upgrading are possible. Furthermore, insofar as they can combine a small capital accumulation with commercial or manual skills, they can make a shaky upward step as independent entrepreneurs. As we shall see below, however, these chances are severely limited. Lacking some dramatic expansion of the economy, the character of the status cleavage of Jamaica does not seem subject to drastic change.[16]

The Ethnics and the Elites

Just as the status cleavage and mobility are the chief topics for studying the undifferentiated elements of the population, the proper study of the highly differentiated elements is function. Table 7–5 summarizes the color

TABLE 7-5

*Color and Ethnic Identity of the
Population, Jamaica, 1943*

	Number*		Per Cent[1]
Black	965,960		78.1
Colored	216,348		17.5
White (unlisted below)	12,550[2]		1.0
Jewish	1,259		.1
Chinese	6,879 ⎱	12,394	1.0
Chinese colored	5,515 ⎰		
East Indian	21,393 ⎱	26,507	2.1
East Indian colored	5,114 ⎰		
Syrian	834 ⎱	1,005	.1
Syrian colored	171 ⎰		
Others and unspecified	1,040		.1
Total	1,237,063		100.0

*Compiled from *Census of Jamaica* (1943), Table 46, p. 92.
[1]*Ibid.*, computed from Table 47, p. 92.

[2]Discrepancies in figures for whites in this table and in Table 7-1 derive from the detailed and summary tables of the Census, from which these data were summarized.

and ethnic identity of the population. In this population, predominantly African in origin, several groups are visible by racial characteristics, cultural characteristics, or simply social identity. This is important because, as we shall see, the more or less visible groups, although quite small, are the very ones which perform distinctive functions in the society.

First, let us reexamine tables 7–2, 7–3, and 7–4 to identify the highly differentiated groups. We note that the whites are educationally the most highly qualified group. Thirteen per cent of the whites had pre-professional or professional schooling, compared with 1.3 per cent of the colored and only .3 per cent of the blacks. To run the percentages the other way, although whites are about one per cent of the population, they account for almost one quarter of the highly educated group; the colored, who are about 18 per cent of the population, and the blacks, who make up 78 per cent, share equally in the remainder. This, however, puts an unduly favorable interpretation on the educational position of the blacks, for a large share of the blacks so classified are pre-professionals and clergymen.

Table 7–3 shows those wage earners getting more than 100 shillings per week (20 dollars U.S.), an income associated with good job stability. Less than two per cent of all wage earners received this amount, but two-fifths of the whites, one-third of the Jews, and almost one-fifth of the

Syrians did. On the other hand, only a fraction of one per cent of East Indians and blacks earned as much as 100 shillings per week.

Table 7–4 tells the same story in the case of large farm operations. About two-fifths of white operators run large farms; indeed a summary of mean holdings would show them in a most advantageous position. One-twentieth of colored operators run large farms, and they account for about half of the larger holdings. Less than one per cent of black farm operators run large farms. The blacks who make up nearly four-fifths of all farm operators run only one-fourth of large farms.

Table 7–6 permits us to assess the differential positions of the several

TABLE 7-6

Male Owners, Managers, and Professionals, Jamaica, 1943*

		Black	Colored	White	Chinese and Chinese Colored	East Indian and E.I. Colored	Syrian and Syrian Colored	Jewish	Total[1]
Total man-agers and profes-sionals	N	3,951	2,712	1,014	1,487	242	162	139	9,819
	per cent	40.2	27.6	10.3	15.1	2.6	1.6	1.4	100.0
Retail trade	N	2,549	1,103	94	1,310	194	124	28	5,429
	per cent	46.9	20.3	1.7	24.1	3.6	2.3	.5	100.0
Exclud-ing retail trade	N	1,402	1,609	920	177	48	38	111	4,390
	per cent	31.9	36.6	21.0	4.0	1.1	.9	2.5	100.0

*Computed from *Eighth Census of Jamaica* (1943), Table 92, pp. 179ff. and unpublished census data. Includes: "Wage Earners and Unpaid Workers," "Own Account Workers," and "Employers." Excludes those engaged in agriculture.

[1]Includes "Not otherwise specified."

ethnic elements in commercial functions. To interpret these data fully we would need to classify by size and type of enterprise. Nevertheless, some clues may be noted—for one thing, the disproportionate representation of colored, whites, and Jews in the non-retail category. Only the blacks and East Indians have less than their "share" in this classification, which includes the strategic urban commercial functions.

In the retail trade category the most striking fact is that the Chinese have a larger share than any other group except the blacks. Moreover, their occupational visibility is not merely statistical, for they are predominant in the retail grocery trade throughout the Island and are very important in the related food processing industry. The opportunity to develop a retail grocery trade lay fallow in the hands of the colored population until the latter nineteenth century when it was taken over by the Chinese with their greater entrepreneurial experience. It would be very difficult now, short of political interference, for the black or colored population to make much headway in this business. As a consequence of their semi-monopoly over the most conspicuous of businesses, the Chinese have come to occupy a difficult position. In scores of towns they stand as strangers who possess the goods most desired by the peasantry and small wage earners. They tend to be ethnically exclusive in their associations, perform few elite functions, and are fairly isolated from the blacks, colored, and the other ethnics. Their conspicuousness could easily be translated into vulnerability. This is suggested in an editorial in a Jamaican periodical:

If the Chinese in Jamaica don't do a *volte face* soon they are going to plunge the whole island into serious racial trouble. As one whose goodwill towards them is no secret, I feel duty-bound to give this note of warning—or these few words of advice. Jamaica's race relations record is too good to be spoilt. So I must warn now before it is too late.

I remember how bitterly they complained to the Moyne Commission of '38 that everybody was against them though they offended no one but merely minded their own business. I remember what wise old Lord Moyne told them. He said in effect: you people are not pulling your weight in the community. You build a wall around yourselves and live within it. People don't like walls, particularly if they get to thinking that what's within is inimical to them. Remove your wall. Integrate with the community, and stop giving the impression that you are only interested in grabbing and scraping all you can out of the island to take back to China. Forget about China. You are Jamaicans. Be Jamaicans—like the Jews, Syrians, Negroes and others whose ancestors also came from alien lands.

That was sound advice. But the Chinese haven't taken it. Instead, they have built a thicker and higher wall. Those who venture out and identify themselves with the rest of the Jamaican people are so few they are lost in the crowd.

The rest of Jamaicans are beginning to look at the Chinese wall. And it is not a friendly look; it is a look that bodes ill, a threat to the continuance of internal peace. If the Chinese keep piling up wealth and hate behind that wall, giving back nothing to the community, they may find it expedient to go back "home" sooner than they hope—if China is still home for any large numbers of Jamaican Chinese. . . .

They hate Negroes more than all ("Nigger" is their favourite word for anybody black), though they have bred more half-Negro children than any other group during the past 50 years. They ostracise any of their group who accept employment with Negro firms. There is the case of a Chinese girl who married a Negro some time ago. Her folks haven't spoken to her since. . . .

. . . The Chinese take full advantage of all the facilities the community offers, yet such facilities as they have as a group are reserved for Chinese only. Examples: only Chinese are employed in Chinese businesses; only Chinese kids are accepted in the Chinese public school; only Chinese are admitted to membership in the Chinese Athletic Club.

Few Chinese even bother to vote. Every public subscription list shows the same few names. . . .

Political control of Jamaica will ever remain in the hands of Negroes. Since it is too late to bar all Chinese—as some other Caribbean countries have done— it is not too late to enact the kind of legislation which will force the Chinese out from behind the wall. . . .[17]

In contrast the Jews, Syrians, and other whites who also perform important commercial functions are involved in varied enterprises, chiefly concentrated in the urban areas. In their exchange functions they have less direct contact with the general public. Like the Chinese, the Syrians are concentrated in commercial activity. Unlike the Chinese, at the turn of the century they entered into competition with the relatively well established dry goods and wholesale firms run by creole whites and colored. In large part through the skill of a single family, the Syrians have become a major economic force, tightly integrated and with close ties to the Syrian community in North America and throughout the Caribbean.

Although a detailed discussion is impossible here, a word must be said about the Jews of Jamaica who have never exceeded a few hundred. They were originally of Spanish and Portuguese origin and were important in the entrepot trade with the Spanish Caribbean. Along with the Scots, they dealt in plantation stores, a large scale business in which sales were made in bulk.[18] In the seventeenth and early eighteenth centuries Jews suffered from discriminatory taxation and civil disabilities. The special taxes were rescinded first, and then, early in the nineteenth century they were relieved of the remaining impediments. As the colored population became urbanized and achieved some vertical mobility, intermarriage and concubinage with Jews as well as with other whites took place. It is not clear to what extent Jews left the Island for England, but they undoubtedly shared in this migration.

As has been indicated, Jews are widely distributed through the urban occupations. Of approximately 200 listed in the Jamaica *Who's Who* (1946), a very inclusive roster, nearly half are in business activities of one sort or another, and most of the remainder are in the free professions or the civil service.

There is not space to report here on current Jewish intermarriage and related problems. It would be safe to assert, however, that despite the observance of religious holidays by Jewish firms and the maintenance of a congregation, the group is the most fully integrated of all the ethnic minorities into Jamaican society. Like the colored, many of their number perform elite functions.

The other whites, especially the English and Jamaica creoles, control most of the largest estates, the finance and the shipping activities. Polite society is dominated by these whites, or more accurately, by the white wives of these men. There are also a number of cliques of high status centering on the colored professionals, but the town clubs, the yacht club, and the country clubs are not racially exclusive. Their memberships, of course, are disproportionately white and light colored as a consequence of the distribution of money, education, and occupation. Perhaps in the country parishes one or two clubs composed exclusively of creole whites might be found, but these are rural survivals of an earlier period.

In Table 7–7 are summarized the data on the ethnic identity and color of samples of doctors and lawyers. The category labelled "White and Light" contains a number of individuals who in the United States could easily "pass" as white but whose ancestry is locally reputed to be in part colored. Although the number of unknowns and the sampling errors require us to treat these figures with caution, once more the monotonous observation must be made that the blacks are under-represented.

TABLE 7-7
Ethnic Identity and Color of Jamaican Professionals *

| | Lawyers, 1951[1] | | Doctors, 1950[2] | |
	Number	Per Cent	Number	Per Cent
Chinese	3	3.1	..	..
East Indians	..	..	1	1.4
Jews	7	7.1	2	2.9
Syrians	..	..	2	2.9
White and light	38	38.8	18	25.7
Olive	10	10.2	7	10.0
Light brown	17	17.3	6	8.6
Dark brown	10	10.2	9	12.8
Black	5	5.1	10	14.3
Unknown	8	8.2	15	21.4
Total	98	100.0	70	100.0

*Chinese, East Indians, Jews, and Syrians are ethnically designated; all others are identified by color. The color of the Jews ranges from white to olive.

[1] Fifty per cent sample drawn from *Handbook of Jamaica* (1951), pp. 136-141. Sample includes only Barristers and Solicitors in residence and in practice.

[2] Thirty-three per cent sample drawn from *Handbook of Jamaica* (1950), pp. 549-554. Sample reduced by two known dead and one known to be off the Island.

What is more impressive is the large proportion who are colored and who by the attainment of professional status have validated an elite identity. A professional occupation has in the past required education abroad[19] as well as the deferment of economic independence. The number of professionals is a measure of the extent to which the educated colored have internalized the values of education and public service. Another measure is the large number of colored who are to be found in the civil service. Both the professionals and the civil servants are highly urbanized, and among their number are the core of the indigenous elite.

The Chinese would not have gained control of the grocery trade so quickly if the educated colored had not become committed to the professions and the civil service as status-bearing occupations. It is ironic that British colonialism, which historically has been so heavily influenced by commercial interests, should have implanted a disdain of commerce among many colonial peoples. This may be in part because a colonial may seek recognition in two places, in the colony and in the metropolitan "home." The dual striving is apparently achieved without conflict of ends most readily in the public service and, of course, some immediate status is acquired by the very identification with official functions.

Table 7–8 reports the color of members of the House of Representatives and of the appointed Legislative Council. The latter traditionally draws heavily on English overseas representation for its membership. The former, elected by universal suffrage under the constitution of 1944, is more representative of the color characteristics of Jamaica than is any other high-status group. Even so, the darker elements are under-represented,[20] if one's sole criterion is proportionality. These elected representatives are the embodiment of a dramatic shift in the locus of power in Jamaica from the white planters and overseas interests to the blacks. The representative of

TABLE 7-8
Color of Public Officials, Jamaica, 1951

		White and Light	Olive	Light Brown	Dark Brown	Black	Total*
House of Representatives	N	3	4	6	12	3	31
	per cent	10	13	19	39	10	100
Legislative Council	N	13	1	—	1	—	15
	per cent	86	7	—	7	—	100

*Includes unknown.

the Crown, of course, held and retains great authority, but he holds far less under the 1944 Constitution than under the earlier Crown Colony government. As the power-shift becomes consolidated, the whites and the ethnically differentiated groups must seek indirect access to power. The Jamaican House in 1951 included in its number men who by training and experience were highly qualified to perform elite responsibilities in a representative government. The cadres of trained personnel, as we have seen, were most numerous in the white, colored and ethnic elements of the population. Jamaica today has two difficult tasks. First, to continue to utilize its resource of personnel with elite qualifications. Second, to train and recruit to the elite a far larger number of blacks. The extent to which these tasks may be accomplished will depend on the appreciation of elite functions by a black electorate with limited schooling.

NOTES

1. An introductory note on the related topic of urbanization has appeared in L. Broom, "Urban Research in the British Caribbean: A Prospectus," *Social and Economic Studies*, 1 (February 1953), pp. 113–119. Published by Institute of Social and Economic Research, University of West Indies, Mona, Jamaica.

2. For example see: W. L. Burn, *Emancipation and Apprenticeship in the British West Indies*, 1937; W. J. Gardner, *A History of Jamaica*, 2nd ed., 1909; L. J. Ragatz, *The Fall of the Planter Class in the British Caribbean, 1763–1833*, 1928.

3. *Op. cit.*, p. 44.

4. Burn, *op. cit.*, p. 25.

5. Cf. M. W. Beckwith, *Black Roadways*, 1929, p. 5 and Ragatz, *op. cit.*, p. 33.

6. Bryan Edwards, *The History, Civil and Commercial, of the British Colonies in the West Indies*, 1793, Vol. II, p. 16.

7. Gardner, *op. cit.*, p. 381.

8. Gardner, *op. cit.*, p. 384.

9. John Stewart, *A Review of the Past and Present State of the Island of Jamaica*, 1823, pp. 333–335.

10. Gardner, *op. cit.*, p. 172.

11. Burn, *op. cit.*, pp. 152–153.

12. John Bigelow, *Jamaica in 1850*, 1851, *passim*.

13. Frank Cundall, *Catalogue of the Portraits in the Jamaica History Gallery of the Institute of Jamaica*, 1914, p. 25.

14. Bigelow, *op. cit.*, pp. 20–22.

15. The separate designation of Syrians here and of Jews later is no attempt to develop a private somatology but simply follows Jamaican custom and census policy. Educational figures for Jews are unavailable. Unless otherwise indicated, in referring to Syrians, East Indians, and Chinese, the colored products of amalgamation are included with these groups, as the census usually does. No separate educational classifications are available.

16. A cautionary note is in order. It would be easy, if inaccurate, to impose on the foregoing discussion a critical estimate of colonial policy. Without going into the matter here, it is only fair to note that Jamaica's difficulties inhere in its very narrow economic base, a weakly differentiated economy, and a severe population pressure. Colonial policies in recent years have made expensive attempts to ameliorate the first two of these conditions. To be sure, the conditions have their history of slavery and the misuse of natural resources and of the drain of capital and talent out of the Island. But these are unrecallable errors, and no panacea is to be found in the simplistic "solutions" of the politically opportunistic or irresponsible.

17. "Occidental Chinese Wall," *Spotlight* (October, 1952), pp. 4 and 7.

18. Ragatz, *op. cit.*, pp. 16–17.

19. The recent establishment in Jamaica of the University College of the West Indies with its medical school has changed this.

20. Fernando Henriques, "Color Values in Jamaican Society," *The British Journal of Sociology*, Vol. II, No. 2, p. 116. Henriques is misleading when he refers to it as a "practically all-black legislature."

PART III

The African Diaspora and Cultural Survivals: The Frazier-Herskovits Debate

Editor's Introduction

Nearly thirty years later, the Frazier-Herskovits debate is still raging, having outlasted both of the principals. Herskovits, an anthropologist with Dahomean experience, spent much of his scholarly energies looking for survivals of African (and especially West African) culture among Afro-Americans in the Western Hemisphere. Frazier, a sociologist, tended to interpret differences in behavior between Afro- and Euro-Americans in terms of the structure of creole European societies, and especially the heritage of slavery and the racist caste system which replaced it. The extent of African survivals varies greatly within the Americas, being perhaps greatest in Brazil (the dueling field for the encounter reproduced here) and Haiti, and smallest in the United States. As far as the United States is concerned, there is no question that a much greater proportion of the relatively minor differences in the sub-cultures of whites and blacks is to be accounted for in terms of structural differences in American society rather than in isolated and questionable instances of African culture traits. It was Herskovits, the white Afrophile, who acted as the sentimentalist antiquarian and Frazier, the black American, who stuck closest to his data and sought to interpret his life experience in the most parsimonious and realistic way. In Brazil, however, Frazier was on weaker ground because African survivals there, especially in the Northeast, are much more evident.

Despite the fact that many of the differences between white and black Americans can be shown to "wash out" if one controls for social class, education, region of origin, place of residence, and similar sociological characteristics, and that nearly all of the residual differences are convincingly explained by the history of slavery and the contemporary experience of racial discrimination, the debate has rebounded into renewed relevance. Frustrated by the slow gains of the integrationist strategy of the civil rights movement, a substantial segment of the black leadership has turned to varying degrees of separatist rhetoric and is asserting the existence of a captive and colonized black nation within the United States. Since the logic of black "nationalism" calls both for an attempt to create a separate culture and for legitimizing myths that the blacks already constitute a nation, there is a substantial African revivalist wing to contemporary black militancy.

As usual, social science is quick to respond to ideological winds, and the thesis that black Americans are very different from white ones has once more supplanted the older liberal-integrationist credo that Afro-Americans are just black Anglo-Saxons. A whole neo-Herskovitsian school spearheaded by urban anthropologists is sweeping the ghettos in search of black culture. As is usual in the social sciences, scholars easily find what they are determined to discover (a great superiority over the physical sciences), but in this particular field they are encountering intellectual opposition from the late Oscar Lewis' "culture of poverty" school. While increasing numbers of sociologists make a living from the sociology of poverty, the time seems ripe, if I may paraphrase Marx, for a searching analysis of the poverty of sociology.

THE NEGRO FAMILY
IN BAHIA, BRAZIL

The title is a misnomer for two reasons: first, this study is based almost entirely upon materials collected on only fifty families in the city of Bahia; and secondly, the designation "Negro family" has certain connotations for Americans which are misleading in regard to race relations in Brazil. Therefore, by way of introduction, I shall indicate first the nature and scope of the materials upon which this study is based and then give a brief account of the racial and cultural background of the population of Bahia. The data upon which our analysis is based consist of one to three interviews with each of fifty-five families during four and a half months residence in the city of Bahia. Forty of these families lived close to the seat or temple (o terreiro) of a religious cult, the Gantois Candomblé, in a semirural area of Bahia, known as Federação.[1] Sixteen of these forty families formed a close community about the Candomblé. In addition to these forty families, fifteen other families were interviewed in order to obtain comparative data on families occupying a different economic and social status. These families included three physicians, a teacher, a law graduate, two stevedores, a weaver, and three leaders of religious cults. Interview materials of a miscellaneous nature, which were obtained from many other persons, helped to give the investigator some general knowledge of the character of the family among certain classes in the population of Bahia.

Bahia, or Salvador, as the city was originally named in 1549, is located in the tropical part of Brazil on a bay 700 miles north of Rio de Janeiro. It was originally settled by a heterogeneous population consisting of adventurers and criminals banished from Portugal, impoverished noblemen, Jews

From E. Franklin Frazier, "The Negro Family in Bahia, Brazil," in *American Sociological Review*, 7 (August 1942), pp. 465–478.

expelled by the Inquisition, Jesuits and Catholic priests, and some gypsies.[2] The males among the indigenous Indian population were killed or driven into the interior and the Portuguese settlers took the Indian women as wives and concubines. During the sixteenth century, Bahia, or the Bay of All Saints, became one of the principal ports for the importation of Negro slaves. So great was the demand for slaves for the cultivation of sugar cane in the rural area surrounding the port that from 1785 to 1806 over 100,000 Negro slaves entered the port of Bahia.[3] On the basis of wealth produced by slave labor, Bahia became the center of Portuguese culture and its aristocracy became powerful in the affairs of the Brazilian state.

In contrast to the situation in the United States, the Portuguese and Brazilians had some knowledge of the tribal and cultural backgrounds of the imported Negro slaves. As stated by Ramos:

At the beginning of the slave trade, the largest number of those imported into Brazil were from Angola, the Congo and Guinea. When more active communication began with Bahia, the leading source of supply was Guinea and the western Sudan. There began a remarkable influx of Yorubas, Minas from the Gold Coast, Donhomans and various Islamized tribes such as the Hausas, Tapas, Mandingos, and Fulahs.[4]

Unlike the Negro in the United States, these Negro slaves were able to re-establish to some extent in the New World their traditional social organization and religious practices. In fact, it was due to this that they were able to organize their revolts which were more successful than similar attempts in the United States. In order to suppress these revolts, it became necessary to expel Mohammedan Negroes from Brazil. Nevertheless, many elements of African culture survived, especially religious practices that are perpetuated in the Candomblé, a religious cult, which embodies a fusion of African practices and Catholicism.

The type of rural civilization which grew up in Brazil on the basis of African slavery has been described by Gilberto Freyre in his celebrated work, *Casa Grande e Senzala*.[5] As indicated in the subtitle of this book, slavery became the basis of a patriarchal economy. Under the patriarchal organization, the Portuguese and the Negro slaves lived in close and intimate association, the racial and cultural background of the Portuguese having facilitated such association.[6] As a result of this association, a large class of mixed-bloods came into existence who enjoyed special privileges because of their kinship with the master class. These mixed-bloods became important in the history of Brazil as the once stable rural patriarchal organization began to disintegrate and urban communities began to dominate the life of the country during the first half of the nineteenth century. In a book describing this process, Gilberto Freyre devotes a chapter to the rise of the bachelor of arts and the mulatto.[7] In the mobile, urban society that came into existence, the mixed-blood found an opportunity to compete on almost equal terms with the pure blooded Portuguese. During this period, the pure-blooded Negroes, especially after emancipation, became more mobile and lost much of their African culture. In the absence of race prejudice, such as exists in the United States, the increasing mobility of the Negroes acceler-ated the mixture of the races. It is impossible to secure accurate figures on the extent of race mixture. Figure 8–1 is based upon the estimates of

FIGURE 8-1
**Estimated Percentage of the Population
of the City of Bahia—White,
Colored, and Black, 1897-1938**

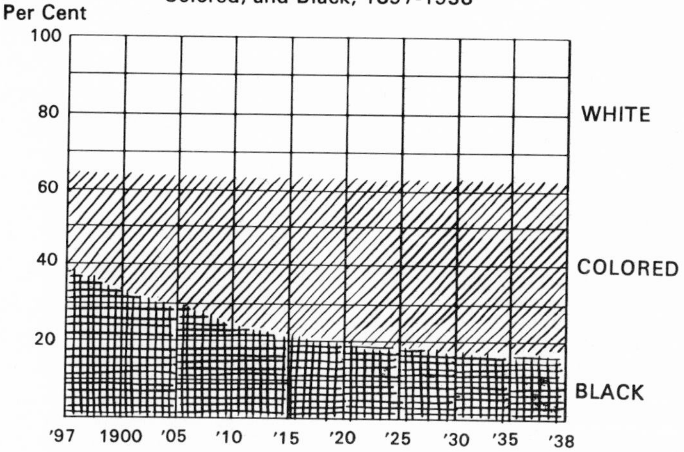

Source: Dr. Adolfo R. Leite
Inspetor Tecnico de Bio-Estatistica
da Cidade de Salvador

Adolfo R. Leite, the statistician in the Department of Health of the City of Bahia, who made his estimates on the basis of the school population and birth and death rates. Leite, realizing the unreliability of these statistics, was reluctant to have them used for scientific purposes, but it is significant that they are practically the same as Donald Pierson's estimates, which were based upon an inspection of 5,000 persons attending a festival in 1936.[8] According to Leite's estimates, from 1897 to 1938 the proportion of whites in the population remained about 33 per cent, whereas the proportion of blacks declined from 38 to 19 per cent. In 1936, Pierson estimated that 32.7 per cent of the population was white and 18 per cent black. Both Leite and Pierson estimated that about 50 per cent of the population was colored or

mulatto.[9] According to Leite's estimates, the black population has remained stationary from the standpoint of numbers, whereas the whites have
doubled and the colored have almost tripled their numbers. (See figure
8–2.) Although Pierson uses the term European for white in his table, in describing the whites he agrees with Leite that he is referring to skin color and
features and not pure white descent. Many whites in Bahia would be classed
as mulattoes in the United States. That the vast majority of the population
is mulatto is indicated in the designation of the city as "A *Velha Mulatta*,"
or "The Old Mulatto Woman."

In his study of racial and cultural adjustment in Bahia, Donald Pierson
has given a brief but excellent account of the history and the present economic and cultural organization of this city.[10] This study indicates that
although the city of Bahia has a population of nearly 400,000, or about the
same as Indianapolis, it is not a highly urbanized community in the sociological sense. In the lower city, there is a cluster of modern stores and banks
on several streets, hemmed in by a medieval market and ancient churches.

FIGURE 8-2
Estimated Growth of White, Colored, and Black
Elements in the Population of the
City of Bahia, 1897-1938

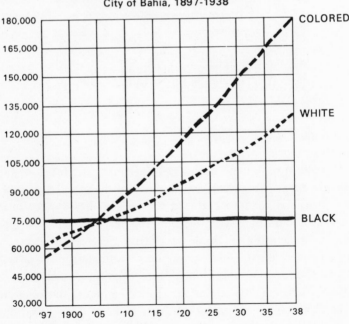

Source: Dr. Adolfo R. Leite
Inspetor Tecnico de Bio-Estatistica
da Cidade de Salvador

When one mounts to the upper city by a modern Otis elevator, one finds a main thoroughfare with a large modern hotel, small shops and a department store. Outside these areas, the richly appointed homes of the wealthy as well as the decayed houses of the poor bear the marks of a medieval civilization in a tropical setting. Within fifteen minutes after leaving the modern hotel, a street car brings one suddenly to semirural areas with mud and clay thatched huts shaded by tropical vegetation. It was in one of these areas, Federação, at the terminus of a streetcar line, that forty of our families lived.

Most of the houses in this section of the city have two rooms and are built of saplings and blocks of mud or clay with roofs of palm fronds. The better houses are covered with clay that is tinted or whitewashed, with wooden or concrete floors and tile roofs. The *seita*, or seat of cult, the Gantois Candomblé, is a one-story building about forty by sixty feet, one half of which is devoted to the ceremonies of the Candomblé, though women work and sew there during the day. This section has only a dirt floor and there are windows with shutters on three sides. The other half of the building has rooms for altars to African gods and Catholic saints and dwelling quarters for the *mãe de santo* (woman head of the cult) and her *filhas de santo* (daughters in saintliness). The *seita* is located on a low plateau surrounded by trees beyond the end of the streetcar line and may be reached by several footpaths. At the time of our study there were all together nineteen family groups living about the *seita*. These families formed a community of neighbors and friends who sought advice and help from the *mãe de santo* in case of need, sickness, or death. Not all of these families were members of the cult. Within the temple or *seita* itself there were three family groups, constituted as follows: a mother with three daughters; three sisters with a brother; the *mãe de santo* with two of her own children and an adopted child. During the course of an analysis of the data on the forty families, these sketchy details will become more meaningful.

From what has been said concerning the racial background of the population of Bahia, it is not surprising that these families showed considerable racial mixture. None of the persons interviewed regarded themselves as Negroes but simply as Brazilians. They used the term black as a means of identifying themselves with reference to color but not as to race. As far as possible, we attempted to construct genealogical trees showing the racial origin of each person interviewed.[11] This information was, of course, limited by their knowledge of their ancestors. About a fourth, or eleven, of the persons interviewed had no knowledge of their grandparents. Only seventeen had knowledge of all their grandparents or earlier ancestors, the remaining twelve knowing only one to three grandparents who were about equally divided between paternal and maternal line. Therefore, for only seventeen of our informants were we able to use genealogical trees in the determination of racial background. The genealogical trees of these seventeen informants showed the following backgrounds: six white and Negro; two Negro and Indian; two white, Negro, and Indian; two white and Indian; one pure white; and four pure Negroes. The remaining twènty-three families interviewed showed in their partial genealogies or physical appearance the same types of racial mixtures. These statistics are not important except that they express quantitatively the fact that these families represent all degrees of mixtures. However, one fact of significance is that the majority of those who did not know anything about their ancestors were black and Negroid enough· in their appearance to be regarded as pure Africans. Another factor of importance in regard to the group of families as a whole is the means of designating the race of their ancestors. Negro ancestors were designated as African or black, African being the term used for those who were born in Africa. The term *Caboclo*, which meant Indian and white mixture, was used interchangeably in two cases with *Cigano*, meaning gypsy. There is reason to believe some of those claiming *Caboclo* ancestors preferred the term to mulatto which implied Negro ancestry.

Our interest in the racial and cultural backgrounds of the persons interviewed was due primarily to our effort to discover the influence of African traditions and culture in the organization and functioning of their families. In attempting such a study, the writer was working in a virgin field, since investigators who have interested themselves in African survivals in Brazil have been concerned with the study of religious practices and beliefs, music, dances, and folklore.[12] This is doubtless attributable to the fact, as pointed out by Ramos, that slavery changed completely the social behavior of the Negro and that African culture survived only in his folklore.[13] That this has been true specifically in regard to the Negro family was borne out in the data which were collected on the families studied.

The first fact that impresses one about the families of our informants as a whole is that they lack the characteristics of a well established institution. This is indicated not only in their lack of knowledge concerning their ancestors but also in the absence of family traditions and continuity in family life. Whatever influence African traditions might have exerted upon the family organization of their African forebears in the New World had evidently been lost through racial mixture and the mobility of these families. Only three of the forty informants had any knowledge of African words and these words had been acquired in the Candomblé. In many of the families, African foods were eaten but such foods were eaten as they are eaten in many families in Bahia and even in the large hotel which is patronized by Brazilian intellectuals, business men, and foreigners. In only three cases were these foods eaten in connection with what might be called African rites and ceremonies. The important fact about such practices is that they were not transmitted through the family but had been acquired in the Candomblé.

The manner in which these practices have been acquired is shown in the case of one of the few informants who were able to trace their ancestry to African origins. (See figure 8–3.) This informant was a big, black, single woman of twenty-three years of age who made her living as a seamstress at fifteen cents a day. She was a *filha de santo* (daughter in saintliness) but went regularly to the Catholic Church. Her great grandfather, whom she described as of Nagô-Gêge or of Yoruba-Ewe mixture, died when she was a "small child." She had a vague memory that he could speak an African language, but she was too young to learn the language. In regard to family ties, the most important person was her mother who had married and had five children who were with her in Rio de Janeiro. After this marriage, her mother had lived *"maritalmente,"* or as the common-law wife, of a man for a few years during which time our informant was born. When our informant was left as an orphan, she was taken into the Candomblé where she learned a few African words, the meaning of which she had no knowledge. When interviewed, she was living with her father's nephew who acted as a father, requiring her to be in the house by dark. She said that she was a virgin and observed her *obrigações*, or certain ceremonies, in regard to foods and other rites connected with the Candomblé. As to the future, she wanted to be married in the Catholic Church and have children if it were the will of God.

Because of the importance of the Candomblé in the social life of certain elements in the black and colored population in Bahia, we shall consider at this point its relation to the families studied. The Candomblé has been studied by several Brazilian anthropologists[14] and by two American scholars, Donald Pierson and Ruth Landes.[15] Briefly described, the Candomblé is a religious institution in which African fetish worship has been fused with Catholic beliefs and practices. In the most important Candomblés in Bahia, the African practices are derived from the Yoruba nation or Nagô according to Bahian speech. The vast majority of the Nagô priests are women because, according to tradition, only women are eligible to render service to the African deities. However, the Candomblé is not only a center for religious festivals and worship; it is also the center of the social life of

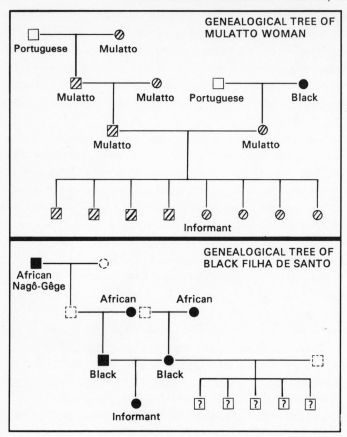

FIGURE 8-3
Genealogical Tree of Mulatto Woman
and of Black Filha de Santo

the neighborhood in which it is located. The families that live about the Candomblé visit the *seita* to gossip and spend their leisure hours. The *mãe de santo*, or priestess, who is regarded as the head of the community, is sought by those in need of physical as well as spiritual aid. Less than half of the forty families studied were connected with the Candomblé in the sense that they participated in its ceremonies. About three fourths of our informants attended the ceremonies of the Candomblé and also went to the Catholic Church; and two thirds of these regarded both as forms of religious expression. The remainder went to the Candomblé in order to enjoy themselves or *"apreciar"* the rites and were not participants. In fact, some of our informants made it clear that they went to the Catholic Church for worship and to the Candomblé in order to enjoy themselves. Of the remaining one fourth of our informants who did not go to the Candomblé, three did not attend even the Catholic Church.

Undoubtedly, in the past the Candomblé played a more important part in the religious life of the Negroes and provided group sanction for familial behavior that had been carried over from Africa. An old black informant said that when she came to Bahia over a half century ago, the Africans were living in a large house under a *pae de santo* (father in sainthood) and had a communistic division of the products of their labor which was carried on individually. They spoke an African language and practiced African rites. However, when she was seventeen years of age, she married the son of a gypsy woman who was opposed to the African way of life. This old woman, now widowed, attends the Catholic Church and the Candomblé.[16] This woman is one of the relatively few living ties with the African past. For example, in the old Candomblé Engenho Velho there are a few very old women living in the temple which was established over a hundred years ago by free Africans. The *mãe de santo*, who is over eighty years of age, is the daughter of two Africans, both of the Yoruba nation, who were brought to Brazil as slaves. She did not remember how many wives her father had but she was sure that his plurality of wives was sanctioned by the Candomblé.

In the family histories of three persons closely connected with the Candomblé, we can see how the African patterns of family life became disintegrated or were lost. In the Gantois Candomblé, which was in the neighborhood we studied, the office of *mãe de santo*, or priestess of the cult, has been filled by four generations of women in the same family. According to the present *mãe de santo*, her great grandfather was born in Africa of the Egba-Arake Tribe and was brought to Brazil as a slave. In Brazil, he married according to Catholic rites an African woman of the Gêge-Mahin Nation or Tribe, though he had another woman as a concubine. His wife was connected with a Candomblé and an African society in Bahia. This great grandmother left the Candomblé and founded the Gantois Candomblé over a hundred years ago. She was the mother of ten children. One of her daughters succeeded her as the *mãe de santo* of the Candomblé. Another daughter, who was the grandmother of the present *mãe de santo*, lived "*maritalmente*" with a musician by whom she had three children, two boys and a girl. When the girl grew to womanhood, she succeeded her aunt as the *mãe de santo* in Candomblé. She also lived "*maritalmente*" with a man who was a carpenter and bore him one child, the present *mãe de santo*. The present informant says that her great grandfather told her stories of Africa and slavery in Brazil. However, it was his daughter who became the *mãe de santo* who taught her African rites and the Yoruba language only a few words of which she knows at present. The present *mãe de santo* lived "*maritalmente*" with a man by whom she had two children.

The second family history is of a black man, sixty-one years of age, who is a *pae de santo* of a Bantu Candomblé.[17] He has little knowledge of his past except that he knew that he was the only child of his mother who was not married to his father. When eight years of age, he was given by his mother to his father who had been born free but had continued in the employ of his father's owner, a white woman. This white woman who became our informant's godmother was a member of a Candomblé. Our informant learned African rites and some knowledge of an African language from the *mãe de santo*, or priestess, who had learned African from an Angola man. Before his marriage 23 years ago, he lived for a time with two women, having had three children by the first and one child by the second woman. These children are living at present with their mothers. By his legal wife, he has had three children who live with him in the Candomblé which he inherited from the *mãe de santo* twelve years ago. Besides his own family, there are also living in the cult house a "*comadre*," or godmother, for the neophytes; three *filhas de santo* including an adopted daughter; and two nephews and two grandchildren. According to the *pae de santo*, when a person is taken into the Candomblé, she is baptized and given an African name. Since these ceremonies are secret and the neophytes swear not to reveal them, the investigator could not learn their nature. According to our informant, since the members of the Candomblé are regarded as brothers and sisters, no intermarriages are permitted between them.

The third informant is a man over eighty years of age who, in the words of one of the leading Brazilian novelists, is "the most noble and most impressive figure among the blacks in Brazil today." His father, who was of the Egba tribe, was brought to Brazil as a slave in the 1820's and freed in 1842. His mother was of the Yoruba Nation and was bought by her husband in 1855. His father and mother were never married either according to Catholic rites or Mohammedan rites, though at the time many Negroes were married according to Mohammedan rites. His grandfather, who was a warrior in Africa, had forty wives and his father, following African polygynous practices had five wives, of whom his mother was the chief wife. Although his father had a child by another woman before setting up his household, this woman was not included in the household. His father had four children, including our informant, by his chief wife. All of the cousins were considered brothers and sisters and, because he was the child of the chief wife, he had a special place in the family. He learned Yoruba from his parents and when around fourteen years of age went with his father to Africa. He remained eleven years in Africa where he perfected his knowledge of Yoruba in an English mission school. When he returned to Brazil he was long a *babalão*, or a sort of "father in saintliness." In former times, the *babalão* was a male connected with the Candomblés who practiced divination and sorcery. The sex life of our informant was of a casual nature until his marriage when fifty years of age. He had one child in Africa and, after returning to Brazil, he had about twenty children but did not know how many different mothers they had. He knows only one grandchild to whom he has given an African name just as he received from his parents an African name in addition to his Brazilian name. He and his first wife, to whom he was married by Catholic and civil rites, lived together fourteen years until her death. Only two years ago, he married another woman, according to Catholic and civil rites, who had been kind to him during an illness.

These three family histories have been presented because they show how African family patterns have disintegrated even when they had the support of a religious cult in which African practices have been perpetuated. However, there are certain facts in the family history of the priestess, as for example, the dominance of the female and the inheritance of the cult house, that might lead one to speculate upon the persistence of African culture patterns. It will be remembered that her great grandmother was of Ewe-Mahin origin, African tribes among which descent is traced in the female line and property is inherited by males on the mother's side. When we examine closely the data on her family, we find no consistent culture pattern but rather an accommodation to Brazilian conditions. The cult house was the property of the great grandmother and, instead of being inherited according to family law, it was given the next priestess. The family arrangements appear to be similar to Negro folk in the southern part of the United States. Likewise, in the case of the *pae de santo* of the Bantu Candomblé, there appear evidences of exogamous regulations concerning the members of the Candomblé which might have African origins. From the studies of Brazilian anthropologists, we know that Bantu culture either disappeared in Brazil or became merged in the Bantu Candomblés with the rituals and beliefs of the Sudanese Negroes. The disorganization of African patterns of family life are clearly shown in the case of the *babalão*. The father of our informant continued the polygynous practices of his African forebears and the system of family relationships according to which all cousins were regarded as brothers and sisters was perpetuated in Brazil. Our informant's sex life did not follow any consistent culture pattern. When he decided to form a marriage relationship, he married according to one in his position in Brazil. His interest at present in African culture is due partly to family tradition and racial pride and he is skeptical of the African beliefs and practices. His many illegitimate children and grandchildren are scattered in the Brazilian population and have not become the inheritors of African traditions. In fact, as fas as I was able to discover, this was generally true of the blacks and persons of African descent. There were no rigid culture patterns governing their family behavior. They exhibited the same characteristics as folk and peasant societies in other parts of the world.[18]

The manner in which the men and women in our families met and mated shows on the whole an absence of a consistent pattern of behavior though the influence of the Portuguese customs is apparent. More than half of the women had met their mates at work, casually on the street, or at the various festivals. The type of associations to which such contacts led is indicated by their marital status. Twenty of the women were married; ten had been married by both civil and church authorities; all except two of the remaining ten had been married by the church authorities alone. There were two women who called themselves widows, one of whom had never been married. Of the five single women, three said that they were virgins, and two were having casual sex relations with men. The remaining thirteen women in our forty families were living *"maritalmente"* with men, or in what we call a common-law relationship. To live *"maritalmente"* is sharply differentiated from a casual relation with a man.[19] It appears to be a customary form of marriage relationship which has grown up among the poorer classes because of the cost of a church or civil marriage. These marriages are evidently relatively stable since some of the couples had been together fifteen to twenty years and had reared large families.

In the organization of the families of our informants, there could be no question concerning the influence of the patriarchal family traditions of the Portuguese. In fact, as Landes has indicated, the position of *ogans*, or male providers, in the Candomblé and the *mãe de santo* bear a striking resemblance to the man's position in his household and the elder woman's position in the Brazilian family.[20] In every family where there was a male, except one, the man was recognized as the head of the house. The one exception was the case of a woman who owned the house. However, the subordination of the woman in these families was not as great as among the upper class Brazilian families. As pointed out by a Brazilian sociologist, the superior position of the Negro woman has been due to the loose family ties which have thrown upon her the responsibility of the family and to some extent to the woman's position in the Candomblé.[21] So far as our forty families were concerned, it appeared that the absence of institutional controls was primarily responsible for the woman's important position in family organizations. Where there had been legal or church marriages, the man was undoubtedly the head of the family. Although the same was generally true of common-law marriage, such relationships were more easily broken and the woman was often left with the responsibility of caring for the children.

Because of the weakness of institutional controls, the family among the majority of our informants tended to assume the character of a natural organization. In the vast majority of our families, the father and husband was an artisan earning about fifty cents per day who rented a house and a small plot of land for his family. In about a fourth of the families, there were three children who were cared for by their mothers during the day while their fathers were at work. Some of these men were known to have affairs with other women but their wives generally regarded this as a masculine privilege in a patriarchal society, but, generally, common interests and bonds of sympathy and affection held the men to their wives and children. As in the southern United States, where the family among many Negroes develops as a natural organization, some of the families included adopted children who had been left as orphans.[22] Only one woman said that she did not like and did not want children. The other wives and mothers regarded children, however numerous, as a gift from God. The children were generally treated indulgently by their fathers as well as their mothers. The girls were subject to the discipline of most girls in the Brazilian household. In a number of families where the girls had escaped parental surveillance to the extent that they could be suspected of sexual relations, they had been expelled from the household. In some cases in which their parents had not been married by civil or religious authorities, such girls had often been forgiven and protected by an indulgent mother. The girl's parents were more likely to be indulgent if the boy intended to live "*maritalmente*" with the girl and assume the obligations of a husband.

Space will not permit a detailed analysis of the black families of a higher social and economic status which were included in our study. The analysis of the family background of a very successful and popular pure Negro professional man will enable us to see how blacks succeed in mounting the economic and social ladder. The paternal grandparents of our informant were free Africans. On his maternal side, his great-grandparents were Africans who were probably slaves but his grandparents were free. His father was a mechanic who, after living seven years "*maritalmente*" with our informant's mother, deserted her and married another woman. When our informant's mother was left with two boys to support, she worked as a dressmaker and endeavored to give them an education which would give them a superior position in the world. Unlike his brother, who cared little for education and was satisfied to become a mechanic like his father, our informant, evidently because of his great devotion to his mother, developed the ambition to enter a certain profession. However, he changed his ambition because he knew that a black man in this particular profession would find it difficult, and decided to enter another profession. In the professional school, he won honors and free tuition. During the ten years that he has followed his profession, he has been highly successful. So far as his beliefs and behavior are concerned, he is a Brazilian, but it is interesting to note that his mother still goes surreptitiously to a Candomblé, which fact she does not openly confess and is regarded with amused indulgence by her son who belongs to another world.

Our investigation of the family life of the blacks in Bahia leads us to some tentative conclusions which should be tested by further study in the same area and other sections of Brazil. Because of the racial mixture which has taken place on a large scale, African patterns of family life have tended to disappear. The dissolution of African family forms was accelerated by the break-up of the rural patriarchal society and the mobility of the population which brought about increased race mixture. Where the black family has assumed an institutional character, it has generally been among those elements in the black and near-black population which have assimilated Brazilian or Portuguese culture. Among the poorer classes clustered about the Candomblés, the family, often based upon a common-law relationship, tends to assume the character of a natural organization. Whatever has been preserved of African culture in the Candomblé has become a part of the folklore of the people and, so far as family relationships are concerned, there are no rigid, consistent patterns of behavior that can be traced to African culture. As Brazil becomes urbanized and industrialized and the mobility of the folk increases, the blacks will continue to merge with the general population.

NOTES

1. Arthur Ramos, *O Negro Brasileiro* (São Paulo, 1940), 57–74.
2. See Donald Pierson, A *Study of Racial and Cultural Adjustment in Bahia, Brazil*, 1–6 unpublished Ph.D. dissertation (University of Chicago, 1939) for an excellent digest of materials on the history of the city of Bahia.

3. *Ibid.*, pp. 30–31.

4. Arthur Ramos, *The Negro in Brazil*, 11 (Washington, D.C., 1939).

5. Gilberto Freyre, *Casa Grande e Senzala* (Rio de Janeiro, 1939). Casa Grande e Senzala may be translated as *The "Big House" and the Slave Quarters*.

6. *Ibid.*, p. 2.

7. Gilberto Freyre, *Sabrados e Mucambos*, São Paulo, 1936. The title of this book may be translated as *Two Storied Town Houses and Huts*.

8. Pierson, *op. cit.*, p. 99.

9. According to Dr. Leite the percentage of colored (*pardos*) in the population increased from 29 in 1897 to 47.4 in 1938.

10. See Donald Pierson, *op. cit.*, chaps. I and II.

11. In nearly all of these forty families, only the wife or mother was interviewed because it was difficult to interview the men who were at work during the day and sometimes at night. Moreover, in arranging the interviews with our informant and his wife, whose home was generally used for the interviews, it was easier to secure the cooperation of the wives and mothers, who were in fact better able than their husbands to give the required information on the family. The investigator interviewed all persons in Portuguese.

12. See Gilberto Freyre e outros, *Novos Estudos Afro-brasileiros*, Trabalhos apresentados ao 1° Congresso Afro-brasileiro do Recife (Rio de Janeiro, 1937) and Varios Autores, *O Negro no Brasil* Trabalhos apresentados ao 2° Congresso Afro-brasileiro (Rio de Janeiro, 1940).

13. Arthur Ramos, "Culturas Negras: Problemas de Acculturação no Brasil," in *O Negro no Brasil*, pp. 153–154.

14. See Nina Rodriques, *Os Africanos no Brasil*, 2.a Edison, São Paulo, 1935 and *O Animismo Fetichista dos Negros Bahianos*, Rio de Janeiro, 1935 and more especially Arthur Ramos, *O Negro Brasileiro*, São Paulo, 1940; and Edison Carneiro, *Religiões Negras* (Rio de Janeiro, 1936) and *Negros Bantus* (Rio de Janeiro, 1937).

15. Donald Pierson, *A Study of Racial Adjustment in Bahia, Brazil* (Chicago, 1939) and Ruth Landes, "A Cult Matriarchate and Male Homosexuality," *Journal of Abnormal and Social Psychology* (1940), 35:386–397.

16. When her daughter began to show signs of possession, some people said that she was crazy but her "husband," who was an *ogan* of the Candomblé, said that she was possessed of an Indian spirit. There are today in Bahia *Caboclo* Candomblés that are organized about the worship of Indian deities. See Landes, *op. cit.*, 391–394.

17. See Edison Carneiro, *Negros Bantus*.

18. Robert Redfield, "The Folk Society and Culture," in *Eleven Twenty-six, A Decade of Social Science Research* (Chicago, 1940), pp. 39–50.

19. The two women who were having casual sex relations exhibited some shame when the said they were not living "*maritalmente*" with men. On the other hand, the women who were living "*maritalmente*" with their "husbands" exhibited the same pride as a woman who had entered a civil or church marriage.

20. Landes, *op. cit.*, p. 391.

21. See Nestor Duarte, *A Ordem Privada e A Organização Political Nacional*, 153 (Rio de Janeiro, 1939).

22. This is a widespread custom among Brazilians and does not appear to have an African origin.

THE NEGRO IN BAHIA, BRAZIL: A PROBLEM IN METHOD

I

Under the same title as the first part of the heading of this paper, Frazier has recently presented a brief analysis of Afro-Bahian family structure, considering its development, present form (or lack of form), and probable future.[1] Frazier's conclusions, which he terms tentative and which "should be tested by further study," are, briefly, as follows:

1. "African patterns of family life have tended to disappear";
2. "Where the black family has assumed an institutional character, it has generally been among those elements . . . which have assimilated Brazilian or Portuguese culture";
3. "Among the poorer classes . . . the family, often based upon a common-law relationship, tends to assume the character of a natural organization";
4. "Whatever has been preserved of African culture . . . has become a part of the folklore of the people and, so far as family relationships are concerned, there are no rigid, consistent patterns of behavior that can be traced to African culture."

It is proposed here to analyze these conclusions, drawing on the results of research in the same city where Frazier worked. Our analysis will be made in terms of a threefold approach, to be phrased in the following questions: What are the "African family forms" and the "African patterns of family life" from which the present-day Afro-Bahian family has evolved? What, in terms of this background, are the forms of the Afro-Bahian family as at present constituted, and, in similar terms, the sanctions of this institution? What methodological problems, as concerns relevance, competence,

From Melville J. Herskovits, "The Negro in Bahia, Brazil: A Problem in Method," in *American Sociological Review*, 8 (1943), pp. 394–402.

and effectiveness of application, arise from the analysis of similarities and differences between Frazier's sketch of the Afro-Bahian family and that to be given here?[2]

II

The study of Negro custom has written an interesting chapter in the history of the methodology of social science in the United States. For in this field, analysis of cultural survivals has been carried on with almost complete disregard of the aboriginal forms of behavior which are variously held to have survived, disappeared or changed form as a result of contact with majority patterns. The documentation of this phenomenon, and an analysis of the reasons why it prevailed have been given elsewhere, and need not here be repeated.[3]

It is but rarely recognized that this procedure is unique to this country. Elsewhere—in Cuba, Haiti, and Brazil, for example—every effort has been made by scholars working in this field to obtain as complete an account as possible of the African baseline of tradition from which their materials are known or are assumed to have been derived.[4] As Frazier observes for Brazil, the concern of Brazilian students was "with the study of religious practices and beliefs, music, dances and folklore," because of their conviction "that slavery changed completely the social behavior of the Negro and that African culture survived only in his folklore."

Frazier felt that Afro-Bahian social structure did offer a field for research, and proceeded to his investigation, bringing the techniques of the North American scholar to the study of his problem. In doing so, however, he imported into Brazil the methodological blind-spot that marks Negro research in this country. No reference to any work describing African cultures is made in his paper, and only oblique references to the forms of African social structure are encountered.

In speaking of a priestess who headed a cult-house whose ownership passed down in the maternal line, we are told that, "her great grandmother was Ewe-Mahin origin (*sic*), African tribes among which descent is traced in the female line and property is inherited by males on the mother's side." Tribes do exist in West Africa where the type of descent and inheritance described here is found, as, for example, the Ashanti of the Gold Coast. But the fact is that Gold Coast slaves were not imported into Brazil in significant numbers, a point established as firmly by documentary evidence as it has been by the findings of comparative ethnography. The social organization of the Dahomean and Yoruban peoples, on the other hand, is patrilineal, not matrilineal.[5] Again, Frazier mentions the polygynous pattern of West African family structure, citing an important figure in the Afro-Bahian cults whose grandfather, "a warrior in Africa" had forty wives, and whose father, "following African polygynous patterns," had five wives. For the rest, variations are rung on the statement that the data show "how African family patterns have disintegrated."

One more point must be made before we proceed to a sketch of West African social organization. As in most works in the American tradition which deal with the survival of African cultural traits, only overt forms, in what is conceived to be the strict African manifestation of a given aspect of social structure, are taken into consideration by Frazier, the underlying sanctions being ignored. That is, where polygyny, under New World stresses, has changed into a series of extra-legal relationships, the sociological reality of this accommodation is overlooked, African polygyny is held to have disappeared, and the psychologically invalid, but legally valid concept of "concubine" is accorded, in the literature, a validity it does not at all have for the people themselves.

The social organization of the Yoruban and Dahomean peoples of West Africa, who have played the most important role in shaping Afro-Bahian culture,[6] is a complex structure. The immediate family, consisting of a man, his wife or wives, and their children, is the fundamental unit. This group inhabits a compound, a series of houses surrounded by a wall or hedge. Each wife has a separate dwelling for herself and her children; the husband has his own structure, where the wives live with him in their allotted turn, cooking his food, washing his clothes, and otherwise ministering to his needs. In the nature of the case, however, the sex ratio being what it is, monogamous matings are by no means rare.

Human relationships within the polygynous household are of a quality that derives from the tensions inherent in the setting. Mother and children are knit by bonds far stronger than those which join father and children, even though descent in these cultures is in the paternal line; one shares one's mother only with one's "own" brothers and sisters, but a father is claimed by the children of all his wives. Each wife therefore uses all her ingenuity to obtain the most favorable position for her own children as against the children of her co-wives.

Even where polygyny is sanctioned, therefore, the life of the group is anything but calm. Songs, bitter songs of "allusion" are on record as sung by one wife against a rival; in the large household cliques intrigue one against the other when occasion arises. "One must be something of a diplomat," was the prescription of the head of one such household known for its smoothness of operation; and in this case, life goes on with no more friction than in any relationship where people are in close and continuous contact.

Typically, compounds are grouped in accordance with the descent of their heads, the compounds of a series of brothers forming what is technically called an "extended family." Sometimes an unmarried younger brother will live in the compound of his elder brother; on occasion, he continues living there even after he is married. The oldest in line of descent from the founder is the head of the group; on his death, the son he designates as heir takes over his compound, while the headship of the extended family passes to the next younger brother surviving the late chief. In certain instances in Dahomey, at least, a woman may be head of an extended family. Marriage types are numerous among this people, and a woman who commands wealth may "marry" an eligible girl, permitting a male friend to cohabit with her, and claiming, as "father," the offspring of her "wife." In this case, the descent unit goes no farther than the extended family, whose physical symbol of unity and whole unique position in society is marked by the rule that, however large, it must always inhabit a single compound, the headship of which is forever retained in the female line.[7]

A group of extended families constitutes a sib or clan, and the unity of this descent-group is validated by its mythologically conceived ancestry. The cult of the dead, as operative in the role of the ancestors in influencing everyday life, must thus be regarded and is actually so regarded by the Africans themselves as the mechanism which, more than any other single cause, gives the significant sanctions to social structures. A man or woman desires many children so that, at death, the proper funeral rites will insure a proper place in the after-world. As a single family grows to be an extended family, the place of the founder will, through eternity, be the more important; should the group attain the stature of a sib, he may look forward to becoming a national, "public" deity.

As in all societies where sib-organization obtains, the role of the sib is to regulate marriage. But, as has been indicated, marriage is an institution which takes many forms. If we refer again to Dahomey—the problem has not been as intensively studied elsewhere, but there is ample evidence to indicate that the Dahomean pattern does not differ widely from that prevalent in all West Africa—thirteen variant forms of marriage are recognized. These types fall into two principal categories, a fact that has implications of considerable importance for the analysis of Africanisms in

New World social organization. It thus merits a somewhat extended description:

> Actually, these forms may be regarded as specialized sub-types of either one or the other of two principal forms of marriage. . . . The French-speaking native denominates these two principal divisions of marriage types as "legitimate" and "illegitimate." The real significance of such classification, however, is revealed in the Fŏn terms for the marriage types which occur most frequently in each category, those in the first being called *akwénúsi*, "money-with women," and in the second *xadudo*, "friend-custody." The point of divergence, then, turns on the fact that marriages in the former category carry an obligation for the bridegroom to give to the father of his wife those traditional payments which, in turn, give him control of the children born of the marriage; while in the latter category these obligations are not assumed and, though the children are members of the sib of their father, control over them remains in the hands of their mother or of her people.[8]

Thus it is to be seen that among this West African folk, and among others where analogous marriage systems are found, there exists an entire series of matings wherein the woman is free to determine the course of her marriage and its permanence. And among these tribes, be it noted, no demoralization of social patterns exists!

Though the control of children rests in the father or mother respectively, in accordance with whether or not the sanctioned payments to the family of the bride have passed, the affiliation of the child, as far as his spiritual being is concerned, is invariably to his father's line, since it is from the father that a child inherits his soul. This is not only the case in patrilineal societies; among the Ashanti, where socio-economic position is determined by affiliation in the maternal line, along which incest prohibitions are drawn, the soul descends from father to child, something so important that it gives rise to a type of preferential mating.

Actually, in West Africa—and, in all likelihood, over all the continent—both parents figure prominently in shaping the destiny of the child. The institutionalized manifestations of this point of view are merely objectifications of attitudes that sometimes take less overt forms. One of these is the attitude, in these societies where unilateral descent is the rule, toward the "off" parent and his family—the parent to whom one is not socially related. Dahomey, again, offers a good instance of this for the area. Here, it will be remembered, the entire "feel" of the descent system is patrilineal; yet the relationship between a person and his mother and her family is extremely close. Where a paternal uncle or grandparent would punish if appealed to by a younger sib-mate in difficulty, a maternal relative will give aid, and help to quiet an embarrassing situation.

III

In the light of the foregoing sketch of West African family structures and their underlying sanctions, let us re-examine the social organization of the Afro-Bahians to see whether or not the picture of almost complete disorganization Frazier presents cannot be resolved into a series of recognizable patterns of both form and sanction. It must be emphasized that what we seek are Africanisms, without reference to their degree of purity; that we are concerned with accommodations to a new setting; that our aim is neither prescription nor prediction, but the understanding of process under acculturation.

In the Brazilian scene, where all the weighting of prestige goes to the modes of behavior of the dominant group, it is natural that the Afro-Bahians, as full citizens of their community, should respond to these values as do their fellows of European descent. All the force of church and state is thrown behind the monogamous mating sanctioned by a marriage ceremony performed in the registry and, later, by the priest before his altar. This is reflected in speech-habits whereby a legal wife is called "Madame" as against the "Senhora" that is the appellation of any mature woman.

Especially among the darker segments of the population are parents jealous to achieve marriage in the legal sense for their daughters. For even under the minimum of interracial tension that exists in Brazil, the black folk, as many of them frankly will tell a listener interested in problems of marriage, feel they must prove their morality in terms of majority values, and that they cannot afford even the liberties the mulatto may take. Black girls are therefore believed to be and, in such cases as could be observed, actually were under a surveillance more strict than were lighter ones.

This feeling goes so far that, it is stated, sex adventures on the part of a black daughter may result in the father's appeal to the law and a forced marriage. Once married, with a ring on her finger and reputation secure, events may proceed as the pair determine. If compatibility develops, the marriage may endure, and on occasion does. If not, husband and wife separate, each free to enter into such new matings as interest and desire dictate.

The patterns of these "regular" marriages are those of the majority of the population, though there are certain sanctions not known to whites, and which the Afro-Bahian will speak of only "to those who have understanding of such things"—to quote his favorite idiom. Reference is had to these steps which assure to the Afro-Bahian that his marriage has the consent of the African deities and the ancestors. These steps are more commonly taken by the woman who, in terms of both European and African patterns, is the more concerned of the two in the consummation and continuation of the marriage. To this end, she consults a diviner to find out whether some other person "blocks the path," and if there is shown to be such a one, Eshu, the guardian of the cross-roads, is invoked to clear the way. Some two weeks before the marriage takes place, a second offering to this same deity is made and another to his master, Ogun, who cares for paths.

From a day to several weeks before the marriage, a cock will be given to the *egun*[9]—for "the ancestors must be fed." In true African fashion they will be called, notified of the impending marriage of their "child," asked to help the match prosper, and then "sent away." If the bride is a widow, the *egun* of her dead husband must be fully propitiated; the diviner is visited to ascertain the wishes of the dead and they are punctiliously fulfilled lest he jealously vent his anger on the new spouse. As a part of this complex, a mass for dead parents of the pair, if they are not living, or even a grandparent, is offered and pilgrimages are made to various special churches on the Sunday following the ceremony. But for one other element, this completes the cycle of ritual. Some time before the marriage, a month or two weeks, the young man and woman, or she alone if he is unable or unwilling to accompany her, go to the cemetery to pray to the souls of their parents, if these are not living. It is asked that they "work with God" for the happiness of the offspring, and to ensure the success of the venture. And a month after the marriage, the couple return to give thanks to the same spirits.

It may be objected that all this is "folklore," and has little or nothing to do with the sociological reality that is the family. The very fact that matings are classified as "legal" or "common-law" marriages, however, indicates that sanctions do figure in setting up categories and evaluating findings. In the situation with which we are concerned, and in other New World Negro groups, what is being studied are the survivals of a non-European culture in a society whose dominant traditions are European in origin and character. Hence, it is critical, even where the overt institutions of the dominant group prevail, to determine whether or not sanctions that derive from another cultural stream have been retained, and the form which these take in the new configuration.

As concerns the Afro-Bahian family, however, we may ask whether, in addition to the non-European sanctions of the dominant, conventional

European marriage form discussed above, survivals of African family types in institutionalized form cannot be discerned. This question may be investigated in terms of possible retentions of the essential points of West African social structure outlined in the preceding section—patterns of polygyny, of sexual independence of women, and of the relations between mother and children as against those between father and children. This, in turn, brings us first of all to a consideration of social as against legally sanctioned types of mating, and to the position of the children in terms of legal and social conceptions of legitimacy.

In Bahia, as elsewhere among New World Negroes, extra-legal matings are common, and have a special designation to distinguish them from legal unions, to which the word "marriage" is given. Thus in Haiti, the system is termed *plaçage*; in Trinidad, a couple who live together as in this way are called "keepers"; in Bahia, the institution termed *mancebia* (concubinage) in literary Portuguese, is locally called by the better known word *amásia* (from which are derived the forms *amasiado, amasiada,* applied to the man or woman living in this relationship).[10] As elsewhere, though it is held in somewhat less esteem than the regular marriage form, it is far from being an index of demoralization.[11] If anything, its continuation can be ascribed, here as elsewhere in Negro America, to economic forces, which have reinforced historical drives and traditional derivations.[12] The *amásia* mating is simple to arrange, solves the problem of the desire for permanent relationship and for children, does all this at an economic level which is within the reach of those concerned, and affords a union that has social sanction.

This last point is essential. As far as the Negroes are concerned, matings of these kinds are marriages. In many cases they last a lifetime.[13] In other instances they take on a less permanent character, enduring for a year, two years, five years; then the man and woman part to find new mates.

The formal investigation into a young man's or young woman's background, personal and family reputation, that is a requisite to marriage in Africa, understandably is absent in the *amásia* mating. This may occur where legal marriages are contemplated, and is not too common even in these cases. If we recall the Dahomean marriage forms of "free" mating, which are often contracted without parental consent, it is apparent that this tradition, and the economic position of the Afro-Bahian woman,[14] explain why "more than half of the women" members of the families interviewed by Frazier, "met their mates at work, casually on the street, or at various festivals." In Bahia, moreover, many of the *amásia* relationships are entered into by persons who had been legally married, but who have left their wives or, more often, their husbands. Divorce, in this Catholic setting, is impossible; the new union is therefore effected on the level of folk-mating, and bigamy avoided.

African patterns of polygyny have by no means disappeared. Plural marriage is not called by this name, and takes some probing to uncover. The *amásia* mating, however, provides the mechanism which permits the tradition to remain a living one. Of course, for a married man to maintain a mistress is no novelty in the European scene, nor must it be forgotten that under slavery a master often had two families, one white and one Negro, and that, in any event, his female slaves were always accessible to him. These are factors which have reinforced aboriginal custom, which finds expression not only in the case of men who have a legal wife and two or three *amasiadas*, each with her children, but in those of men who visit more than one *amasiada* in turn, and are not legally married at all.

The common finding among New World Negroes, that children are closer to their mothers than to their fathers, applies to the Afro-Bahians, and is most clearly indicated by the fact that when a union is broken, the children almost invariably go with the mother. So regularly does this method of disposing of children occur, and so recognized is it by the people as the proper procedure, that it demonstrates the presence of a living, functioning pattern which governs this particular aspect of social behavior. Where the children belong in such cases is not even open to question, and few instances contrary to the rule were encountered among the many observed or discussed.

It is important to understand the role of the father and the attitudes toward him. Where broken homes represent a pathological phenomenon, and the children are retained by the mother, the father disappears from the scene. But in the Afro-Bahian convention, the role of the father, most important while the family remains intact, is often continued when he leaves. It is rare for a mother to teach her children to hate their father even when parents have become bitter enemies on parting; it is held to be spiritually harmful to the child for her to impart such an attitude. In the same way, though she may strong resent a man with whom she lives having another mate, her children will not be permitted to quarrel with the offspring of their father's other wife. Even after separation, the children visit and may be visited by their father.

Instance after instance of this was observed, or came out in conversation, as when a man would say, "Of course, my father and mother don't live together any more, but I go to see him now and then," or when a half-brother and -sister would come with their common father, amicably to discuss their Afro-Bahian ways of life, or to record the songs of their African cult-groups. A woman is expected to call in the husband who no longer lives with her when his child merits a major punishment; a man customarily provides clothing and contributes toward the maintenance of his child by a woman from whom he has separated; and woe to the child who speaks ill of his father before his mother!

Most revealing of all are the duties wives and children owe the spirit of a dead husband and father. The *egun*, the ghost, exacts its tribute in almost complete African fashion. Though only a widow wears mourning, and an *amasiada* does not, all of a man's children, by no matter what women, must wear full mourning. The oldest son of the legally married wife, if there is one, or of the oldest *amasiada*, becomes family head, and must see to it that the junior members do not want. There is none other than the moral obligation to do this, yet belief is strong and, in any event, a man would fear his father's *egun*.

Offerings to the dead man's soul expresses the inner unity of the group which had a common husband and father. These offerings are given at the death-rites which separate a member of an African religious sect from his cult-groups, and on the first, third, and seventh anniversary of his death. On these occasions all must contribute—the wife, the *amasiadas*, their children. A woman who has remarried or remated will, if necessary, ask her new husband to aid her in amassing the necessary sum; and he must contribute for fear of the dead if he refuses. Here there is no quarreling; all the women and children, under the leadership of the man's senior mate or oldest son unite amicably to see that the death-rites, not alone of the African cults, but in the form of masses for the souls of the dead, are adequately provided for.

IV

It is apparent that the picture of the Afro-Bahian family drawn by Frazier differs widely from that sketched here. And this brings us once more to the methodological problem raised at the outset of this discussion. On the basis of considerable experience among Negro groups, it is to be doubted whether the kind of interview technique he describes as having been employed in his study can yield very satisfactory results when applied to these folk. The point is best documented in terms of the very persons whose family histories are given by Frazier. For in a city the size of Bahia, it is not difficult to recognize descriptions of individuals, even when they are treated anonymously.

The case we are to analyze is that of the "big, black single woman" twenty-three years old, a *filha de santo* (cult initiate);[15] a seamstress; a member of the Catholic church; living in the family of her father's nephew, who is a strict disciplinarian. As far as it goes, this checks with the findings of this research, if the total impression given by the phrasing of the description is disregarded. This matter of shading is important, as is to be seen from the following; our subject, as has been said, is a cult-initiate, "but went regularly to the Catholic church"; when, as a young orphan, she was taken into the cult "she learned a few African words, the meaning of which she had no knowledge." "She said she was a virgin and observed her *obrigações*, or certain ceremonies, in regard to foods and other rites connected with the Candomblé." Finally, "As to the future, she wanted to be married in the Catholic church and have children if it were the will of God."

One of the objectives of this research in Bahia was the recording of Negro songs. Most of the records were made by teams who became familiar with the technique employed, each group being composed of singers and drummers, usually consisting of members of a single family. One of these teams was the family to which this girl belongs.

If there is any other family in Bahia which, on the surface, is more acculturated to European ways of life, and at the same time more devoted to African cult-practices, it would be difficult to find it. The husband and father, this girl's father's nephew, is a renowned drummer at the cult rites, and has been principal *ogan*, or male official, of one of the most orthodox Afro-Bahian cult-groups. His wife, who dresses carefully in the European manner and never wears the traditional Bahian Negro woman's costume except in her house, is herself a priestess; though at the time of Frazier's visit, she only functioned as a diviner and curer, and had not attained this higher status. In the house of this family are numerous shrines, all skillfully concealed from casual visitors.

The "big, black single woman" plays her full rôle, in this scene. In singing for the recording instrument, she was the soloist, since her knowledge of cult-songs is wide and her voice good. At one quite esoteric rite witnessed at this house, she led the singing as she did at the laboratory. She knows, and gave a list of, over one hundred words and phrases in Nago, the West African Yoruban tongue, and their translation; the words of almost all the dozens of songs she recorded are in this language. Like all members of the Afro-Bahian cults she is a good Catholic; but she is already preparing for her seventh anniversary cult-rites, which are the most elaborate an initiate must give, and after which she becomes a senior cult-member. Our subject does indeed wish to marry "in the Church" and have children. But she has another ambition. This is to become a *mãe pequena* in a good cult-house; that is, she desires to be an assistant priestess. She is a modest young woman; her god, she says, has not yet manifested the knowledge or power to permit her to be a future *mãe de santo!*

This example has been considered at some length, because it so clearly illustrates the methodological deficiencies of the interview technique as employed by Frazier. This is especially the case when its user is handicapped, as in the study of New World Negro groups, by the acceptance of an hypothesis concerning the disappearance of African traits which renders it difficult for him to discern them when he comes on them, or to evaluate their importance if he does see them.

On the basis of the materials in the preceding section, it would seem that Frazier's statement, "African patterns of family life have tended to disappear" is something less than fact, and that the "either-or" position implied in Frazier's second conclusion cited at the outset of this paper overlooks the well-recognized process of syncretism that provides the means to reconcile African and European divergencies in tradition.

Frazier's third conclusion is difficult to understand. What, indeed, makes of the Afro-Bahian family a "natural organization"?

In the vast majority of cases, the father and husband was an artisan earning about fifty cents per day who rented a house and a small plot of land for his family. In about a fourth of the families, there were three children who were cared for by their mothers during the day while their fathers were at work.

Are these its characteristics? The untenability of the hypothesis of the "weakness of institutional controls" has been demonstrated in the preceding section. If one but knows where to look for these controls, or how to analyze them when one finds them, they are not difficult to describe. Is the "natural family" indeed, to be considered as one manifestation of them?

The final point, concerning the absence of "rigid, consistent patterns of behavior that can be traced to African culture" where family relationships are concerned, involves a concept of culture open to serious objection. How "rigid" is any series of socialized behavior patterns? Have not the lessons taught by years of studying social institutions in various cultures demonstrated that variability in behavior, rather than rigidity, is the rule? Is it possible that Frazier implies that the customs of nonliterate folk (Africans are, from this point of view to be classed as "primitives"), are in the nature of the outmoded concept of the cultural strait-jacket? As far as the consistency of the Afro-Bahian patterns of family life is concerned, it must at least be recognized that they are consistent enough to permit their being outlined in the manner in which they have been here. If one goes back over the data in Frazier's paper itself with this point in mind, these same patterns can be found either implicit in the materials, or explicitly stated.

THE NEGRO IN BAHIA, BRAZIL: PROBLEM IN METHOD

In the final analysis, we are dealing with an acculturative situation, and the past of the Afro-Bahians being what it is, greater variation in any phase of custom is to be looked for than in the indigenous cultures either of Africa or Europe. But in studying this situation it must never be forgotten that variation does not mean demoralization, and that accommodation, institutional no less than psychological, is not prevented by the fact of cultural syncretization.

NOTES

1. *American Sociological Review*, Vol. VII (August 1942), pp. 465–478. The term "Afro-Bahian" is an adaptation of "Afro-Brazilian," a designation commonly used by Brazilian students of the Negro.

2. The materials incorporated in this paper were gathered in 1941–42, during a field trip to study the Brazilian Negro. This research was undertaken with the support of a grant from the Rockerfeller Foundation. The field-work was carried on by Mrs. Herskovits and the writer. It is a pleasure to record my indebtedness to Dr. José Valladares, Director of the Bahian State Museum, who gave so liberally of his time in aiding this research, not only as interpreter, but as friend and fellow-student.

3. M. J. Herskovits, *The Myth of the Negro Past*, passim, but especially pp. 54–61.

4. *Cf.*, for example, the works of Fernando Ortiz on the Cuban Negro, of Price-Mars for Haiti, of Nina Rodrigues, Arthur Ramos, Gilberto Freyre, and others for Brazil.

5. For the Yoruba, *cf.* P. A. Talbot, *The Peoples of Southern Nigeria*, Vol. II, pp. 539, 683, *inter alia*; for Dahomey, *cf.* M. J. Herskovits, *Dahomey*, Vol. I, pp. 137 ff. See also for the Gã, M. J. Field, *Social Organization of the Gã People*, pp. 1–65. For the Ashanti matrilineal system, wherein, however, descent on the father's side also assumes importance, *cf.* R. S. Rattray, *Ashanti*, pp. 22 ff., 37 ff., 45 ff.

6. The Congo-Angola influences are not taken up here, since their weight in this process cannot as yet be evaluated. Frazier's statement (p. 475), that, "From the studies of Brazilian anthropologists, we know that Bantu culture either disappeared in Brazil or became merged in the Bantu Candomblés with the rituals and beliefs of the Sudanese Negroes," is unacceptable; on the very pages he cites (in note 13) of an article by Ramos, this student gives a list of aspects of Afro-Brazilian cultural traits imported from the Congo area. The literature from this region is, on the whole deficient, but we have enough information to indicate that the unilateral descent pattern, polygyny, and the ancestral cult, are among the aspects it had in common with the Dahomean-Yoruban cultures, which means that these traits would be reinforced under contact with European tradition. *Cf.*, for example, W. D. Hambley, "The Ovimbundu of Angola," Field Museum Pub., Anth. Ser., 21 (1934), pp. 179–199.

7. *Cf.* M. J. Herskovits, "A Note on Woman Marriage," *Africa*, 10 (1937), pp. 225–341. It is to this convention, rather than to a rule of matrilineal descent, that the inheritance of the Bahian cult-center in the matrilineal line noted by Frazier is to be referred.

8. M. J. Herskovits, *Dahomey*, Vol. I, pp. 301–302.

9. The *egun* cult of the dead is practiced in Nigeria today as it was when the Africans brought it to Brazil.

10. This is presumably the type of mating Frazier means when he speaks of a woman "living 'maritalmente' " with a man.

11. Frazier's finding that a "weakness of institutional controls" exists for Bahian social structure is not strengthened when he tells us that only two out of the forty women he interviewed were living casually with men, and they were ashamed of the fact; while "the women who were living 'maritalmente' with their 'husbands' exhibited the same pride as a woman who had entered a civil or a church marriage" (p. 476, n. 19).

12. This fact is recognized by Frazier: "It appears to be a customary form of marriage relationship which has grown up among the poorer classes because of the cost of a church or civil marriage."

13. Frazier's material amply documents this, some of the couples he studied having been living together fifteen to twenty years, and having reared large families.

14. *Cf.* M. and F. Herskovits, "The Negroes of Brazil," *Yale Review*, 32 (1943), pp. 264–266.

15. Frazier's acceptance and use of the translation "daughter in saintliness" is unfortunate; so is his use of "father in saintliness" for *pae de santo*. This latter term, for instance, is actually a literal translation of the Yoruban babalorisha ("father of the gods"), and the English equivalent is "priest."

REJOINDER: THE NEGRO
IN BAHIA, BRAZIL

This rejoinder to Professor Herskovits' criticism of my article is written simply because the facts which I gathered in Brazil do not support his conclusions. It is not written because, as he has stated in his *The Myth of the Negro Past* (p. 31), I belong among those Negroes who "accept as a compliment the theory of a complete break with Africa." It is a matter of indifference to me personally whether there are African survivals in the United States or Brazil. Therefore, if there were a "methodological blind spot imported from the United States," it was due to my ignorance of African culture or my lack of skill in observing it. However, it should be pointed out that Professor Herskovits was interested in discovering Africanisms and that I was only interested in African survivals so far as they affected the organization and adjustment of the Negro family to the Brazilian environment.

I must emphasize here what I stated in my paper, namely, that the majority of the families that I studied represented all degrees of racial mixtures involving whites, Negroes, and Indians. Therefore, when the designation Negro was used, it was used in the sense in which we use the term in the United States. I did not find in Bahia any group of Negroes of pure blood or blacks who were isolated from white, yellow, and brown people. It is possible, of course, that Professor Herskovits found such groups and among such groups African culture traits were apparent in their family life. I was careful to state that my conclusions should be tested by further research. But even if allowance is made for the possibility that Professor

From E. Franklin Frazier, "Rejoinder," in *American Sociological Review*, 8 (1943), pp. 402–404.

Herskovits studied a different group of Negroes, there are certain phases of his criticisms which cannot go unanswered.

First, I would like to point out that if what I said about the woman who stated that her great grandmother was of Ewe-Mahin origin is read in its context, his remarks about Gold Coast Negroes are irrelevant. I know as well as Professor Herskovits that Gold Coast Negroes were not imported into Brazil in large numbers. My remark was simply that the manner in which the candomblé was inherited might lead one to speculate upon the influence of African culture. Secondly, I would like to emphasize that it was not my intention to give a picture of complete family disorganization among the so-called Negroes. As I undertook to show in my article, the family among these people did not have an institutional character but grew out of association of men and women in a relationship which was based upon personal inclinations and habit. Although it is customary for men and women to initiate family life in such a manner, I found no evidence that their behavior was due to African customs. White men and women of the lower class form exactly the same type of unions. This behavior has grown up among lower class Brazilians because of certain social and economic factors. As stated in my article, these people speak of themselves as living together "maritalmente" or "marriedly." For some reason Professor Herskovits does not seem to be acquainted with this term. He states that I must be referring to the relationship of "amasiado." My informants as well as persons acquainted with family relations among this group assured me that there was an important difference between the two relationships. The relationship known as "amasiado" is more of a free love relationship, whereas when people live "maritalmente" their relationship is regarded as conjugal. In the former relationship a man may only visit his "amásia," but when a man lives "maritalmente" with a woman he lives with her and assumes the responsibility for the support of her and her children. As stated in my article, these so-called "common-law marriages" (my term) often grow out of pregnancy or when a man has deflowered a girl and he either voluntarily or at the demand of her parents makes a home for her and assumes the responsibility of a husband. In such practices one can observe the influence of Brazilian culture which is intensely patriarchal. Moreover, I found no evidence for Professor Herskovits' statement that blacks exercise more surveillance over the sex behavior of their daughters than persons of lighter color. The amount of surveillance is a matter of class, the members of the upper and middle classes—black, brown, or white—showing more regard for the sex behavior of their daughters than members of the lower class.

Professor Herskovits has objected to the case which I cited as an illustration of the manner in which the African heritage has disintegrated and has been lost. In my analysis I made clear that when my informant's father took five wives and built houses for them, he was behaving in accordance with his African heritage. But when my informant first had a child in Africa (where incidentally he learned some of his Yoruba in a Mission school) and later in Brazil had about twenty children as the result of casual sex relations, the African heritage had begun to disintegrate and lose its meaning. The children whose mothers were of diverse racial origin and for whom no home was provided by the father had no opportunity to take over his African heritage. The sex behavior of my informant was obviously promiscuous; and certainly Professor Herskovits would not say that promiscuous sex behavior, except where it was ritualistically controlled, was an African culture trait. During his residence in Brazil, my informant was becoming a Brazilian, for when he got married he married in the Catholic church and settled down as a respectable Brazilian. I am not prepared to say how far my informant's attitudes toward sex and marital relations were still influenced by his African heritage but his overt behavior conformed to Brazilian standards.

The mobility of this informant provides a good transition to what I have to say concerning another claim which Professor Herskovits makes concerning the persistence of African traits in the families of Brazilian Negroes. In my paper I showed that the spouses in the families which I studied had met casually at work, at festivals and even in the street. To me this meant that the increasing mobility of Brazilian life had caused marriage or mating to be a fortuitous affair. But according to Professor Herskovits this is an African culture heritage! Moreover, in regard to my assertion that there is no consistent pattern of marriage and mating Professor Herskovits offers the objection that I have a mistaken notion of culture among primitive people; that in fact primitive culture shows variations. If culture is defined as patterns of behavior there must be some consistency in behavior or otherwise behavior is the result of the fortuitous operation of impulses. In fact, it seems that Professor Herskovits rules out human impulses, spontaneous emotions, and sentiments generated through the association of members in the same household. He seems to ridicule the idea that the family may come into existence as a "natural organization." From my studies of the Negro family in the southern states I am convinced that without the operation of institutional controls, the family group often develops as the result of the interaction between spouses and children in the same household.

Professor Herskovits thinks that he has identified the young woman whose genealogy I gave in my article and contradicts my statement that she knew only a few African words which she had learned in candomblé. After going over my records I have found that he has not identified the young woman though I have a record of the young woman he mentions. Concerning the foster parents of the young woman whom he mentions he makes the statement: "If there is any other family in Bahia which, on the surface, is more acculturated to European ways of life, and at the same time more devoted to African cult-practices, it would be difficult to find it." I visited this family nearly every day and I knew its members very well. I was acquainted with the shrines which were "all skillfully concealed from casual visitors." I knew also that the "wife" who is a mixed-blood was originally possessed by an Indian god and that people said that she was crazy; but that her "husband" when he secured her to live "marital-mente" with him convinced her that it was an African god. Moreover, her husband who is black and knows nothing of his parents did not receive his knowledge of African lore and skill in beating the drums through his parents. These facts as well as others which I have cited have been checked with the findings of Dr. Ruth Landes who spent over a year in Brazil and was intimately acquainted with this family.

Although problems of anthropology and ethnology cannot be settled by analysis of grammatical forms, I would like to answer Professor Herskovits' criticism of my translation of pae-de-santo which is the designation of the cult leader of the candomblé. According to Professor Herskovits my translation of this term as "father-in-saintliness" is unfortunate because it really means "father of the god." In the Portuguese language, the preposition "de" without the article is used with a noun to denote quality. Therefore, I translated the terms pae-de-santo, mãe-de-santo, and filha-de-santo as "father-in-saintliness" (sainted father or holy father), "mother-in-saintliness" and "daughter-in-saintliness." In the Portuguese dictionary the term pae-de-santo is incidentally given as an example of the use of *santo* as an adjective. (See Pequeno dicionario brasiliero da lingua portuguesa. 2. Ediçâo. Rio de Janeiro, 1939, p. 923.) Professor Herskovits made the mistake (see his *The Myth of the Negro Past*, p. 220) of writing *filha-do-santo* instead of *filha-de-santo*. The term filha-do-santo, translated literally would be daughter of the god because "do" is the contracted form of the preposition "de" and the definite article "o." But filha-de-santo means "holy daughter" just as "uma casa de madeira" means "a wooden house." A Brazilian and an American anthropologist have both translated the term pae-de-santo into English as "father-in-saintliness." (See Ruth Landes,

"Fetish Worship in Brazil," *The Journal of American Folklore*, Vol. 53 (October–December, 1940), pp. 261–270; and Edison Carneiro, "The Structure of African Cults in Bahia," *ibid.*, pp. 271–278.) However, I wish to emphasize that I did not depend upon the Portuguese grammar for a translation of these terms. I tried to find out what the terms pae-de-santo, mãe-de-santo, filha-de-santo meant to the people themselves. In no case did I find that these terms meant father-, mother-, or daughter-of-the-god. So far as I was able to get their meaning, *santo* meant a quality which they acquired. In fact, one pae-de-santo told me that he was really only a *zelador* or *zealot* because there was only one who was *santo* or holy and he dwelt on high. This remark undoubtedly revealed the influence of Catholicism which has been fused with the beliefs and practices of cult.

After reading Professor Herskovits' paper I see no reason to change the conclusions started in my article, though they are tentative and should be tested by further research. There may be some ritualistic practices of African origin connected with the sex and family life of the Negroes which I did not discover. It is not without interest that there can be no dispute about African survivals in the candomblé. In the case of the candomblé it is easy to observe and record African survivals, whereas Professor Herskovits' statement concerning African family survivals are chiefly inferences based upon speculation. Even in the candomblés, as Carneiro points out (*loc. cit.*, pp. 277–278), African traditions and practices are disappearing. So far as the pattern of the family is concerned, I am still convinced that African influences have on the whole disappeared and that the type of family organization which we find among the Negroes whom I studied has grown up in response to economic and social conditions in Brazil. The African survivals which one finds among the upper class black families such as the eating of certain foods and in their music is a part of the national culture of Brazil.

PART IV

Endogamy and Exogamy

Editor's Introduction

Of the many manifestations of race and ethnic relations, rules of endogamy have been among the most studied. Nearly ubiquitous in all multi-ethnic and multi-racial societies, endogamy tends to be *preferential* in cases of ethnic groups and *prescriptive* in cases of racial groups. The rule of prescriptive endogamy characteristic of many racist societies became, along with the criteria of hierarchy and completely ascribed membership, the basis of the analogy to caste so frequently used in the race literature. Introduced by Alfred Kroeber in anthropology, the notion of racial castes was extensively used by W. Lloyd Warner, Gunnar Myrdal, and the entire "caste and class" school of race relations. It was criticized at length by O. C. Cox and many Indianists who insisted that the Hindu caste system is so unique as to make the analogy with multi-racial societies misleading.

Whatever the merits of the concept of racial caste, the rule of prescriptive endogamy is a key feature of nearly all racist societies. Especially in Western societies which have a bilateral rule of descent, the social definition of racial group membership would become quickly blurred if extensive intermarriage took place. An important point to note, however, is that intermarriage and miscegenation are two quite distinct phenomena. Extensive concubinage between men of the dominant group and women of the subordinate group is characteristic of all slave regimes, despite strict rules of endogamy. Miscegenation in this case is the result of sexual exploitation of subordinate group women and is totally unrelated to alleged liberalism or absence of racial prejudice. Intermarriage, on the other hand, is symptomatic of a more equal status. Generally, it can be said that the amount of interracial or interethnic concubinage is *inversely* related to status equality between groups, while intermarriage is a direct function thereof. Since the quantitative data about intermarriage are much more readily available than data on other forms of sexual unions, most studies deal with intermarriage. It is essential to keep in mind, however, that intermarriage data cannot allow one to infer the incidence of miscegenation.

The three articles included in this collection cover a wide geographic range (Hawaii, North and Central America, and Europe) and deal both with interracial and interethnic marriage.

Milton L. Barron

THE INCIDENCE OF
JEWISH INTERMARRIAGE
IN EUROPE AND AMERICA

The community utilized as the point of departure for this survey of in-termarriages is Derby, Connecticut, the smallest in area of the 169 town-ships in the state. Its population, according to the United States Census of 1940, totals 10,287. Located in the lower Naugatuck Valley eight miles west of New Haven, Derby is an industrial community noted for its pro-duction of textiles and light metal commodities. Approximately 32 immi-grant groups of the Caucasoid race are represented there, along with a few Negroes and Chinese. The pattern of their arrival was essentially the same as that found in hundreds of other towns and cities along the Eastern Sea-board. Six Protestant churches, two Roman Catholic churches, and an orthodox Jewish synagogue, as well as several other churches and synagogues in neighboring communities serve the religious needs of the people.

The original Jews in the community arrived from Germany during the late nineteenth century. Here they peddled their merchandise from door to door and subsequently opened clothing, jewelry, and millinery stores in the central business section of the city as soon as they had accumulated some capital. It was not until the turn of the century that Jews immigrated in numbers sufficient to constitute an independent religious group. Most of these later immigrants were orthodox Jews from Russia and Poland; a few came from Hungary and Rumania. Almost all of them were merchants, catering to the needs of the immigrant gentiles whose languages they spoke. In 1905 the Jews organized a congregation, hiring the hall of a fraternal

From Milton L. Barron, "The Incidence of Jewish Intermarriage in Europe and America," in *American Sociological Review*, 11 (1946), pp. 6–13.

organization for Sabbath and Holy Day services. Previously they had attended synagogues in nearby communities or had formed prayer groups in their own homes. In 1916, when there were approximately fifty Jewish families in Derby, plans for the erection of a synagogue were begun. The building was completed in 1918. A resident rabbi was secured, a "Jack-of-all trades" who not only conducted religious services but also taught the children, served as cantor, slaughtered poultry and cattle, circumcized the male children, and married and buried the adults.

To what extent have these "small town" Jews intermarried? How does their intermarriage incidence compare with the rates of other communities and areas in Europe and America?

The Jews of Derby, 110 families in all, have had a high rate of inmarriage, none intermarrying in 1929–1930 and only one, a female, in 1940. Local informants asserted that there have been very few cases in the last twenty years. Several orthodox Jews of Derby have recently married conservative and reformed Jews, most of them residents of the larger neighboring communities of New Haven and Bridgeport. The Derby Rabbi, whose other attitudes were ultra-conservative, had no objection to these interdenominational unions. When the writer asked him if he approved of these marriages, he replied: "Why not? Jews are Jews, whether orthodox, conservative or reformed. The lines are really meaningless."

The premarital relations of Jewish boys and girls in Derby with gentiles are similar to some caste relations, especially in regard to the sex taboo. They afford insight into the high rate of Jewish endogamy. For example, although it is quite common for a Jewish boy in Derby to have friends of his own sex among gentiles, it is only rarely that he will have a gentile "girl friend." One or two "dates" of this sort are sufficient for the relationship to become a topic of gossip in the community. In such cases, word usually reaches Jewish parents quite rapidly and they plead with their wayward sons to "stop bothering with 'Shikses' because there are plenty of fine Jewish girls in town."

More or less the same is true of Jewish girls. In fact, it is even more difficult for them than for unmarried Jewish males to cross the religious line heterosexually. The male friends of Jewish girls are very carefully checked, more so than in the case of gentile girls. Whereas Jewish boys are also closely guarded in this respect, they take advantage of the wider mobility which is a prerogative of their sex to sow their wild oats among gentile girls "out of town." Jewish girls are notably chaste in their premarital years, but it is common knowledge in the community that many if not most single Jewish males who engage in premarital intercourse resort to "Shikses."

Two Yiddish rhymes reflecting this situation are often expressed in Jewish "stag" groups. One is attributed to the average chaste Jewish girl whose guiding principle in premarital sex relations is summed up in these transliterated Yiddish words: "No Chuppe, no Shtuppe," or "No wedding (Canopy), no sex." The other rhyme which concerns the Jewish bachelor's relations with Gentile girls is as follows:

> In die Torah ist geschrieben,
> Mit a Shikse kennst du liegen,
> Wenn die Shikse lass nit toppen,
> A Cholere soll sie choppen!

or

> In the Torah it is written,
> That you may lie with a Gentile girl,
> But if the girl does not let you "have" her,
> May she be afflicted with Cholera!

To be sure, endogamy prevails among Derby Jews. Yet it is rare to find the individual Derby Jew marrying another Jew of the same community. In short, there seems to be a conflict between the taboo against intermarriage and the almost incestuous repulsion against marriage with members of the in-group with whom contact has been intimate and prolonged. This conflict is resolved by community exogamy combined with religious endogamy. The same phenomenon was noted by Mandelbaum in "Urbana,"[1] a neighboring small community. There, it was pointed out, "the young men are averse to keeping company with the local girls and the young women seek their husbands from other places. A group as small and compact as is Urbana Jewry comes to take on some of the aspects of an extended family. Its members are so familiar with each other's history and foibles that there is little room for romantic interest. Moreover, young men desiring to be fetter-free, feel themselves enmeshed by local gossip, if they pay particular attention to an Urbana girl."

One fact which is incompatible with this analysis, however, is that it does not apply to many other Derby groups, most of whom practice both religious and community endogamy. Possibly their larger numbers provide the answer.

Jewish Intermarriage in Europe

Until late in the nineteenth century, European Jews inmarried almost entirely, so that one of their scholars[2] recently remarked that inmarriage "formed the strongest bond . . . making them into a homogeneous ethnic unit, able to show a unique power of resistance against the assimilating forces of Christianity and Islam. Even Jews who have become indifferent to their religion often remain adverse to marrying outside their community; this is perhaps the last remnant of their national consciousness. They feel that, although they have dropped the Jewish ritual, they will remain Jews so long as they and their children intermarry with Jews, and that only a mixed marriage would finally separate them from their people. Indeed, intermarriage, as soon as it appears on a large scale, marks the end of Judaism."

From the latter part of the nineteenth century until the advent of Hitler, Jewish intermarriage with non-Jews increased steadily throughout Europe and the United States. The gradual increase was true only when all incidents were combined, but not in each specific country, as Table 11-1 demonstrates. That no necessary pattern of gradual increase in Jewish intermarriage exists is further corroborated by the observation that throughout Jewish history Jews have intermarried more in prosperous times than in times of economic depression and social oppression.[3]

Generally, in the western European countries where Jews have been numerically few and "emancipated" in the sense of enjoying full civil rights and of practicing a relatively diluted form of Judaism, they have intermarried proportionately more and at a faster rate than Jews elsewhere in Europe. Jewish women nearly everywhere have been more conservative than Jewish men in entering intermarriage.[4] For example, the Jews of Switzerland in the course of 32 years have more than doubled their rate of intermarriage. In 1888, the first year for which statistics are available, they intermarried in 5.39 of every 100 marriages in which they participated; two years later, in 1900, the rate increased to 6.89 per cent. By 1910 the rate was 8.84 per cent and in 1920 it rose to 11.66 per cent. Both sexes showed an increasing tendency to intermarry, but the women, except in 1888 when they outnumbered the men slightly, constituted the smaller element of Jews entering intermarriage. From 1888 to 1920, the men were 52.1 per cent of the Jews who intermarried whereas the women supplied 47.9 per cent.[5]

TABLE 11-1

Summary of Studies of the Incidence of Jewish Intermarriage

Student	Locale	Period	Rate of Intermarriage per 100 Marriages in Which Jews Were Participants[n]
Engelman[a]	Switzerland	1888	5.39
Engelman[a]	Switzerland	1900	6.89
Engelman[a]	Switzerland	1910	8.84
Engelman[a]	Switzerland	1920-	11.66
Fishberg[b]	Hungary	1895-1904	5.83
Ruppin[c]	Hungary	1907-1908	8.30
Ruppin[c]	Hungary	1925	20.46
Ruppin[c]	Hungary	1935	24.46
Fishberg[d]	Germany	1901-1904	14.72
Fishberg[d]	Germany	1905-1907	17.72
Ruppin[e]	Germany	1910-1911	21.36
Drachsler[f]	Germany	1915	51.00
Ruppin[g]	Germany	1928	34.96
Ruppin[g]	Germany	1933	43.78
Ruppin[g]	Germany	1934	23.89
Ruppin[g]	Germany	1935	15.46
Ruppin[g]	Russia in Europe	1924-1926	12.73
Ruppin[g]	Lithuania	1931	0.39
Ruppin[g]	Czechoslovakia	1933	20.45
Ruppin[g]	Latvia	1933	5.14
Silcox and Fisher[h]	Ontario	1920-1930	5.06
Silcox and Fisher[h]	Quebec	1926-1931	2.99
Silcox and Fisher[h]	Canada (excl. Quebec)	1920-1931	6.52
Silcox and Fisher[h]	Canada (all)	1926-1931	4.82
Drachsler[i]	New York City	1908-1912	2.27
Brickner[j]	Cincinnati	1916-1919	3.60
Kennedy[k]	New Haven	1870	0.00
Kennedy[k]	New Haven	1900	1.18
Kennedy[k]	New Haven	1930	2.99
Kennedy[k]	New Haven	1940	5.68
Koenig[l]	Stamford	1938[m]	7.16
Barron	Derby	1929-1930	0.00
Barron	Derby	1940	16.67

[a]"Intermarriage Among Jews in Switzerland, 1880-1920," *American Journal of Sociology*, 34 (November 1928), p. 518.

[b]*The Jews: A Study of Race and Environment* (New York: The Walter Scott Publishing Co., 1911), p. 197.

[c]*The Jewish Fate and Future* (London: The Macmillan Co., 1940), p. 108.

[d]*Op. cit.*, p. 197.

[e]*Op. cit.*, p. 108.

[f]*Democracy and Assimilation* (New York: The Macmillan Co., 1920), p. 126.

[g]*Op. cit.*, p. 108.

[h]*Catholics, Jews and Protestants* (New York: Harper & Bros., 1934), p. 265.

[i]*Op. cit.*, p. 128.

[j]Silcox and Fisher, *op. cit.*, p. 264.

[k]"Single or Triple Melting-Pot? Intermarriage Trends in New Haven, 1870-1940," in *American Journal of Sociology*, 49 (January 1944), p. 333.

[l]"The Socioeconomic Structure of an American Jewish Community," *Jews in a Gentile World*, edited by Isacque Graeber and Steuart Henderson Britt, 1942, Chap. VIII, pp. 235-237.

[m]Data were collected in 1938. The years of marraige varied.

[n]The percentages of intermarriage incidence are shown in terms of each 100 marriages in which Jews participated. For example, if the Jews in Area A had representatives in 150 marriages, 50 of which were intermarriages, the percentage of intermarriage incidence was 33.33 per cent. Intermarriage percentages in other studies were not comparable with percentages for Derby, because *different bases* were used in the percentages. That is, some scholars used the total of marriages as a base, some used inmarriages, and others used marrying individuals. In order to have all incidences of intermarriage on a comparable level, the meanings of the percentages of the other studies were translated into a uniform meaning; namely, the cases of intermarriage per 100 marriages in which Jews participated.

In Hungary, the Jews over a period of forty years almost quintupled their intermarriage rate. In the period from 1895 to 1904, 5.83 per cent of the marriages involving Jews were intermarriages.[6] In 1907–1908 the rate was 8.30 per cent. This increased to 20.46 per cent in 1925 and 24.46 per cent in 1935.[7]

Scandinavian Jews in the early years of the twentieth century were only a very small fraction of the population and they experienced almost as many intermarriages as inmarriages. Indeed, in Sweden the number of Jewish intermarriages exceeded the inmarriages. In that country the rabbis protested so violently that they refused to officiate at the intermarriage ceremonies or to circumcize the children of intermarried couples. However, the Jewish laymen authorized several physicians to perform the circumcisions.[8]

In France and Italy, where Jews also constituted a very small minority and were treated tolerantly, intermarriages prevailed. Almost all Jewish families in Italy had Christian relatives through intermarriages.[9] This process was terminated by Italian legislation in 1938 which prohibited intermarriages between Christians and Jews.[10] English Jews of Spanish and Portuguese origin have almost disappeared through intermarriage with Christians, although the recent immigrant Jew in England of the Orthodox faith has remained relatively steadfast in endogamy.[11]

Of special interest is the pattern of incidence in Germany. For the first ten years after the legalization of intermarriages in Prussia in 1875, only 9.14 per cent of the marriages in which Jews participated were intermarriages.[12] This increased to 14.72 per cent in 1901–1904, 17.72 per cent in 1905–1907,[13] 21.36 per cent in 1910–1911,[14] and 51.00 per cent in 1915.[15] After the World War, however, the intermarriage rate declined considerably, the rate being 34.96 per cent in 1928 and 43.78 per cent in 1933. The coming to power of Hitler and the enactment of the Nuremberg Laws which included restrictions against intermarriage were responsible for another decline in the ensuing years, the rates being 23.89 per cent in 1934 and 15.46 per cent in 1935.[16]

Czechoslovakia in 1933 had a Jewish intermarriage rate of 20.45 per cent, but in Eastern Europe, except in Soviet Russia, intermarriages by Jews who are mostly Orthodox never reached large proportions. Lithuanian Jews in 1931 had a rate of only 0.39 per cent and Latvian Jews a rate of 5.14 per cent. Jews in European Russia were affected by emancipating influences of the Revolution to the extent of having an intermarriage rate of 12.73 per cent in 1924–1926.[17]

Jewish Intermarriage in Canada and the United States

In Canada, where Jews are largely of the first and second generation and of Eastern European stock, intermarriage rates have been low, more so in Quebec because of French Catholic cooperation with Orthodox Jews in aversion to intermarriage and stringency of regulation. In Ontario during the period 1920–1930, the rate was 5.06 per cent; in Quebec during the years 1926–1931, the rate was 2.99 per cent; in Canada, excluding Quebec, from 1920 through 1931, 6.52 per cent of the marriages participated in by Jews were intermarriages. In all Canada during the period 1926–1931 the rate was 4.82 per cent. The year-by-year rates in the above mentioned places and periods of Canada did not show a pattern of increase, which is further evidence against the alleged existence of an inevitable trend in that direction.[18] Indeed, there was some indication of a generally diminishing rate of Jewish intermarriage. Silcox and Fisher not only discount the theory that intermarriage must progressively increase, but they also claim that in the case of the Jews at least, there should be a trend in the opposition direction. In Canada, they pointed out, "there does tend to be a hardening of Jewish communalism as the group is longer domiciled, and after the second generation has broken loose for a time, it tends to find its life more largely within its own cultural group. Indeed, there is evidence that a very large proportion of the intermarriage which takes place concerns Orthodox Jews; as the Jew becomes successful, he is apt to attach himself to the liberal synagogue and finds there a social status more acceptable than he may discover either outside of Judaism or in Orthodox Judaism. He then finds his friends and his mates in that circle."[19] Jewish males in Canada, as elsewhere, have been found to intermarry more frequently than the women, despite the balanced sex ratio.[20]

During the colonial period in what is now the United States, Jews intermarried at a higher rate than they have ever since that time, probably because of the scarcity of Jewish women.[21] The first Jewish intermarriage on record occurred in 1660 when a well-known Jewish doctor in Maryland, Jacob Lumbrozo, took a Christian wife.[22] The Jewish pioneers who lived in Kentucky before 1836 disappeared through intermarraige, "the descendants of the early settlers . . . known only by their Jewish family names and their oriental features."[23] Jewish families in New York, Pennsylvania, Connecticut, and Massachusetts all intermarried extensively in pre-Revolutionary times, thus accounting in large part for the virtual disappearance of the Sephardic Jews in America.[24] Many Sephardic Jews who have gained prominence in American public affairs since the Civil War have married Christians.[25]

The German Jews who followed the Sephardic Jews to America likewise began to intermarry very frequently after a number of years of residence, more so in the southern and western states where they were few in number than in the eastern states.[26]

The third wave of immigrant Jews who came from Eastern Europe have not as yet intermarried with gentiles to the extent that their preceding co-religionists have. Indeed, the three divisions of Jews in the United States, until recently, married very little with one another, the earlier arrivals scorning the later ones as crude, superstitious, and economically indigent, and the latter despising the former as snobs and religious renegades.[27] As recently as 1925, one student of immigrant groups[28] asserted that "intermarriage between a Sephardic Jew and a Russian Jew, for instance, is as rare, if not rarer, than intermarriage between Jew and gentile." Even within each of these divisions of Jews there was at first aversion to marriage with some of the sub-divisions. Bavarian Jews hesitated to marry with those German Jews who came from the area near the Polish border, derisively labelled "Pollacks." The Russian Jew looked down on the Polish and Galician Jews and refused to marry them or to permit his children to do so.[29] Although these intra-Jewish barriers to marriage have largely disappeared in recent times, first generation Jewish parents may still go through the motions of expressions of embarrassment when their children marry the sons and daughters of a ridiculed sub-group.

The Eastern European Jews, by reason of their overwhelming numerical superiority over other Jews, have been the main subject of intermarriage statistics during the last thirty years. In New York City during the years 1908–1912 only 2.27 per cent of the marriages involving Jews were intermarriages. Of all groups Jews and Negroes ranked lowest in intermarriage percentages. German and French Jews, the nearest to Gentiles in cultural traits, had the highest intermarriage rates of all Jews. Next in rank were the Jews from Hungary and Holland, and last of all those from Eastern Europe.[30] Smaller Jewish communities in the United States whose intermarriage records are available also show low incidences. According to Rabbi Brickner's analysis of Jewish marriages in Cincinnati between 1916 and 1919, only 3.60 per cent of the cases were intermarriages.[31] In New Haven statistics are available beginning in 1870 when no Jewish intermarriages took place. In 1900 the rate was 1.18 per cent; in 1930, 2.99 per cent of Jewish marriages were intermarriages; and in 1940 the rate was 5.68 per cent.[32] In Stamford in 1938, 7.16 per cent of the Jewish marriages functioning at the time, regardless of the years of their consummation, were intermarriages. In the overwhelming majority of these intermarriage cases, 40 out of 59, the Jewish partners were male.[33] In "Buna," another community studied recently, Jewish males were also found to be more likely to intermarry than Jewish females. However, in the higher income brackets and among the Reformed Jews, the number of Jewish women entering intermarriage was proportionately higher.[34]

Although the Burlington study compiled no data about the intermarriage incidence of both sexes among the Jews, it did reveal that of the 180 Jewish male householders in the community whose wives were living, only seven had intermarried.[35] This was the lowest intermarriage rate of all groups in Burlington. In attitude, too, Burlington Jews were very conservative, for 53 of the 57 persons interviewed were of the opinion that Jews should not intermarry, their main reasons being the dangers of assimilation, family conflict and child disorganization that would ensue.[36]

Two students of Jewish intermarriage have attempted to define the social psychological types of Jews who intermarry, using terms suggested by University of Chicago sociologists, especially Park and Miller,[37] and correlating them with W. I. Thomas' "four wishes." The first attempt, by Reuben B. Resnik,[38] classified intermarrying Jews in four types: (1) the emancipated person who has freed himself from the religious influence of Judaism and who thus acquires a greater tendency to intermarry, (2) the rebellious person who deliberately intermarries in order to remove his Jewish identity, (3) the detached person who has broken away from the Jewish primary group, thus experiencing a weakening of the old restrictions against intermarriage, and (4) the adventurous person who looks at marriage as a new experience and does not care about the identity of his spouse. No type is pure, each having some characteristics of the other. The types are correlated with "the four wishes," according to Resnik, as follows:[39]

We see in the *desire for new experience* the *adventurous* person seeking a mate for a new thrill. The cultural background and other factors may influence his choice but do not in any vital way appear to motivate his decision. In the *desire for security* we see, for example, Jews in some cases marrying non-Jews because the former seem to feel a greater social security when they are accepted in marriage by members of the non-Jewish group. The *desire for response* is clearly brought out by the sex factor that enters into the decision of one mate to choose another regardless of the fact that that person has or has not the same background. The *desire for recognition* takes form in the devices for securing position and distinction in the eyes of the social group and, as a result, an enviable and advantageous social status. This wish in marriage is exemplified by the rich Jews of France intermarrying with some of the decadent aristocracy of that country.

The second attempt to define intermarriage types among Jews was made by J. S. Slotkin[40] who added four to the original four presented by Resnik. They are: (1) the unorganized or demoralized person who is a product of the deteriorated ecological areas of the city and one of whose modes of expressing non-conformity to the culture at large is intermarriage; (2) the promiscuous person who first has a casual sexual relationship outside his own religious group which he hesitates to form within his group for fear of "entangling alliances," and affection for the partner in promiscuity develops, followed by intermarriage; (3) the marginal person, who, having absorbed the culture of the dominant Gentile group although he is still nominally a member of the subordinate Jewish group, intermarries in order to raise his status or that of his children to that of the dominant group; and (4) the acculturated person, who having become "Americanized" and having assumed Gentile standards, intermarries because no one among his own Jewish group is acceptable according to his newly acquired standards.

These concepts and types appear to have little value because they overlap considerably. Furthermore, they are nebulous to the extent that they may be used in classifying almost any individual, whether he inmarries or intermarries, in one or more types. The writer fails to see where any patterns or types of intermarrying individuals exist, either among Jews or any other groups.

Conclusions

Generalizations concerning an ever-increasing rate of Jewish intermarriage in America are not substantiated by comparative analysis of the facts available here and abroad. Jewish intermarriage does not necessarily adhere to a pattern of increasing incidence. It varies in time and place according to the fluctuations of social conditions.

There is endogamous strength in numbers. However, unlike some other numerically small religious groups in Derby, such as the Greek Orthodox and Greek Catholics, the Jewish rate of intermarriage has been low. Two explanations to account for this discrepancy are the following:

1. The Jews are heavily concentrated in the merchant and professional economic classes, whereas the Greek Orthodox and Greek Catholics are

recent immigrants from peasant Europe and unskilled and semi-skilled laborers. A higher economic status provides the Jews with horizontal mobility to the larger neighboring Jewish communities, permitting them to overcome the handicap of small numbers.

2. The longer, more varied history of migration by the Jews, and their centuries of existence as a minority in proximity to gentile majorities enabled them to develop attitudes and techniques of intermarriage resistance long before their arrival in America.

NOTES

1. "A Study of the Jews of Urbana," *The Jewish Social Service Quarterly*, 12 (December 1935), p. 230.

2. Ruppin, *op. cit.*, p. 106.

3. Coon, Carleton S., "Have the Jews a Racial Identity?" *Jews in a Gentile World*, edited by Isacque Graeber and Steuart Henderson Britt, 1961, chap. I, p. 28.

4. Ruppin, *op. cit.*, p. 111.

5. Engelman, "Intermarriage among Jews in Switzerland, 1880–1920," *American Journal of Sociology*, 34 (November 1928), pp. 518–519.

6. Fishberg, *The Jews: A Study of Race and Environment* (New York: The Walter Scott Publishing Co., 1911), p. 197.

7. Ruppin, *The Jewish Fate and Future* (London: The Macmillan Co., 1940), p. 108.

8. Fishberg, *op. cit.*, pp. 196–198.

9. *Ibid.*, pp. 201–202.

10. Ruppin, *op. cit.*, p. 109.

11. Fishberg, *op. cit.*, p. 203.

12. Ruppin, *op. cit.*, p. 108.

13. Fishberg, *op. cit.*, p. 197.

14. Ruppin, *op. cit.*, p. 108.

15. Drachsler, *op. cit.*, p. 126.

16. Ruppin, *op. cit.*, p. 108.

17. *Ibid.*, p. 108.

18. Silcox and Fisher, *op. cit.*, p. 265.

19. *Ibid.*, p. 263.

20. *Ibid.*, p. 266.

21. *Ibid.*, pp. 265–266.

22. *Publications of the American Jewish Historical Society*, Vol. I, p. 29.

23. *Ibid.*, pp. 99–101.

24. *Ibid.*, Vol. I, pp. 57–58; Vol. II, p. 91; Vol. VII, p. 43; Vol. XII, pp. 68–69; Vol. VI, pp. 92–93.

25. Davie, Maurice R., *World Immigration* (New York: The Macmillan Co., 1936), pp. 161–162.

26. Fishberg, op. cit., pp. 203–204.

27. Stern, Elizabeth, *I Am a Woman and a Jew* (New York: J. H. Sears & Co., 1926), p. 183.

28. Bercovici, Konrad, *On New Shores*, (New York: The Century Co., 1925), p. 211.

29. Broun, Heywood, and Britt, George, *Christians Only* (New York: The Vanguard Press, 1931), pp. 299–300.

30. Drachsler, *op. cit.*, pp. 121–124.

31. Silcox and Fisher, *op. cit.*, p. 264.

32. Kennedy, *op. cit.*, p. 333.

33. Koenig, *op. cit.*, pp. 235–237.

34. Bloom, Leonard, "The Jews of Buna," *Jews in a Gentile World*, edited by Isacque Graeber and Steuart Henderson Britt, 1961, chap. VII, pp. 190–191.

35. Anderson, *op. cit.*, p. 188.

36. *Ibid.*, pp. 192–193.

37. *Old World Traits Transplanted* (New York: Harper & Bros., 1927), pp. 81–119.

38. "Some Sociological Aspects of Intermarriage of Jew and Non-Jew," *Social Forces*, 12 (1933), pp. 94–102.

39. *Ibid.*, pp. 98–99.

40. "Jewish-Gentile Intermarriage in Chicago," *American Sociological Review*, 12 (February, 1942), pp. 34–39.

ADJUSTMENT OF INTERETHNIC MARRIAGES ON THE ISTHMUS OF PANAMA

An interethnic situation makes it possible and necessary to view marriages as points of contact and adjustment between groups rather than—the usual approach—between the spouses as individuals. Therefore along with factors general to marriage, such as age at time of marriage and number of children, there are two situational factors specific to interethnic marriage: the intergroup situation, and the diverse ethnic norms of the two groups.

The intergroup situation involving native Americans and an ethnic minority in the United States is different from the intergroup situation involving Panamanians and Americans on the Isthmus. The native Panamanian ingroup has relatively low prestige, but is well organized on both informal-primary and formal-secondary levels, e.g., has long-established kinship and friendship groups and also its own government; whereas the American outgroup is poorly organized on informal-primary but well organized on formal-secondary levels, e.g., has few long-established kinship and friendship groups but separate government and high degree of industrial discipline. Ownership and operation of the canal, achievements in tropical sanitation, military and naval establishments, and consequent domination of Panamanian economy all give the American outgroup high prestige and require a high degree of formal-secondary organization.

Thus the constants in any intergroup situation are the ingroup and the outgroup; the variables are the relative degrees of prestige, relative degrees of organization on the informal-primary level, and relative degrees of organization on the formal-secondary level.

From John Biesanz and Luke M. Smith, "Adjustment of Interethnic Marriages on the Isthmus of Panama," in *American Sociological Review*, 16 (1951), pp. 819–822.

Effect of the Intergroup Situation upon
General Factors in Marital Adjustment[1]

Some of the general factors in marital adjustment operate in the same way as they do in ethnically homogeneous marriages in the United States; others are affected by the intergroup situation; while still others operate differently because of specific differences between Panamanian and American cultures rather than because of the intergroup situation.

AGE AT MARRIAGE; SOCIO-ECONOMIC STATUS; EDUCATION

These general factors operate in approximately the same way as they do in ethnically homogeneous marriages in the United States[2] and therefore are not clearly affected by the intergroup situation on the Isthmus. Happiness tends to increase with age at marriage,[3] with socio-economic status,[4] and with education.

LENGTH OF COURTSHIP; TIME MARRIED; NUMBER OF CHILDREN

Contrary to general marriage findings (those dealing with factors general to marriage) in the United States, comparatively short courtships do not result in adjustment difficulties. Couples commenced courtship almost as soon as they met; most of them married within a year.[5] Panamanian women are predisposed in favor of the high prestige American husband, while the American male migrant to the Zone is socially unorganized at first and hence more likely to marry outside of his ethnic group. The longer he waits the more he is likely to establish social relationships with his ethnic group; and the more he learns that Americans look down upon Panamanians and resist their attempts to break into the monopoly of American positions and possessions. It may be deduced that if he marries early upon arrival, later relationships with his compatriots will not greatly affect the happiness of his Panamanian marriage. *When the outgroup spouse is socially unorganized on the informal-primary level, marriage into an organized ingroup tends to restructure the situation for him and to prevent unhappiness in marriage,* even though later he becomes more integrated into his own group.

As would be expected, then, there is no significant decrease of unhappiness with length of time married.[6] This is contrary to some general marriage findings in the United States.

Happiness increases with the number of children.[7] General marriage studies in the United States show that the number of children does not increase marital happiness unless they are wanted. Since Panamanian women normatively desire a number of children, it may be concluded that the presence of children keeps the social situation of the husband structured toward the wife's ethnic group and in this way aids marital adjustment.

RURAL-URBAN ORIGIN; PREVIOUS MARITAL STATUS

Contrary to general marriage findings in the United States, which show the greatest marital adjustment when the spouses are of rural origin, the Isthmian data show Panamanian-American spouses to be happiest when the Panamanian wives are from urban areas. The two large cities of Panama are contiguous to the urban areas of the Zone and therefore allow a greater degree of assimilation than would be true of rural areas, while Panama's rural culture is little removed from its primitive Indian background. Mere urban origin in itself, however, is not the important factor, but rather the degree of assimilation to the group of the high prestige spouse. Thus when racial background and education are held constant, there are no significant rural-urban differences.

Previous marital status findings are incomplete. The mores do not sanction divorce;[8] and in addition to legalized marriage there is the consensual union, where couples live together without civil or religious ceremony, and the mistress system. These patterns being only semi-institutionalized, it is difficult to obtain intimate data about them.

Diverse Ethnic Norms and Their Operation Within the Marriage

Because spouses are culture bearers, diverse ethnic norms operate within the marriage as well as through pressure of culture bearers outside the marriage.

LANGUAGE

Wives are more often bilingual than husbands. Americans usually reveal disdain for Panamanians by refusing to learn Spanish; Panamanians who desire to profit by contacts with Americans must learn English. Panamanians feel sensitive over such concessions, which define them as the low prestige group on their own soil. Bilingual spouses have the highest marital adjustment. Where only one language is spoken higher adjustment occurs when that language is Spanish, because the American husband is able to participate with his wife's well-established circle of friends and relatives, who desire contact with him; whereas he has few friends and relatives of his own on the Isthmus, and these do not desire contact with the low prestige group.[9]

CUISINE

Adjustment problems do not arise. Urban Panamanian diet includes many high prestige American foods, and the privilege of buying at low cost Zone commissaries reinforces this tendency.

RELIGION

Such differences also produce few problems.[10] Marriages of Catholics are only a little happier than mixed marriages. The explanation may lie in the socially unorganized position of the Protestant spouse. On the Isthmus, away from the controls of his family of orientation, there is little pressure from Protestant in-laws. Furthermore, Panamanian men are rarely expected to go to church except for family rituals such as weddings and funerals.

INSTITUTIONALIZED ROLES OF HUSBAND AND WIFE

Norms in each ethnic group relieve the strains caused by parallel norms in the other. American husbands typically give their wives more liberty, attention, and faithfulness than do Panamanian husbands; and Panamanian women often admittedly prefer American husbands for these reasons. Panamanian wives typically are more passionate, home loving, and submissive than American wives, and are willing to grant their husbands greater liberty. Marital happiness is positively correlated with sharing activities, husband's help about the house, and wife's participation in management of income.[11]

Where a Panamanian man marries an American woman, the different institutionalized roles increase marital strain. It is generally agreed that these marriages have a far smaller chance of success than the former type. Furthermore, in the comparatively few intermarriages of this type on the Isthmus, the courtship and wedding usually occurred in the States, the

American wives entering the marriage with little understanding of Panamanian culture.

ATTITUDES OF THE SPOUSES TOWARD THE ETHNIC DIFFERENCES

Happy as well as unhappy wives tend to attribute their happiness or unhappiness to the fact that their husbands are American, and husbands do the same with respect to their Panamanian wives.[12] One American says his wife is neat, another complains his is slovenly; both say, "Panamanians are like that." The same is true of thrift and extravagance, jealousy and understanding, diligence and laziness.

Adjustment of the Intermarried Couples to the Intergroup Situation

On the Isthmus, the most important extraneous factor interfering with adjustment of Panamanian-American couples is American prejudice against other nationalities and races, and the tendency to categorize all Panamanians as colored "Spiggotties." The high prestige American outgroup, of course, desires to keep its relationships and possessions for its own members, and therefore strongly disapproves of any move to break into this monopoly. Hence the rationality of the prejudice. Panamanians, on the other hand, not only desire the prestige of relationships and things American, but also as members of the ingroup feel entitled to greater consideration.

KINSHIP RELATIONS

In the intergroup situation in the United States, marital adjustment may be difficult because the families of orientation exert pressure upon mixed couples to swing them over to one ethnic group or the other. On the Isthmus the intergroup situation may actually aid adjustment. American in-laws are usually far away, and if they disapprove—as they are very likely to do where racial mixture is involved—they can do little about it. However, they often make their disapproval felt when the husband takes his bride home for a visit or tries to settle in the States—where she looks darker than she did on the Isthmus. Wives are seldom taken back to the States on visits to in-laws.[13] Indirect relationships through correspondence, however, are positively correlated with marital happiness.[14]

As for the husband's relationships with his Panamanian in-laws, nearly all husbands visit them and receive them at home. They usually approve of him,[15] and change to disapproval only in distinctly unhappy cases. In view of the advantages of obtaining relationships with the high prestige Americans, one would expect this tolerant behavior.

FRIENDSHIPS

Shared friendships are positively correlated with happiness.[16] Yet, most wives also say they and their husbands have most of their friends among their respective nationalities. Apparently sharing friends is less important to adjustment than is liking and respect for the other spouse's nationality.

STATUS IN THE COMMUNITY

These marriages carry little or no stigma in the Republic, whereas in the Zone they are condemned and the couples snubbed. A man may find a job promotion blocked by his marriage to a Panamanian. Wives who are rated as "colored" tend to be unhappier than those rated as "white."[17]

In view of these manifestations of prejudice, would it not seem likely that marital adjustment would be more difficult in the Zone? Yet the sample shows the opposite to be true: Zone dwellers are rated as happier. Also, nearly half the wives (18 out of 41) living in the Republic prefer the Zone from the standpoint of economy, quiet, and convenience. It may be concluded that Panamanian women prefer the Zone, in spite of the prejudice against them there, because it is the territory of the high prestige group, and residence there is a symbol that the Panamanian woman is successful in achieving the ends for which she married an American.

Furthermore, it is easy for the Panamanian wife to retain her kinship and friendship relations in the Republic, which is just across the street from Zone territory. On the other hand, even if the couple lives in the Republic, the American husband usually works in the Zone, retains his ties with compatriots, and feels the pressure of their prejudices.

Summary

Adjustment of interethnic marriages depends, in addition to general factors in marital adjustment, upon the intergroup situation and the diverse norms of the two ethnic groups. The intergroup (ingroup-outgroup) situation comprises three variables for each group: relative degrees of (1) prestige, (2) informal-primary organization, and (3) formal-secondary organization.

In one combination of these variables, the high prestige group is the outgroup and relatively unorganized on the informal-primary level, whereas the low prestige group is the ingroup and well organized. In this combination strong prejudice is exhibited against the intermarried couple by outgroup members wishing to retain their monopoly of high prestige positions and possessions. The ingroup wife is able to obtain prestige symbols of her husband's group without losing security in her own—because *her* group has stronger informal-primary organization. Prejudice of the high prestige group, then, has little effect upon marital adjustment. The husband is able to use the relationships in his wife's group to restructure his situation, and his resultant feeling of respect for his wife's group contributes to her security there. It is these attitudes toward the other spouse's ethnic status as a *total* status which are basic to adjustment.

Diverse norms of the two ethnic groups are important only when they symbolize this total status, happiness as well as unhappiness being attributed to the other spouse as a typical bearer of his ethnic norms. Even those norms which relieve or heighten strains caused by parallel norms in in the other culture are effective mainly because of the total status meaning given to them.

Reduction of these ethnic differences through assimilation is successful chiefly if it is in the direction of preserving the wife's security with her relatives and friends (e.g., *husband's* linguistic and religious assimilation), while on the other hand allowing her to obtain some of the prestige of the outgroup to which her husband belongs (e.g., outgroup norms giving the wife greater liberty and respect than afforded by ingroup norms).

NOTES

1. This analysis is based primarily on schedule interviews of 66 Panamanian women married to Americans, 41 of whom reside in Panama City or its suburbs and 25 in the adjacent Canal Zone. For method, and social data on the spouses, see John Biesanz, "Inter-American Marriages on the Isthmus of Panama," *Social Forces*, 29 (December, 1950), pp. 159–163.

Inasmuch as the study is focused upon interethnic relations rather than marital relations *per se*, it was not useful to have a representative sample of all Panamanian-American marriages. Therefore the sample was not enlarged beyond the relatively stable unions which happened to be selected by the middle class students who did the interviewing. Thus the specific effects of the interethnic marriages could be studied in isolation from other factors. Cases of desertion were omitted as abnormalities.

Happiness ratings: (1) *By interviewer:* very happy, 9; happy, 36; average, 14; unhappy, 3; very unhappy, 2; no answer, 2. (2) *By interviewee:* very happy, 23;

happy, 30; average, 10; unhappy, 2; very unhappy, 1. Where there is a discrepancy, the *interviewer* rating is used, as it is more conservative by one point in the scale and possibly more objective. *Computations are based on the 64 interviewer happiness ratings.*

2. Ernest W. Burgess and Leonard S. Cottrell, Jr., *Predicting Sucess or Failure in Marriage* (New York: Prentice-Hall, 1939); Lewis M. Terman *et al.*, *Psycholological Factors in Marital Happiness* (New York: McGraw-Hill, 1938); Clifford Kirkpatrick, *What Science Says about Happiness in Marriage* (Minneapolis: Burgess Publishing Company, 1947); Harvey J. Locke, *Predicting Adjustment in Marriage* (New York: Henry Holt and Company, 1951).

3. Happiest, above 30; less happy than majority, below 20; least happy, 26–30.

4. Couples with servants show greatest marital happiness. Only half the wives of skilled workers are happy or very happy. Nine-tenths of the professionals are in happy categories, the white collar group almost as high.

5. Largest group—the happy—typically courted about a year, all others about 8 months (range: 2 weeks to an atypical case of 6 years).

6. Couples were married from less than one up to 26 years (average 4.2; median 5.3 years).

7. Very happy: 0.45 children per year of marriage; happy 0.30; average 0.28; unhappy 0.18; very unhappy 1.0 (each couple with one child and married only a year). Children per couple: very happy, 1.6; happy, 1.4; average, 1.0; unhappy 2.3 (these 3 couples include one married 26 years with 4 children); very unhappy, 1.0.

8. Only 6 Panamanian wives were divorcees. None was very happy, none very unhappy; only one was unhappy, 2 average, and 3 happy.

9. While 7 out of 10 happy husbands know Spanish, only 4 out of 10 average and unhappy do. Nine out of 10 happy wives and 8 out of 10 average and unhappy ones know English. Children are more likely to be bilingual in the happier homes.

10. In 40 cases both spouses are Catholic; in 3 both Protestant; in 20 husband is Protestant, wife Catholic; no data on religion and happiness in 3 cases. It may be that many couples do not marry because of these differences, so that those who do are not typical adherents of their respective faiths. Cf. Burgess and Cottrell, *op. cit.*, 87–88.

Arrival of children makes adjustment more difficult, although the sample is too small to warrant generalization. More Protestant husbands disapprove of Catholic baptism for their children in average than in happy homes.

11. All except unhappy wives share much leisure time, more so in happier cases. In 39 cases husbands share household tasks. In the happy categories, 4 out of 5 help their wives, only half in the less happy categories. Fourteen of the 15 who plan expenditures jointly, and 21 of the 30 in which the wife holds the purse strings, are happy or very happy, but only 2 of the 17 whose husbands manage the money are so rated; no data on 2 cases.

12. Only 5 wives (2 of them unhappy) say that Panamanians make better husbands.

13. Only 14 of the wives report such visits.

14. All but one of the very happy wives correspond regularly with in-laws; two thirds of the happy, one sixth of the average, and none of the unhappy wives.

15. He has won over all but 3 of the 9 disapproving families in the happier marriages and 2 of the 4 in the average.

16. Seven of the 9 very happy report mutual friendships, 22 of 36 happy, 6 of 14 average, 1 of 3 unhappy, and neither of the 2 very unhappy.

17. Of the 21 "white," 19 are happy or very happy, but only 26 of the 41 "mixed"; no data on race or happiness in 4 cases.

Robert C. Schmitt

INTERRACIAL MARRIAGE AND OCCUPATIONAL STATUS IN HAWAII

Do interracial marriage rates vary by occupational group? Although several authors have offered opinions on this subject, statistical evidence has heretofore been extremely limited. Recent data from Hawaii now suggest that intermarriage rates vary considerably by occupation, ranging from 24 per cent for technical and professional workers to 49 per cent for farm laborers.

Earlier research was inconclusive. Reuter,[1] Hoffman,[2] and Baker[3] speculated that most interracial marriages involved persons of low socio-economic status, but were unable to find statistical confirmation. Drachsler, defining intermarriage to include partners of different national (as well as racial) origins, concluded from his study of New York data that a greater probability of intermarriage existed among the higher-status occupational groups.[4] Barron suggested that equality of the partners' occupational status, rather than its level, encouraged intermarriage.[5] Earlier writers on intermarriage in Hawaii (an area long noted for high interracial marriage rates) offered little or no data on occupational differentials.[6] A recent sample survey, limited to the heads of mixed and unmixed households in metropolitan Honolulu, has indicated the likelihood of such differentials.[7]

New evidence, based on official registration statistics, has now become available for Hawaii. For many years, all marriages licensed in the state have been tabulated by the ethnic group ("race") of each partner, using

NOTE: The author gratefully acknowledges the assistance of Charles G. Bennett, Lillian Louis, Rose E. Strombel, and George H. Tokuyama.

From Robert C. Schmitt, "Interracial Marriage and Occupational Status in Hawaii," in *American Sociological Review*, 28 (1963), pp. 809–810.

a ten-group breakdown based on United States Census definitions. More recently, marriages have been tabulated by the usual occupation of bride and groom, using an eleven-category occupational classification likewise modeled on the U.S. Census. The present analysis is based on a special cross-tabulation of the 1960 and 1961 data on race and occupation, provided on request by the Research, Planning and Statistics Office of the Hawaii State Department of Health. Data from this cross-tabulation appear in tables 13–1 and 13–2.

TABLE 13-1

*Marriages, Total and Mixed, by Usual Occupation
of Groom, for Hawaii: 1960 and 1961*

Usual Occupation of Groom	All Marriages	Mixed Marriages	
		Number	Per Cent
All grooms	10,535	3,721	35.3
No occupation, or not stated	534	162	30.3
Civilian occupations	7,459	2,672	35.8
Professional, technical, and kindred workers	1,023	243	23.8
Managers, officials, and proprietors, including farm	701	210	30.0
Clerical and kindred workers	565	189	33.5
Sales workers	374	120	32.1
Craftsmen, foremen, and kindred workers	1,943	655	33.7
Operatives and kindred workers	1,310	588	44.9
Private household and service workers	544	235	43.2
Farm laborers and foremen	195	95	48.7
Laborers, except farm and mines	804	337	41.9
Armed forces	2,542	887	34.9

White-collar grooms were far less likely than blue-collar grooms to marry outside of their own ethnic group. Rates ranged from 23.8 per cent for professional, technical, and kindred workers to 48.7 per cent for farm laborers and foremen. For all groups combined, the interracial marriage rate was 35.3 per cent.

Although overall rates differed widely among grooms of different ethnic stocks, white-collar workers had lower intermarriage rates than blue-collar workers in four of the six ethnic categories used in the analysis. Only the Hawaiian (including part Hawaiian) and "other" (Puerto Rican, Korean, Negro, and miscellaneous—combined because of the small number of cases) grooms failed to follow the general pattern.

Correlation analysis provides an index of this occupational differential. Marriages were dichotomized by usual occupation of groom (white-collar

TABLE 13-2

Marriages, Total and Mixed, by Race and Usual Occupation of Groom, for Hawaii: 1960 and 1961

| Subject | All Grooms | Usual Occupation of Groom | | |
		"White Collar"[a]	"Blue Collar"[b]	Armed Forces, None, or Not Stated
All marriages, total	10,535	2,663	4,796	3,076
Caucasian groom	3,806	921	767	2,118
Hawaiian groom[c]	1,958	328	1,408	222
Chinese groom	446	213	171	62
Filipino groom	1,217	147	878	192
Japanese groom	2,482	971	1,212	299
Other groom[d]	626	83	360	183
Mixed marriages, total	3,721	762	1,910	1,049
Caucasian groom	1,384	244	422	718
Hawaiian groom[c]	806	187	530	89
Chinese groom	233	99	107	27
Filipino groom	606	71	461	74
Japanese groom	327	105	174	48
Other groom[d]	365	56	216	93
Per cent mixed, total	35.3	28.6	39.8	34.1
Caucasian groom	36.4	26.5	55.0	33.9
Hawaiian groom[c]	41.2	57.0	37.6	40.1
Chinese groom	52.2	46.5	62.6	43.5
Filipino groom	49.8	48.3	52.5	38.5
Japanese groom	13.2	10.8	14.4	16.1
Other groom[d]	58.3	67.5	60.0	50.8

Sources of tables 13-1 and 13-2: Research, Planning and Statistics Office, Department of Health, State of Hawaii, special tabulation.

[a]Includes professional, technical, and kindred workers; managers, officials, and proprietors, including farm; clerical and kindred workers; and sales workers.

[b]Includes craftsmen, foremen, and kindred workers; operatives and kindred workers; private household and service workers; farm laborers and foremen; and laborers, except farm and mine.

[c]Includes part Hawaiians.

[d]Includes Puerto Rican, Korean, Negro, and other races.

or blue-collar; military personnel and persons without occupation were excluded) and ethnic group of bride (same as that of groom or different). The coefficient of correlation computed from the resulting 2 × 2 table was −.11. It was −.29 for Caucasian grooms, −.16 for Chinese grooms, −.05 for the Japanese, −.03 for Filipinos, +.15 for Hawaiians, and +.06 for all others.

These correlation coefficients followed much the same order as the rank of each race in occupational status and median income. The occupational differential was most marked among the higher status and income groups, and least marked (or evident in reversed form) among the lower status and income groups. Coefficients of rank correlation with the preceding coefficients for each race, signs considered, were −.71 for occupational status[8] and −.66 for median income.[9]

NOTES

1. Edward Byron Reuter, *The Mulatto in the United States* (Boston: Richard G. Badger, 1918), pp. 131, 136, and 139.

2. Quoted in *ibid.*, pp. 136–137.

3. Quoted in *ibid.*, p. 139.

4. Julius Drachsler, *Intermarriage in New York City: A Statistical Study of the Amalgamation of European Peoples* (New York: Columbia University, 1921), pp. 38–39 and 60.

5. Milton L. Barron, *People Who Intermarry: Intermarriage in a New England Industrial Community* (Syracuse: Syracuse University Press, 1946), pp. 291–296.

6. See, for example, Romanzo Adams, *Interracial Marriage in Hawaii* (New York: The Macmillan Co., 1937), Chap. V.

7. Robert C. Schmidt and Robert A. Souza, "Social and Economic Characteristics of Interracial Households in Honolulu," *Social Problems*, 10, No. 3 (Winter 1963), pp. 264–268.

8. As measured by the per cent of employed civilian grooms classified as white collar.

9. From the Hawaii Department of Planning and Research, *Statistical Abstract of Hawaii*, 1962 (Honolulu, 1962), p. 71.

PART V

Race and Ethnic Attitudes

Editor's Introduction

During the 1950's and early 1960's, one of the main thrusts of research in the area of race and ethnic relations was the study of prejudicial attitudes. Prejudice was widely seen as the root of the evil of racial and ethnic discrimination and as being a form of social pathology. Many of these attitude studies had implicit or explicit therapeutic aims. It was held by most well-meaning academic liberals that prejudice was sustained by ignorance and irrationality, and that if only people could be educated to understand how silly prejudice was, attitudes toward "out-groups" would improve, and discrimination would diminish. The genesis, growth, and cure of prejudice thus became central concerns for research, and a multiplicity of questionnaires, social distance scales, F and E scales, and countless other instruments purporting to measure prejudice and its relationship to age, sex, socio-economic status, social mobility, education, and many other variables were developed and applied to a multitude of captive groups within the grasp of researchers, with students in introductory sociology and psychology classes being natural victims.

Ethnic and racial attitudes were also studied through observation and experimentation in situations of intergroup contact under both "natural" and "laboratory" conditions. Starting with the "common sense" notion that people would get along much better with one another if only they understood each other, and that they would understand each other better if only they interacted, numerous studies were undertaken trying to define the situational conditions under which prejudices grow or decline. Attempts were made to assess or manipulate conditions of interaction, treating prejudicial attitudes as the dependent variable. Was the contact situation between status equals; was it competitive or threatening; did experimentally induced frustration lead to enhanced bigotry, and so on.

Of growing interest was the relationship between prejudice and discrimination. Under what conditions did individually held prejudices express themselves as overt discrimination? In those days when double dichotomies became transposed into two-by-two tables, which in turn generated instant typologies and theories, respondents were classified into prejudiced versus unprejudiced discriminators and non-discriminators. The commonly accepted theory was that while prejudice and discrimination stood in a relationship of reciprocal causation, thereby producing a vicious circle, there was a certain measure of independence between the psychogenesis of prejudice (held to be at least partly determined by personality characteristics and idiosyncratic life experiences) and the overt practice of discrimination (believed to be largely a function of the legitimacy of social norms). If the norms favored and rewarded discrimination, then even unprejudiced persons would discriminate; conversely, if the norms were tolerant, even bigots would often refrain from discrimination.

The question of the relationship between prejudice and discrimination was, of course, central to policy questions. Over time, it became increasingly obvious that educational campaigns aimed at the reduction of prejudice were an expensive and quite ineffective way of reducing actual discrimination. Since the direct aim of the policy was to eradicate not so much prejudice itself but its concrete behavioral manifestations, it followed that a direct attack on discrimination would be more effective than an indirect attack via the reduction of prejudice. This reorientation of research was, not coincidentally, related to the growth of the civil rights movement in the mid-1950's to mid-1960's with its heavy emphasis on anti-discriminatory legislation. Starting with the 1954 Brown versus the Board of Education Supreme Court decision, the social sciences saw themselves drawn into a consultant relationship in the drafting of remedial legislation.

It is interesting to note that now that American race relations have moved away from the integrationist model buttressed by civil rights legislation and toward confrontation tactics based on a power conflict model, the research of the 1950's and 1960's seems *passé*, and social scientists are once more reorienting themselves (with some time lag) toward the latest ideological whimseys with a characteristic inability to make good their claims to objectivity and to detachment from the political process.

The following articles represent a rather diverse sample of the research of the 1950's and early 1960's, ranging in methods from questionnaire studies to field observation.

STEREOTYPES, NORMS, AND INTERRACIAL BEHAVIOR IN SÃO PAULO, BRAZIL

Although the racial situation in Brazil differs markedly from the situation in the United States, there is nevertheless a racial problem in Brazil.[1] Large scale industrialization and urbanization in the great metropolises of the South such as Rio de Janeiro and São Paulo have brought about changes in the traditional attitudes and behavior between the various ethnic and racial groups.[2]

Lucila Hermann, from the Faculty of Economics of the University of São Paulo, devised a questionnaire to determine the patterns of race relations in the white middle class of São Paulo.[3] The questionnaire includes four parts:

1. A list of 41 stereotypes derived from the list of Johnson[4] for comparative purposes with the United States, from a content analysis of Brazilian literature, and from oral folklore. For each listed trait (foresight, suggestibility, self-control, intelligence, etc.) the subject was asked whether he considered, first Negroes, then mulattoes, as inferior, equal or superior to whites.

2. A series of 27 questions on social norms of behavior. For example, should white and Negro children play together? Should whites and Negroes exchange courtesy visits? Should they intermarry? etc.

3. A series of 16 questions on actual behavior of the subjects, similar in content to some questions of part 2.

4. A series of 16 questions on hypothetical personal behavior put in the conditional form: Would you marry (fall in love with, go out with) a Negro? A light-skinned mulatto? etc.

From Roger Bastide and Pierre van den Berghe, "Stereotypes, Norms, and Interracial Behavior in São Paulo, Brazil," in *American Sociological Review*, 22 (1957), pp. 689–694.

The sample is neither random nor proportional. It consists of 580 "white" students from five different teachers' colleges in São Paulo. We have good reason to believe that the questionnaire was applied to whole classes of students in a "captive" class-room situation. The percentage of refusals is unknown, but we think it was very low. We had to reject only one almost blank questionnaire. Most schedules were very conscientiously and completely filled out. The age distribution varies from 15 to 44, but it leans on the young side with a mean age of 19.9 years; 483 subjects are women, 97 are men. Socio-economic data on parents of the subjects are incomplete but they indicate a predominantly lower-middle and upper-middle class background. Seventy-five per cent of the fathers have non-manual occupations. For the 296 subjects who answered the question on family income the mean is 7,000 cruzeiros a month. As concerns ethnic origin of parents, 384 subjects are children of Brazilians, 102 have one foreign parent, 85 have both parents foreign. Of the 384 children of nationals 232 have at least one foreign grandparent. This ethnic situation seems representative of the middle class of São Paulo where third generation Brazilians dominate only in the upper and in the lower class.[5] The results of this study hold only for the "white" middle class of São Paulo.

ANALYSIS OF THE DATA

The questionnaire was subjected to a two-fold analysis. First, each question was treated as an entity and the answers of all subjects to each separate question were added together and reduced to percentages. Behind this procedure lies, of course, the assumption that the same answer has the same meaning for all subjects. Although some errors have undoubtedly been introduced, in particular by certain questions intended as "traps," we do not think that the conclusions have been altered.

The second part of the analysis is logically independent of the first and permits a corroboration of the conclusions. Each of the 580 subjects was treated as an entity. An arbitrary score was assigned to each subject for the various parts of the questionnaire, by simple unweighted addition of responses. The two underlying postulates behind this procedure are (1) that qualitative answers may be quantified and (2) that the same score means the same thing for different subjects. From these two postulates there is derived a classification of subjects on six scales treated as unidimensional variables. Four of these variables corresponding to each part of the questionnaire are treated as components of a general prejudice-tolerance continuum. Variable a is a measure of acceptance or rejection of stereotypes. Variable b measures tolerance or prejudice in social norms. Variable *c* measures actual interracial behavior as reported by the subjects. Variable *d* measures willingness to enter into specific personal relationships with Negroes or mulattoes. The other two variables are secondary variables on part 1 of the questionnaire. The higher the score on each of the four main variables, the more tolerant is the subject. For the sake of brevity, the great mass of descriptive statistics has been eliminated. The tabular material has likewise been reduced to the bare minimum. Only the salient conclusions have been retained.

Stereotypes against Negroes and mulattoes are widespread. Seventy-five per cent of the sample accept 23 or more stereotypes against Negroes. No one rejects all stereotypes against Negroes. For mulattoes the overall picture is somewhat more favorable, though very similar. Mulattoes are judged inferior or superior to whites on the same traits as Negroes but with somewhat lower percentages. The most widely accepted stereotypes are lack of hygiene (accepted by 91 per cent for Negroes), physical unattractiveness (87 per cent), superstition (80 per cent), lack of financial foresight (77 per cent), lack of a morality (76 per cent), aggressiveness (73 per cent), laziness (72 per cent), lack of persistence at work (62 per cent), sexual "perversity" (51 per cent), and exhibitionism (50 per cent).

Fifty-five per cent of the sample think that Negroes are intellectually equal to whites (only 43 per cent consider Negroes less intelligent than white), and only 22 per cent of the sample accept Negroes as musically gifted. The similarities with the North American stereotypes are more numerous than the differences, particularly as concerns the association of racial prejudice with sexuality.

Going back to the comparison between stereotypes against Negroes and stereotypes against mulattoes, one very important difference appears behind the overall similarity. Two hundred sixty-nine subjects judge Negroes as they do mulattoes; 268 subjects are more favorable to mulattoes than to Negroes; finally, a small group of 43 subjects is more favorable to Negroes than to mulattoes. We compared this last group with the 45 subjects having the most extreme differences in the second group of 268. This comparison between the two extreme groups reveals no statistically significant differences for age, sex, nationality of the parents, or family income. But significant differences appear on the means of variables *b*, *c* and *d* ($p<.05$ for each of the three variables). Those differences are further confirmed by the answers to the questions on intermarriage ($p<.05$).

The group more unfavorable to mulattoes shows much more prejudice against *both* Negroes and mulattoes in social norms, in behavior, and in willingness to intermarry, than the group more unfavorable to Negroes.

We may hypothesize that there are two contrasting "schools of thought" in the sample. These two "schools" share a belief in the superiority of the white "race." But the group more favorable to mulattoes considers the latter superior to Negroes because mulattoes are nearer to whites. It is thus less opposed to miscegenation and in general more tolerant. The group more favorable to Negroes expresses a much more virulent form of racism. It judges Negroes superior to mulattoes because the former are a "pure race." Any miscegenation is rejected and the other manifestations of prejudice are likewise stronger. If our hypothesis is correct, there is in Brazil, at least among part of the population, an extreme form of racial prejudice rather than a milder aesthetic prejudice of "physical appearance," which has been propounded by certain students of Brazilian racial relations.[6] There is no indication from our data that this extreme form of racial prejudice where people think in terms of "pure races" has been introduced in Brazil by European immigrants, as some maintain. A research done in Rio de Janeiro also points to more prejudice against mulattoes than against Negroes, thereby giving partial confirmation to our findings.[7]

The question remains entirely open whether the genesis of such extreme racial prejudice goes back to slavery or to the dynamics of social mobility and of the labor market, where mulattoes might be considered more dangerous competitors than Negroes. Further research on this problem would be highly desirable.

STEREOTYPES, NORMS AND BEHAVIOR

The ideal norms of behavior contrast in their relative tolerance with the wide acceptance of stereotypes. A theoretical equality of opportunities for whites and Negroes is accepted by 92 per cent in accordance with the Brazilian democratic ethos. Over 60 per cent accept casual relations between whites and Negroes. The color line is found at the level of closer emotional relationships: 62 per cent are opposed to a degree of intimacy with Negroes beyond that of simple comradeship; 77 per cent are opposed to miscegenation with Negroes, 55 per cent to miscegenation with mulattoes.

In actual behavior as reported, and in hypothetical relationships, the sample leans heavily on the segregation side (although lack of actual contact does not necessarily mean prejudice). One hundred four subjects report no contacts with either Negroes or mulattoes. Ninety-five per cent of the sample would not marry a Negro; 87 per cent would not marry a light skinned mulatto.

TABLE 14-1

Table of Intercorrelations

Variable a Stereotypes	Var. b Norms	Var. c Behavior	Var. d Hyp. Rel.	
	+.60	+.25	+.37	Variable a stereotypes
+.60		+.51	+.68	Variable b norms
+.25	+.51		+.49	Variable c actual behavior
+.37	+.68	+.49		Variable d hypothetical relationships

The linear correlation coefficients (Pearsonian r) between the four main variables are all positive, which vindicates at least partially our statistical treatment. Particularly noteworthy is the low correlation between stereotypes and actual behavior (+.25).

A paradox appears in comparing these four variables or dimensions of prejudice. On the one hand, we find a wide adherence to democratic norms, and, on the other hand, a high degree of stereotypy, a great amount of segregation at the intimate personal level, and a practically complete endogamy. This ambivalence constitutes a real "Brazilian Dilemma," different though it may be from the "American Dilemma."[8]

DIFFERENCES BY SEX, SOCIO-ECONOMIC STATUS AND ETHNIC ORIGIN

Manifest differences appear between men and women in our sample. Men accept more stereotypes than women but are much more tolerant for the three other variables. The differences between the means are significant at the level $p < .01$. These differences appear for practically all questions taken separately but particularly for the question on intermarriage. Men are much more ready to marry light-skinned mulattoes than women. This finding is in agreement with the study of Pierson in Bahia,[9] and with Brazilian folklore, which emphasizes the erotic appeal of the "morena." Several hypotheses to be tested empirically may account for these differences. Women are certainly less free in their associations than men. The penalty put on interracial mingling may be greater for women than for men. There may be a sub-conscious fear of sexual aggression by Negroes on the part of some women as indicated by the question on "sensuality": 40 per cent of the women think that Negroes are more sensual than whites as opposed to 4 per cent for men ($p<.01$). On the other hand, as women enter less in economic competition with Negroes than men, there may be less need for women to develop the racial superiority myth as a defense mechanism.

The most tenable hypothesis is perhaps to be found in the Brazilian racial education which rests on two opposite foundations: on the one hand, opposition to miscegenation; on the other hand, avoidance of racial tensions and of open expression of prejudice.[10] As women remain longer than men under the family influence, they absorb more of this racial indoctrination. From the rejection of miscegenation results the greater intolerance of women; from the etiquette of racial "good manners" results the greater self-censorship on the verbal expression of stereotypes.

The criterion of income alone gives a very poor index of socio-economic status. Our conclusions on this point are very tentative. In comparing the two extreme groups on the income distribution (incomes under 4,500 cruzeiros and over 14,500 cruzeiros), the high-income group accepts more stereotypes than the low-income group but is more tolerant in its social norms and actual behavior. Only the first finding on stereotypes is significant at the level $p<.05$.

No definite assertions can be deduced from such uncertain results. The upper-income group is perhaps more "traditional" and paternalistic. In the low-income group there may be developing a more acute "competitive" type of discrimination and segregation comparable to that of the "poor white" in the post-bellum South in the United States. These historical-dynamic considerations are beyond the scope of our study. In any case, our findings invalidate for São Paulo two conclusions of Pierson in his Bahia study:[11]

1. That prejudice in Brazil is more a class prejudice than a racial prejudice. Although we have not been able to isolate the effects of class and racial prejudice and, although the two are certainly linked together, we can definitely assert that, after having eliminated the effects of class prejudice against colored people, there would remain an important residue of properly racial prejudice. The latent subjective relationship between sexuality and prejudice would among other facts be incomprehensible if there were only a class prejudice.

2. That prejudice against Negroes is directly proportional to socio-economic status. Our study fails to confirm this statement for the middle class of São Paulo. The relationship between status and prejudice is certainly not as simple and direct as Pierson formulated it.

171

When the group of first generation Brazilians as a whole is compared with the group of older-stock Brazilians, no significant differences appear. However, mutually canceling differences are found when the various ethnic groups are separated. The group of Japanese descent is much less prejudiced against Negroes than the general sample, perhaps because it suffers itself from some discrimination. The group of descendants of Syrians and Lebanese is much more prejudiced for reasons explained elsewhere.[12] The Italian group responds like the low-income group in the general sample, which is in accordance with the socio-economic level of a majority of its members. The Portuguese group shows the same patterns as the high-income group. This fact may be explained by the common cultural heritage of Portuguese and Brazilians. The "high-income" type of response may come from the more traditional and paternalistic heritage of the past. All these ethnic-group differences cancel each other and are obscured when the descendants of immigrants are lumped together.

SUMMARY AND CONCLUSION

The existence of racial prejudice against Negroes and mulattoes has been established. Opinions vary greatly from relative tolerance to relative intolerance; freedom of attitudes and, to a lesser degree, of behavior is relatively great: social norms are directive rather than compulsive. Equality of opportunities is largely accepted, casual relations are widely tolerated but intimate relationships with colored people are frowned upon. Mulattoes are generally less discriminated against than Negroes but a small minority "prefers" Negroes to mulattoes. This small minority exhibits a much more virulent form of prejudice against both Negroes and mulattoes than does the general sample. Sex is an important determinant of prejudice. So is socio-economic status, although our data are too uncertain and incomplete to determine the exact relationship. Ethnic origin of the parents likewise plays an important role.

The weaknesses of our study are many and obvious. As we have pointed out, the sample is not random nor proportional; the postulates underlying the analysis are debatable, etc. Our conclusions must be accepted with all caution, and we have raised more problems than we have solved. Although our findings largely confirm previous studies, certain revisions of the literature seem in order. Should our study only stimulate criticism, further research, and a few working hypotheses, we should be highly satisfied.

NOTES

1. For our purposes a "race" is a human grouping socially and subjectively defined in a given society. This grouping considers itself different from other groupings similarly defined by virtue of innate and visible physical characteristics, or, in the extreme case, defined, rightly or wrongly, as biologically separate sub-groups.

The same terms such as "Negro" and "white" may, in different societies, cover objectively dissimilar groupings as exemplified by Brazil and the United States. In this research, we shall use the Brazilian definition. "Racial prejudice" is the totality of reciprocal relations of stereotypy, discrimination, and segregation existing between human groupings that consider themselves and each other as "races."

2. On Brazilian racial problems see: Gilberto Freyre, *Casa Grande e Senzala* (Rio de Janeiro, 1934); Gilberto Freyre, *Sobrados e Mucambos* (São Paulo, 1936); Donald Pierson, *Negroes in Brazil* (Chicago, 1942); Charles Wagley, editor, *Races and Class in Rural Brazil* (UNESCO, 1952); Thales de Azevedo, *Les élites de couleur dans une ville brésilienne* (UNESCO, 1953); L. A. Da Costa Pinto, *O Negro no Rio de Janeiro* (São Paulo, 1953); R. Bastide, F. Fernandes, V. Bicudo, A. M. Ginsberg and O. Nogueira, *Relacões Raciais entre Negros e Brancos em São Paulo* (1955); René Ribeiro, *Religião e Relacões Raciais* (Rio de Janeiro, 1956).

3. The present study was undertaken under the auspices of the UNESCO but was not included in the final report because of the death of Lucila Hermann. We received the filled-out questionnaires in Paris a few years later.

4. Guy B. Johnson, "The Stereotype of the American Negro" in O. Klineberg, editor, *Characteristics of the American Negro* (New York: 1944), pp. 1–22. For the complete questionnaire see: R. Bastide, "Stéréotypes et préjugés de couleur," *Sociologia*, 18 (May 1955).

5. Samuel H. Lowrie, "Origem da populacão de São Paulo e Diferenciação das classes sociais," *Revista do Arquivo Municipal*, 42 (São Paulo), pp. 195–212.

6. Oracy Nogueira, "Preconceito racial de marca e preconceito racial de origem," *Anais do XXXI Congresso International de Americanistas* (São Paulo, 1955), pp. 409–434.

7. Costa Pinto, *op. cit.*, pp. 203–208.

8. G. Myrdal, *An American Dilemma* (New York: 1944), pp. 21, 39, 84–89, 460, 614, 899.

9. D. Pierson, *op. cit.*, pp. 136–137.

10. R. Bastide *et al.*, *op. cit.*, p. 126.

11. D. Pierson, *op. cit.*, pp. 348–349; and D. Pierson, *Bulletin International des Sciences Sociales*, vol. IV, n°2 (UNESCO, no date), p. 488. For statements more in agreement with our conclusions see: T. de Azevedo, *op. cit.*, pp. 34–45; C. Wagley, *op. cit.*, pp. 147, 150, 159; R. Bastide *et al.*, *op. cit.*, pp. 11, 123–124, 133–139.

12. R. Bastide *et al.*, *op. cit.*, pp. 128–129.

ALIENATION, RACE, AND EDUCATION

One of the problems empirical studies of alienation must confront is the multiplicity of meanings attached to the concept. Seeman has suggested that there are five major meanings: powerlessness, meaninglessness, normlessness, isolation, and self-estrangement.[1] Most studies have dealt with only one of these variants of alienation—or at most two or three, singly or in combination—and there is little evidence regarding the relative frequency of different types of alienation in the population or of their differential association with various causal factors. We shall adopt, with some modifications, Seeman's variants of alienation and examine their incidence in a small southern city.

On the basis of the theoretical formulations of the classic social theorists as well as the fragmentary previous empirical research, we hypothesize that the different types of alienation are highly correlated with one another. Further, we hypothesize that each type of alienation is directly related to those disabling social conditions that limit or block the attainment of culturally valued objectives. We shall test this hypothesis with regard to two of the most important disabling conditions in American society: subordinate racial status and low educational attainment.

One possible exception to the general hypotheses is suggested by the vast literature pointing to the alienation of the intellectual from the dominant culture. Awareness of the more subtle ways in which this dominant culture may thwart human potentialities probably requires a relatively high level of education and sophistication. Cultural estrangement may therefore

From Russell Middleton, "Alienation, Race, and Education," in *American Sociological Review*, 28 (1963), pp. 473–477.

be inversely related to the disabling conditions specified and less highly correlated with the other types of alienation.

Method

This study was conducted in a central Florida city of 18,000 during the summer of 1962. All residents above the age of 20 were enumerated, and a simple random sample of 256 persons was drawn. Since the number of Negroes in this sample was inadequate for extensive analysis, an additional 50 Negro subjects were randomly drawn. The final sample thus consisted of 207 whites and 99 Negroes. Generalizations about the community as a whole, however, are based on the original sample of 256.

This study constituted a part of a larger cooperative survey of attitudes on a variety of subjects: civil defense, mental illness, political leadership, and the employment of married women. Since exigencies of the larger study permitted us to include only a few items dealing with alienation, a single attitude statement was formulated for each of the variants of alienation. It would have been desirable to construct scales for each type of alienation, but the single items are useful at least for exploratory analysis.[2]

The types of alienation and the attitude statements associated with each are as follows:

1. *Powerlessness.* "There is not much that I can do about most of the important problems that we face today."

2. *Meaninglessness.* "Things have become so complicated in the world today that I really don't understand just what is going on."

3. *Normlessness.* "In order to get ahead in the world today, you are almost forced to do some things which are not right." The most commonly used measure of a sense of normlessness is Srole's anomia scale.[3] The manifest content of this scale, however, appears to be a combination of cynicism and pessimism—or, as Nettler and Meier and Bell maintain, despair.[4] Although pessimism and cynicism or despair may ordinarily accompany anomia, they do not in themselves constitute it, and the degree of association is an empirical question. The concept of normlessness has also been used in several other senses,[5] but here we follow the more restricted usage of Merton and Seeman, emphasizing the expectation that illegitimate means must be employed to realize culturally prescribed goals.[6]

4. *Cultural estrangement.* "I am not much interested in the TV programs, movies, or magazines that most people seem to like." Seeman refers

to this variant of alienation as "isolation," but to avoid the traditional connotation of social isolation, we use the more explicit term "cultural estrangement." Like many of the questions in Nettler's scale for alienation,[7] the present item focuses on the individual's acceptance of popular culture.

5. *Social estrangement.* "I often feel lonely." Although Dean, working with Seeman, developed a scale to measure social isolation,[8] Seeman later decided that this was "not a very useful meaning" and abandoned social isolation as a type of alienation.[9] In doing so, however, he has abandoned a significant part of the tradition associated with the concept of alienation. Nisbet,[10] Pappenheim,[11] and Grodzins,[12] for example, follow Tönnies and Durkheim in emphasizing the loss of community in modern society as the source of alienation. On the other hand, Seeman's point that social isolation cannot readily be separated from differences in associational style—the fact that some men are sociable and some are not—makes clear the desirability of distinguishing social isolation from social estrangement. In his study of the aged, Townsend makes such a distinction: ". . . to be socially isolated is to have few contacts with family and community; to be lonely is to have an unwelcome *feeling* of lack or loss of companionship. The one is objective, the other subjective and, as we shall see, the two do not coincide."[13] Eric and Mary Josephson also comment that not all isolates are socially estranged, nor are all nonisolates free from alienation.[14] It is, then, the feeling of loneliness that is crucial to alienation, and the present item is designed to tap this subjective sense of social estrangement.

6. *Estrangement from work.* "I don't really enjoy most of the work that I do, but I feel that I must do it in order to have other things that I need and want." One of the oldest themes in the literature of alienation is that man may become estranged from himself by failing to realize his own human capacities to the fullest. Seeman suggests the absence of intrinsically meaningful activity as an indicator of self-estrangement.[15] As used by social theorists from Marx to Fromm, however, the concept of self-estrangement is considerably broader—as broad, in fact, as the concept of human nature. Fromm, for example, discusses most of the other types of alienation as aspects of self-estrangement or as conditions leading to self-estrangement.[16] As Seeman points out, the notion of self-estrangement also begs the question in that it implies certain assumptions about human nature and the ideal human condition. Nevertheless, the notion of alienation from meaningful work has an important place in the literature and deserves separate treatment. We thus include the present item to measure estrangement from work, though one may choose to interpret it as an index of self-estrangement.

Russell Middleton

TABLE 15-1

Intercorrelations of Types of Alienation *

	Meaning-lessness	Norm-lessness	Cultural Estrange-ment	Social Estrange-ment	Estrange-ment from Work
Powerlessness	.58	.61	.06	.54	.57
Meaninglessness	—	.59	.17	.46	.81
Normlessness	—	—	.31	.48	.67
Cultural estrangement	—	—	—	.08	.20
Social estrangement	—	—	—	—	.71

*The number of cases is 256; the measure of association is Yule's Q. The values of χ^2 for all relationships for which Q exceeds .30 are significant at the .05 level.

In the interviews the six items dealing with alienation were interspersed with a large number of unrelated questions. The respondents were given the following instructions: "Although you may not agree or disagree completely with any of the following statements, please tell me whether you tend more to agree or disagree with each statement." Each agreement was taken as an indication of alienation.

The chi-square test of significance, with the rejection level set at .05, and Yule's coefficient of association (Q) were utilized in the statistical analysis of the data.

Findings

Intercorrelations among the types of alienation are presented in Table 15–1. With the exception of cultural estrangement, the association between each type of alienation and each other type is moderately strong, with Q's ranging from .46 to .81.[17] As expected, cultural estrangement is not highly correlated with the other variants of alienation; the only statistically significant relation is with normlessness, and even here the Q is a relatively low .31. The type of alienation most highly correlated with the other types is estrangement from work. This suggests that it may indeed be a useful index to self-estrangement, if, as Marx and Fromm have maintained, self-estrangement is at the core of the phenomenon of alienation.

If cultural estrangement is excluded, the five remaining items constitute a Guttman scale with a coefficient of reproducibility of .90. Although these five types of alienation may be distinct on a conceptual level, there is apparently an underlying unity. Studies employing a measure of generalized alienation thus may be feasible, though the nature of the relation of cultural estrangement to the other types of alienation perhaps needs further clarification.

Our present purpose, however, is to determine whether each of the varieties of alienation is associated with conditions of deprivation. The importance of racial status as an alienating condition is immediately apparent from the figures in Table 15–2. The percentage of Negroes who feel

TABLE 15-2

Alienation, by Race

| | Per Cent Who Feel Alienated | | |
Type of Alienation	Negroes*	Whites	Total Community
Powerlessness	70	40	47
Meaninglessness	71	48	52
Normlessness	55	16	24
Cultural estrangement	35	34	35
Social estrangement	60	27	35
Estrangement from work	66	18	28
Number of cases	(99)	(207)	(256)

*The Negro sample is augmented by an additional 50 cases chosen randomly from the enumeration of Negro adults in the community. Figures for the total community do not include the 50 additional cases.

alienated is far higher than the percentage of whites for every type of alienation except cultural estrangement. Approximately two-thirds of the Negro subjects agree with most of the items indicating alienation, whereas a majority of whites disagree with every item. The racial difference is statistically significant in every instance except cultural estrangement.

The difference is largest with respect to estrangement from work. No doubt this reflects the occupational structure of the community, for 72 per cent of the employed Negroes are working in semiskilled or unskilled jobs, as compared to only 14 per cent of the whites. A marked difference between Negroes and whites also occurs in the case of normlessness. More than half the Negroes but only 16 per cent of the whites perceive a conflict between success goals and ethical means. This difference may stem in part from the Negroes' recognition that discrimination leaves few legitimate avenues to success open to them. Observation of the discrepancy between the whites' professed ideals and their actual behavior, particularly in relation to Negroes, may also give Negroes a rather cynical perspective on society.

In Table 15–3 we may examine the effect of education on alienation within each racial group. Among the Negroes, those who have had 12 or more years of education are in every instance less likely to feel alienated than those with less education, though the differences are statistically significant only for social estrangement and estrangement from work. There is a similar pattern among the whites, with significant differences for powerlessness, meaninglessness, and estrangement from work.

TABLE 15-3

Alienation, by Race and Years of Education

| | Per Cent Who Feel Alienated | | | |
| | Negroes* | | Whites | |
Type of Alienation	Less Than 12 Years Education	12 or More Years of Education	Less Than 12 Years Education	12 or More Years of Education
Powerlessness	73	60	57	34
Meaninglessness	76	56	80	35
Normlessness	59	40	22	14
Cultural estrangement	39	24	42	31
Social estrangement	67	40	37	24
Estrangement from work	73	44	33	12
Number of cases	(74)	(25)	(60)	(147)

*The Negro sample is augmented by an additional 50 cases chosen randomly from the enumeration of Negro adults in the community.

As one would expect, the inverse relation between education and a sense of meaninglessness is particularly strong, but much more so among the whites than among the Negroes. The percentage difference between high and low educational groups among the whites is more than twice that for the Negroes. Why is education not a more significant factor in relieving Negroes of the sense that they "really don't understand just what is going on?" We might speculate that the Negroes' greater sense of powerlessness is responsible. Even educated Negroes may feel little interest in attempting to understand things they believe are beyond their control. This interpretation is supported by the fact that education has more effect on powerlessness among whites than it does among Negroes. For each of the other types of alienation, however, the percentage difference between educational groups is greater among the Negroes than among the whites.

179

Use of the scale for general alienation, which consists of all of the items except cultural estrangement, permits us to gain an overview of the relation between alienation and race and education. If, on the basis of this scale, the sample is divided at the median into groups of high and low alienation, the association between subordinate racial status and alienation is $Q = .79$. Approximately 6 per cent of the Negroes and 23 per cent of the whites show no alienation with regard to any of the five types in the scale; 28 per cent of the Negroes and only 1 per cent of the whites feel alienated in every respect.

The association between education and general alienation is $-.67$ for the white group and $-.44$ among the Negroes. Thus, education appears to be of somewhat greater significance among whites than among Negroes. For Negroes in a southern community racial status is far and away the most salient fact; the whites tend to treat Negroes categorically, regardless of education, occupation, or reputation. Yet, education affects most types of alienation, even among the Negroes. On the other hand, there is no significant educational difference among Negroes in the incidence of pessimism. The highly educated Negroes are almost as likely as the poorly educated to agree with the statement, "In spite of what some people say, the lot of the average man is getting worse." Killian and Grigg report similar findings for Florida Negroes in connection with Srole's anomia scale, of which this item is a part.[18]

Conclusion

Among the adults of a small city in central Florida five types of alienation —powerlessness, meaninglessness, normlessness, social estrangement, and estrangement from work—are highly intercorrelated, but a sixth, cultural estrangement, is not closely related to the others. The hypothesis that social conditions of deprivation are related to alienation is generally supported. Subordinate racial status and limited education are strongly associated with all but one type of alienation. Several other factors, such as occupation of head of household, family income, sex, marital status, and size of community of origin, also tend to be related to alienation, but the coefficients of association are not as high as for race or education.

By far the most striking finding of the study is the pervasiveness of alienation among the Negro population, a point which is also dramatically clear in James Baldwin's essay, "Down at the Cross." In addition to each of the other types of alienation, Baldwin senses a cultural estrangement among American Negroes so extreme that "there are some wars . . . that the American Negro will not support, however many of his people may be coerced. . . ."[19] William Worthy, correspondent of the *Baltimore Afro-American*, has pointed out that the greatest amount of pro-Castro sentiment in the United States is to be found in Harlem among lower-class Negroes, and Black Muslim publications have advocated a policy of "Hands Off Cuba!" This evidence of estrangement from American culture is not consistent with the findings of this study, which show that Negroes are no more likely to be culturally estranged than whites. The discrepancy may be due to the circumscribed nature of the item used here to determine cultural estrangement, since it deals only with attitudes toward the popular culture of the mass media. Negroes may feel a deep estrangement from basic aspects of American culture and yet turn to the soporific fare of the mass media as a means of escape from the problems and tensions of life.

NOTES

1. Melvin Seeman, "On the Meaning of Alienation," *American Sociological Review*, 24 (December 1959), pp. 783–791.
2. Prior to the study the six items were presented without identification to 14 graduate students in a seminar in sociological theory who had previously read and discussed the work of Durkheim, Merton, Srole, Nettler, Meier and Bell, Seeman, and Dean on the subjects of anomie and alienation. The students, working independently, showed little hesitation in classifying the items, and they were in unanimous agreement concerning the type of alienation represented by each of the six items.
3. Leo Srole, "Social Integration and Certain Corollaries: An Exploratory Study," *American Sociological Review*, 21 (December 1956), pp. 709–716.
4. Dorothy L. Meier and Wendell Bell, "Anomia and Differential Access to the Achievement of Life Goals," *American Sociological Review*, 24 (April 1959), pp. 190–191.
5. See, for example, Dwight G. Dean, "Alienation: Its Meaning and Measurement," *American Sociological Review*, 26 (October 1961), pp. 754–755.
6. Robert K. Merton, "Social Structure and Anomie," in *Social Theory and Social Structure* (Glencoe, Ill.: Free Press, 1957), and Seeman, *op. cit.*, pp. 787–788.
7. Gwynn Nettler, "A Measure of Alienation," *American Sociological Review*, 22 (December 1957), pp. 670–677. In addition to questions dealing with political, religious, and familial norms, Nettler asks such questions as the following: "Do you enjoy TV?" "What do you think of the new model American Automobiles?" "Do you read *Reader's Digest?*" Do national spectator sports (football, baseball) interest you?"
8. Dean, *op. cit.*, pp. 755–756.
9. Seeman, *op. cit.*, p. 789.
10. Robert A. Nisbet, *Community and Power* (New York: Oxford University Press), 1962.

11. Fritz Pappenheim, *The Alienation of Modern Man* (New York: Monthly Review Press), 1959.

12. Morton Grodzins, *The Loyal and the Disloyal* (Chicago: University of Chicago Press, 1956), p. 134.

13. Peter Townsend, *The Family Life of Old People* (London: Routledge and Kegan Paul, 1957), p. 166.

14. Eric and Mary Josephson (eds.), *Man Alone: Alienation in Modern Society* (New York: Dell, 1962), p. 14.

15. Seeman, *op. cit.*, pp. 789–790.

16. Erich Fromm, *The Sane Society* (New York: Holt, Rinehart and Winston, 1955). See also Erich Fromm, *Marx's Concept of Man* (New York: Frederick Ungar), 1961.

17. For comparison purposes, phi coefficients (ø) were also calculated. Since ø involves a more restrictive definition of association than Q, the coefficients are uniformly lower, but the patterns of relationship among the variables are almost identical.

18. Lewis M. Killian and Charles M. Grigg, "Urbanism, Race, and Anomia," *American Journal of Sociology*, 67 (May 1962), pp. 661–665.

19. James Baldwin, *The Fire Next Time* (New York: Dial Press, 1963), p. 117. At an informal meeting between Attorney General Robert F. Kennedy and James Baldwin and a group of his friends, ". . . a once-injured, often-jailed young Freedom Rider waggled a finger in the astonished Kennedy's face and told him he wouldn't take up arms against Cuba. 'He was surprised to hear there were Negroes who wouldn't fight for their country,' Baldwin said later in his two-room downtown Manhattan flat. 'How many Negroes would fight to free Cuba when they can't be freed themselves?' That was precisely the message the Negroes wanted to get across—a message of anger, of quickening urgency, of deepening alienation." "Kennedy and Baldwin: The Gulf," *Newsweek*, 61 (June 3, 1963), p. 19.

16   *Melvin L. Kohn and Robin M. Williams, Jr.*

SITUATIONAL PATTERNING
IN INTERGROUP RELATIONS

There is now abundant research evidence of situational variability in intergroup behavior: an ever-accumulating body of research demonstrates that allegedly prejudiced persons act in a thoroughly egalitarian manner in situations where that is the socially prescribed mode of behavior, and that allegedly unprejudiced persons discriminate in situations where they feel it is socially appropriate to do so.[1] It is also well known that patterns of "appropriateness" in intergroup behavior have been changing with increasing tempo in recent years. The unthinkable of a short time ago has in many areas of life become the commonplace of today. For a brief period the transition from unthinkable to commonplace arouses extreme emotional fervor; but as the new definition of the situation becomes the socially prescribed, the fervor soon diminishes. What was for the moment an "unpatterned" situation becomes, in Karl Mannheim's terms, "built into the framework of the society."[2]

Unpatterned situations, in which definitions of appropriate conduct are in process of change, occur infrequently, and it is even more infrequent that they occur at the convenience of the research observer. Yet their importance for social change is likely to be great. In the multitude of unambiguous, patterned situations we have the raw material for documenting existing patterns of intergroup behavior. In the relatively rare unpatterned situations, however, we may hope to find important information concerning social change. It appears, for instance, that one of the most basic changes in race relations in the South is the growing uncertainty of all concerned about what is appropriate, "proper" intergroup behavior. This, along with the

From Melvin L. Kohn and Robin M. Williams, Jr., "Situational Patterning in Intergroup Relations," in *American Sociological Review*, 21 (1956), pp. 164–174.

decreased personal interaction between whites and Negroes (especially middle- and upper-class Negroes), is compounded with the relative impersonality of the new urban South, to create an unprecedented situation in which further changes can occur with a rapidity that would have been thought impossible only a few years ago.

The social scientist who wishes to study the processes by which unpatterned situations come to be defined by their participants is faced with several major problems, not the least of which is the difficulty of finding situations that can be studied systematically. It is not sufficient to create hypothetical situations and to ask people how they think they would behave in them. People's responses to hypothetical situations are patterned in the same way as ordinary opinion-items—for example, they can be ordered into unidimensional scales. But behavior studied in actual intergroup situations has not proven scalable; such behavior encompasses factors idiosyncratic to the particular situation, that cannot be foreseen by the person asked to predict his probable behavior.

Since hypothetical situations are not adequate, and actual unpatterned situations occur but rarely, the research worker is left with little choice but to initiate new situations. The procedure must be covert, for if the participants knew that the situations were created for research purposes, their definitions would be radically altered. Many problems are necessarily created, on both ethical and practical levels: the procedure involves a degree of manipulation; it poses a degree of danger to the participant observers and perhaps to other participants as well; it creates barriers to observation and interviewing. In the absence of preferable alternatives, however, we felt justified in initiating a series of forty-three situations in which we could observe and interview in a reasonably systematic fashion.

These situations were initiated in social contexts that were neither so intimate as automatically to exclude Negro participation, nor so functionally specific as to make acceptance of Negroes unproblematic. In particular, we focused on service establishments, such as restaurants and taverns. In white neighborhoods infrequently visited by Negroes, for example, we found many restaurant and tavern managers who had never faced a situation where it was necessary to decide whether or not to serve Negro patrons. Frequently the manager, when confronted by a Negro customer, was caught in a serious dilemma. On the one hand, it is illegal in the communities studied to refuse to serve Negroes. On the other hand, these establishments are often informal neighborhood social centers, and the managers' fears that their customers would object to the presence of Negroes militate against serving. For the manager who has no already established policy, this can be a highly problematic situation.

Within the restricted area in which it was possible to initiate situations—in public service establishments, voluntary organizations, and the like—we attempted to vary the situational conditions to the maximum degree possible. Even so, it must be recognized that our conclusions are based on studies in a very limited range of social institutions; e.g., we could not initiate new situations in industrial organizations or in schools. Thus we cannot assert that the present findings are directly applicable to institutions outside of the range studied. It seems probable, however, that though the processes by which unpatterned situations arise in these institutions are different from those of the present research, the processes by which they come to be defined by participants are similar.

Procedure

Before initiating a situation, we attempted to assess the usual patterns of behavior in the particular setting. The formality of our procedure depended on the social context: in formal organizations we were able to attend meetings, and to interview leaders and a sample of the membership; in service establishments we could only visit frequently enough to establish informal relationships with the staff and a few steady customers. Only after we felt we had some basis for predicting their probable reception, did we introduce Negro "stimulus-participants." White observers, located at strategic positions, observed the reactions of the principal participants.

Immediately after the Negroes withdrew from the scene, these "stimulus-participants" recorded the chronological sequence of events, and in addition filled out recording forms that had been designed to elicit their interpretations of the events. The white observers remained behind long enough to observe after-the-fact reactions, and then recorded their observations and interpretations in similar fashion. Thus we were able to secure the definitions held by non-participant observers and by Negro participants, as well as data on the overt behavior that occurred. In most cases we were also able to secure retrospective reports from white participants (organizational leaders, bartenders, customers) by formal interviewing procedures.

As an example of the procedure followed, let us consider one of these situations in some detail. A Negro couple (members of the research staff) entered a working-class tavern that was believed to discriminate. White observers, some of whom had visited the establishment frequently enough to be able to ask questions without arousing undue suspicion, were seated at strategic spots throughout the tavern. The following are the chronological accounts written by one of the Negro "stimulus participants" and one of the white observers:

THE REPORT OF THE "STIMULUS-PARTICIPANT"

Entered at 10:15. People looked around, but we strode dauntlessly to table near fire. Most people seemed to look around, notice us, and comment. I needed a match and went to the couple in the first booth. The fellow had a lighter. I asked for a light. He replied eagerly, "Yes sir," and flicked his lighter for me. Testing the afternoon hunch on restrooms, I went to the men's room. As I passed the lady's room, the bartender blocked my way.

BARTENDER: "What did you say?"

RESEACHER: "How do you do. I didn't say anything. I'm looking for the men's room."

BARTENDER: "I'll show you." He leads me to the men's room, stands at the next urinal in a grand rapport gesture, and says confidently, "Now, mind you, I don't have anything against you people. I went to school with you folks and I've got a lot of friends among you. But some of my customers don't like to see you in here. Five or six of them have already complained to me and left. Now I can't have that. I hope you'll understand if I ask you to leave."

RESEARCHER: "It's pretty hard to understand. I went to war for these people."

BARTENDER: "Yeah, I went to war too. But some of our people are funny. They don't like to see you in here. So I'll have to ask you to go." He leaves, and another young Caucasian enters. I am pretty damn upset.

I: "I suppose you're one of these fine people who wants me to leave."

HE: "No, no, everybody's all right with me. What's the matter, you have some trouble?"

I: "You're damned tootin'!" I go back to the table. Several people are entering and leaving for no apparent connected reason. No one comes to wait on us. Ten minutes later I go to the cigarette machine.

BARTENDER: (stops me again): "Say, are you going to leave or are we going to have some trouble? Some of the boys are pretty hot. Now I suggest that you get out of here before something happens. We don't want your kind. Remember, I've told you." I go back to the table. L (the Negro girl) is enthusiastic. The waitress comes near to clean off a table and L calls her three times. Waitress tosses her head and leaves. Band returns from intermission and begins to play. After about five danceless numbers, three couples move out on floor. We go to dance. Here comes bartender again.

BARTENDER: "Now look, I've told you three times. War or no war, now you get out of here. We don't want you. I've got my customers to think of. Come on, get off the floor and get out of here before you have trouble."

I ask him to call the cops if there's trouble, but he demurs and shoves us off dance floor. We leave. Must have been a great side-show to the white customers and observers, but I'm boiling so much I could kill every white face. Decide I'm through with this stunt. As we left, a fellow standing in front of the cigarette machine said, "Hell, we're all Americans. I'm all for you." Bartender was just behind us, shepherding us out, and he stopped and asked, "What did you say?" I didn't hear the rest, but the fellow was evidently championing us in a weak but determined way. Maybe there is some hope for some white folks.

THE REPORT OF ONE OF THE WHITE OBSERVERS

I arrived to find the bar crowded. D and J (observers) arrived, went through barroom to dancehall, just as I was climbing on a recently vacated stool at the bar. Proprietor was serving a tray of drinks to blonde waitress. The bartender was standing akimbo at north end of the bar, waiting for electric mixer to finish stirring drink for him. Door opened, Negro researchers walked in, going through barroom and into hallway to dance floor. Blonde looked around at them, staring, then looked back at proprietor with her mouth open.

PROPRIETOR (amazed): "Well, how do you like that!"
BARTENDER (turning): "What?"
PROPRIETOR AND BLONDE (simultaneously): "Those two jigs that just walked through here." "Two colored people just went in."
BARTENDER (in surprise): "Where'd they go?"
BLONDE: "Into the dance hall."

Enter Jane, a second waitress, from kitchen.

JANE: "I'm not going in there. What can we do? This never happened before. (To proprietor) "What'll we do? (Anguished) Do I *have* to serve them?"
PROPRIETOR (peering through service peephole from bar to dance floor): "Let 'em sit."
BARTENDER: "Yes, stay away from them. I didn't see them. Where'd they go?"
BLONDE: "They're at the table for six. What are we going to do?"
JANE: "I'm not going in there. This is awful."

Proprietor ducks under the lift-up gate at the end of the bar, takes a quick look into dance hall, then back under the gate board to his station behind the bar.

PROPRIETOR: "Just let them sit." For the next several minutes, the proprietor inquired anxiously, from time to time, "What are they doing now? Did they go?" Each time he looked more amazed. Said to me, "Never in my time here did we have any of them at the bar." After a wait of perhaps 15 to 18 minutes:
PROPRIETOR: "Well, I'm going to see that they leave." He took off apron, started to duck under the bar gate again, then said to bartender: "You better go in and get them out of there. I don't think I should go, because my name's on the license . . . if there's any trouble."
SCHOOLTEACHER (sitting with husband at the bar): "How can you get them to leave? (then to me) She was an attractive little thing, wasn't she?"

PROPRIETOR (again): "I wish they'd go. (Then to blonde waitress) Are any of your customers leaving?"

BLONDE: "A couple, but I think they were leaving anyway. They'd asked for their check. Others are looking around at them, and they're all talking about it . . . it gives me the creeps to have to walk in there, and know they're staring at me, expecting me to come over and wait on them."

JANE (to me): "We never had colored people here. This is the first couple that ever went in there. (Shrugging) I'm just not going in. What a time they picked to come! Saturday night—our busiest time! Why didn't they make it some week night?—there aren't so many people here."

By this time the bartender had taken off his apron, left the barroom, and a few minutes later returned and went directly into the men's room, followed by the Negro researcher.

PROPRIETOR (after a minute or so): "Where did the bartender go?"

JANE: "In the men's room."

TEACHER: "They've been in there quite a while."

PROPRIETOR (ducking under gate, apron and all): "I'd better see what's going on. He may have a knife." Goes and peers through four inch opening, as he holds the door ajar. Returns. "They're o.k." Bartender returned to bar, researcher to the dance hall.

BARTENDER: "He wanted to give me an argument. Said he was a veteran."

PROPRIETOR: "They all have something like that to say, I guess. I want them to get out. What did he say?"

BARTENDER: "He said yes."

I (turning to man on stool beside me): "This is some situation, isn't it?"

MAN (venomously): "It stinks!"

BLONDE (watching Negroes through doorway): "He's sitting down. It's a good thing the orchestra is having intermission."

PROPRIETOR: "Yes, I suppose they'd be dancing."

BARTENDER: "That looks like that Robeson stuff."

WAITRESS: "I can't think of any time I've seen colored people in here."

BARTENDER: "Stay away from them. Don't look at them. Don't let them catch your eye." Waitress departs for dance hall again.

YOUTH (at bar, to proprietor): "Maybe you can get a date." Proprietor snorted, ready to blow his top.

TEACHER: "He's getting cigarettes."

BARTENDER: "Where is he?"

JANE: "At the cigarette machine."

BARTENDER (apron and all, under the bar gate again): "I'll tell him to get going." Went and spoke to researcher, then back to bar. "They'll leave, I think. I told him there were a couple of fellows were going to see about it, if they didn't." Just about this time the orchestra's intermission was over; they returned to the bandstand.

PROPRIETOR: "There goes the band. I suppose they'll start to dance now. I wish I'd thought to hold up the orchestra until they got out of here. (To blonde) Watch them now. (To Jane) Jane, get me a sandwich, will you?"

Melvin L. Kohn and Robin M. Williams, Jr.

TEACHER: "You're in a tough spot, aren't you? Are you going to serve them?"
PROPRIETOR: "No."
BARTENDER: "We'll have to put them out for causing a disturbance."
BLONDE: "Four of my couples have left."
PROPRIETOR: "That does it! Go in and get them out of there, NOW!"

Bartender went into dancehall, one man followed him, and three or four other men gathered around. The Negro researchers walked out through the bar. Bartender went back behind the bar and the man resumed his seat.

PROPRIETOR (who had followed, with his eyes, the Negro girl as she left): "Did you see the cute little smile she had on?"
BARTENDER: "Well, that buck thinks he's tough, I guess. Robeson stuff."
CUSTOMER: "You could have served them. They got rights!"
BARTENDER: "You want to make something of it? Are you with them?"
CUSTOMER: "No, I'm not with them. They got a right to have a drink. You all stink."
BARTENDER (threateningly): "Pick up your change and drift. You want to drink with them? Go on down to the C.D. bar. Lots of them there." Man picked up his change and stalked to door, mumbling.
PROPRIETOR: "What the hell do you suppose is the matter with him? He's not drunk."
TEACHER: "Maybe he's one of those people who has Negro friends."
ANOTHER CUSTOMER: "In Germany those black bastards got everything they wanted. Excuse me, ma'm. (To teacher) Two or three of them would come along and take a white soldier's girl right away from him. I hate their guts. They want to stay away from me. I just wish you'd told me, I could have thrown them out. . . ."
PROPRIETOR: "You can if they come back. You can throw out their whole gang. They've probably gone to get the bunch. I don't think they came in just to get a drink."
TEACHER'S HUSBAND: "No, I think they came here deliberately to get served or make trouble. If they dropped in for a drink, they would have left when the bartender talked to him. I think this must be planned somehow."
BARTENDER: "Yeah, Robeson stuff. Spooks! Little Peekskill, they wanted to make out of this place."
TEACHER: "I feel sorry for them. (To me) She looked like a real nice girl. I have to teach my children tolerance and things like that. . . ."

Defining Unpatterned Situations

In these situations, it appeared that the participants attempted to achieve cognitive clarity by striving to assimilate the situation to their past actual or vicarious experience, that is, to categorize it as one of a type of situation with which they knew how to cope. The process, of course, was rarely as rational or as purposive as this formulation would imply. Yet the behavior manifested in these situations can be interpreted as an attempt to see a socially unstructured situation in terms of one or possibly even of several alternative socially acceptable structures. For example, in the illustration above, the bartender and waitress perceived the situation as one that could be categorized in either of two ways:

1. Here are two Negro out-of-towners who do not realize they are not welcome here.
2. Here are a couple of troublemakers who are trying to create another Peekskill riot here.

The importance of being able to categorize the situation is suggested by their dilemma. If the situation were the first type, they could expect the Negroes to leave when asked politely. If the situation were the second type, they could expect resistance to such a request—the Negroes might cause an immediate disturbance, "come back with their gang," or file suit for violation of the State Civil Rights Statute.

In this example two reasonably clear-cut alternative definitions of the situation were possible. At the extreme, even this degree of structure was missing. Here participants reacted by confusion: either the situation was so totally outside the range of their experience, or it partook of so wide a variety of possible definitions, that these participants were initially unable to see any structure to the situation at all.

It seems useful to distinguish these two possible reactions to an unpatterned situation. In one, the individual is confused about what behavior to expect from others and what is appropriate action to take himself. In the other, he has reasonably definite, but contradictory, expectations of how others will act and how he himself should act. These two types of reaction differ in degree only, and it is difficult to distinguish them in some concrete situations. Nevertheless, the distinction is useful because the probable future actions of the person whose orientation is primarily marked by *confusion* are different from the probable future actions of the person whose orientation is primarily marked by *contradiction*.[3]

In the situations studied, the participants who were primarily *confused* actively sought cues from others' behavior that could be useful in clarifying their own definitions of the situation. Where formal leadership roles existed, other participants turned to the presumed leaders for clarification. Members of organizations almost invariably took their cues from the presiding officers—if the club president greeted a Negro lecturer warmly, the members were likely to listen to his speech attentively. Similarly, waitresses and bartenders studied the reactions of owners and managers for hints as to whether or not service to Negro patrons was in order.

But in the nature of the case it most often happened that the people in leadership positions were themselves confused; for them the situation was not structured enough even to suggest where to turn for clarification. In consequence, action on the part of *any* participant became disproportionately important in determining their definitions. Expressions of discomfiture on the part of *any* customer were taken as an index that "the customers" objected to the presence of Negroes. Direct intervention on the part of a customer almost invariably proved decisive. If any white undertook to act as intermediary for a Negro patron, by ordering a drink for him, or buying him a drink, the bartender served the Negro. Even if the white were a disheveled drunk with a friendliness born of liquor, the bartender was likely to take his action as an index that the customers did not object to his serving Negroes. The possibility that the drunk's attitudes were atypical of the attitudes of other customers was for the moment ignored.

Initial behavioral cues, of course, could be variously interpreted. The cues themselves were often ambiguous, allowing of several alternative interpretations even to similarly situated persons. Furthermore, some persons seemed to be more sensitive to nuances of behavior than were others, for reasons that did not seem related to their roles in the situation. However, the most important factor in how participants interpreted behavioral cues appeared rather clearly to be their prestige-status in the situation. Negro participants were typically far less secure in these situations than were whites. They were more likely to be sensitive to minimal cues, and to interpret cues as indices of prejudice or lack of prejudice. A casual reference by a white to "you people" was frequently taken by Negro participants as an indication that the white was categorizing them as Negroes, and was therefore prejudiced. The white would have no idea that his statement—often made in the form of a testimonial meant to communicate good will—was so interpreted.

Finally, in some situations there were almost literally no appropriate behavioral cues to guide the confused participant. A white woman who taught a theatrical make-up class was thrown into a flurry of aimless excitement for almost ten minutes when a Negro girl who unexpectedly attended the practice session of her class asked her for an appropriate shade of face powder. She knew which shade would be best, but she had no idea of how to react to having a Negro girl attend the class. The reactions of the other members of the class did not help to resolve her confusion, and there were no other adults present. The consequence was that she persisted in her confusion for several minutes.

These interpretations apply only when the impediment to a satisfactory definition of the situation is confusion or ambiguity. Where the problem is that two alternative definitions are applicable to the situation (i.e., where the problem is one of *contradiction* or *conflict*), different behavioral consequences ensue. Usually, in such situations, it is possible to resolve the conflict by *exempting* the particular situation from all but one definition—in effect, by assigning one definition of the situation a higher priority than that accorded to the others. Two forms of exemption were apparent in the observed situations:

1. A particular *type of event* can be exempted from a more general definition: for example, a restaurant-owner, who in other contexts does not discriminate against Negroes, does discriminate against them in his restaurant because he feels that "business" takes precedence over other values.

2. A particular *individual* can be exempted in a range of situations: for example, a white treats a particular Negro as "different from other Negroes" and therefore acceptable in contexts where other Negroes would be unwelcome. One bar-owner served former high school classmates, although he refused to serve other Negroes.[4]

On occasion, however, neither of the alternative definitions can be avoided—the situation constrains the participants to act on the basis of both definitions simultaneously. For example, at a dinner-meeting tendered to party workers of a major political party, many of the white participants wished to avoid eating with the Negro party-workers, but at the same time did not wish to rebuff them and risk losing Negro votes. Their common mode of behavior was to act in a friendly fashion toward these Negroes, but not to sit at the same tables with them. When all other tables were fully occupied, some of the whites waited for new tables to be set up, rather than sitting at tables already partly occupied by Negroes. This we interpret to be a common mode of behavior by which the whites attempted to act in partial conformity to both definitions of the situation—the definition that this was a solidary group of party members, and the definition that this was an inter-racial situation. They had to eat at tables adjoining the tables at which Negroes were seated, but they did not have to eat with Negroes. Although they rebuffed these Negroes, they did not entirely alienate them. It appears that when an individual is constrained to act on the basis of two or more mutually incompatible definitions of the situation, he will seek a compromise solution by which he deviates as little as possible from the action appropriate to each of these definitions.

Finally, there are situations in which the alternative definitions cannot be reconciled. For example, the dilemma of the bartender who does not know whether or not to serve Negroes and feels: if I serve them, the white customers will object; if I don't, they may create a disturbance. In such a situation, the typical response is withdrawal from the situation, as when the bartender "looks the other way" or the prejudiced club-member leaves upon discovering that the lecturer of the evening is Negro. But withdrawal is not always possible. The bartender may "look the other way" when a Negro patron enters, but he cannot continue to do so when the Negro walks up to the bar directly in front of him. Then the result is usually an inconsistent series of actions, marked by a good deal of wavering. The bartender may begin to serve the Negro quite cordially, then appears to be unwilling to serve the Negro, then once again is quite cordial. If an observer asks him about it, he will be quite frank in stating that he feels impelled first towards one course of behavior, then towards the other. This inconsistent behavior may perseverate for an extraordinarily long time, until the individual is finally able (often for apparently irrelevant reasons) to give one or the other definition a higher priority.

Modification of Definitions

Although these covertly initiated situations enabled us to study the processes by which unpatterned situations are initially defined, they did not provide adequate data on the processes by which initial definitions are modified in interaction. The very conditions required for initiating unpatterned situations precluded our continued observation once the single event had transpired. To study the processes of change, it was necessary to find naturally occurring situations, or series of situations, in which changes of definition were taking place. We wanted to be able to observe a group of people engaged in a continuing series of situations; to interview these people at regular intervals, in order to elicit their interpretations of each situation; and to secure data about their behavior in past situations that might prove useful in interpreting their present behavior. Our procedure was to search for a group that had formed in response to a particular problem in which all were interested. We found the group we sought engaged in a rather dramatic endeavor—a civil rights law suit.

Two Negro men had been refused service in a country tavern, in the presence of Negro waiters. The men left the tavern quietly in spite of the fact that one of the waiters quit his job in protest. Two days later, the wife of one of these men telephoned the president of the local chapter of the National Association for the Advancement of Colored People, who in turn suggested that the men re-visit the tavern in the company of the executive committee of the NAACP chapter.[5] A first visit was, from their point of view, ineffectual: the proprietor was absent, and his son equivocated. A second trip found the proprietor prepared. After protesting his own lack of prejudice, he argued that he could not risk a boycott by white customers. When this argument fell on unresponsive ears—the NAACP president waved a copy of the State Anti-Discrimination Statute in his face—he argued that he didn't care what the law said, he simply was not going to serve Negroes. Then ensued a long debate on whether or not minority groups should insist on service where they were not wanted, ending in an impasse.

The NAACP leaders attempted, without success, to interest the local district attorney in taking court action. Then, with tacit approval by the prospective plaintiffs, they established contact with the state NAACP legal department. Initial plans for court action were made, followed by a delay of several months before the case was tried. The period of quiescence was marked by the plaintiff's loss of interest in the case.

The weekend preceding the case brought feverish activity on the part of the NAACP lawyer and two members of the executive committee, first in questioning witnesses, and later in detailed "cross-examination" of one waiter who reported that he would testify for the defense. Other members of the executive committee, the second waiter, and another participant-observer were brought in during the last stages of this examination—at a time of open conflict, with the lawyer and NAACP president accusing the dissident waiter of "selling out the race." The incident ended in excited denunciation of the "turncoat" by the waiter who had quit his job in protest against discrimination.

To this point, the plaintiffs had not participated. They and their wives joined the group at a meeting that evening, called to plan strategy for the trial. The first order of business was a dramatic account of the afternoon's activities. Then the lawyer interrupted abruptly to ask for his clients' minimum demands. He added that cash settlements generally weren't very high in this type of case. The plaintiffs said nothing. But the president jumped in to aver that "these men aren't in this for cash. They're in it for the principle of the thing!" He paid tribute to "men who have the guts to stick it out." A member of the executive committee spoke about the effects that this case would have on the Negro community generally. Others spoke *for* the plaintiffs. One asked that the men be given a chance to speak for themselves

—but he too congratulated them "for having the courage to go through with the case *for the principle of it!*"

The lawyer asked the plaintiffs directly: "How do you feel about this?" A long silence. Then one plaintiff answered. He said that he and his friend were fighting for the good of the race. He said that he hoped this action would benefit the Negro community as a whole. He said that he believed in *action* to improve the position of Negroes. He added that he was a poor man.

At once the president exclaimed that he too was a poor man, but that even if it meant losing his job, he would stick it through. There was no further ambiguity about money. The lawyer congratulated the plaintiffs for not seeking monetary retribution, and then asked the group as a whole for a statement of minimal demands. Almost all members of the group spoke up now, including the heretofore-silent plaintiffs and their wives. All agreed to a policy enunciated by the president: the demands were to be a full public apology, together with a statement by the proprietor that he would not discriminate in the future.

Succeeding events need not be described in detail here. The defendant, upon pressure from the judge, settled the case in court on the plaintiffs' terms.

For present purposes, the most striking aspect of this series of events was the radical change in the behavior of the plaintiffs. Their behavior in the discriminatory situation had been passive; upon their return to the community they did nothing to institute action against the bar-owner. Personality studies of the two men, based on detailed life history data, indicate that this passive acceptance of the intergroup relations status quo was entirely in keeping with their behavior in other situations. In fact, they had but a few weeks before this incident predicted (in response to a questionnaire-interview administered to a cross-section of the Negro community) that in such a situation they would leave the establishment without saying anything, and take no further action. Yet in the course of these situations the positive or negative evaluation of their behavior by a militant group of Negro leaders became important to their own evaluations of their behavior; their self-conceptions changed to those of "race men," or fighters for the good of the Negro community; their definitions of the discriminatory incident and of their own subsequent behavior were enlarged to include an evaluation of how these actions affected other Negroes in the city; and their passive behavior was transformed into militancy.

In broadest outline, this change can be viewed as the consequence of a long series of successive redefinitions of the situations in which they participated. When the bartender refused to serve them, they quickly developed an initial definition on the basis of which they hurriedly left the tavern. Their definition of this original situation held important consequences for their behavior in subsequent situations. Although each of these, too, contained idiosyncratic elements, there was a significant degree of continuity in their definitions of succeeding situations. The plaintiffs did not define each situation anew, solely on the basis of its idiosyncratic elements, but developed their definitions of particular situations from their definitions of preceding situations. It was as if they tried on their previous definitions for fit, modified them to meet the exigencies of the present, then modified them anew as these exigencies changed. Since new elements entered these situations almost continuously, this process never ceased. In the end, a revolution in definition and in behavior had been produced. But seen as a step-by-step process, this "revolution" was never more than a minor change in a preceding definition, with its apropriate behavioral consequences.[6]

The most readily apparent change in the plantiffs' orientation was their coming to depend upon the NAACP leaders as referents.[7] But why did the NAACP come to play this role?

It would seem that the plaintiffs must have been predisposed, at least to a limited degree, to see the NAACP definition of the situation as legitimate—even if not the only legitimate definition. It seems further that they must have felt constrained to co-operate with the NAACP leaders, provided that this did not entail a major commitment of time. Otherwise, the president could not have prevailed on them to participate even to the extent of a discussion with the tavern proprietor. Once they were involved in the NAACP activities, several factors conspired to commit them more and more firmly to the NAACP group: the NAACP leaders could and did shame them by holding out the threat that they would be regarded by the community as "quitters"; at the same time, these leaders were able to argue the logic of their philosophy, and to demonstrate by their own action how their philosophy worked in practice; continued group enterprise brought the emotional satisfactions of group *esprit de corps* and of participation in "something important"; finally the plaintiffs' behavior brought approbation from some other members of the Negro community.

At the same time, other pressures generated by the situations served to bring the plaintiffs' definitions into harmony with that of the NAACP leaders. Perhaps the most important event here was the "cross-examination" of the dissident waiter. The NAACP leaders could not have asked for a more compelling demonstration that the point at issue was a moral principle, with all other considerations irrelevant. A clear dichotomy was drawn between those who "sell out the race" and those who "fight for the race." If the dissident waiter stood as the symbol of selling out, his courageous colleague embodied the virtues of the man of principle. In the face of his sacrifice of his job, who could undertake to do less?

Even then, the plaintiffs were not fully committed. Interviews with the major participants indicate that the men hoped to be able to fight for the race and exact some monetary retribution as well. But this was exactly what the NAACP leaders wished to avoid; they did not want it said that the case was merely a matter of Negroes "trying to con a white man out of his money." It had to be a matter of principle, and principle alone! Here the introduction of new information enabled the plaintiffs to redefine the situation: if cash awards were generally not very high in these cases, it was considerably easier to forego the possibility of a windfall. Even so, foregoing cash was not easy. It took some time for a plaintiff to make the offer, and even then his offer was hardly forth-right. His statement did, however, allow of slight reinterpretation; once this occurred, the men were hardly in a position to backtrack.

For the plaintiffs, acceptance of the NAACP position brought a change in self-conception: they now thought of themselves as "race men." It also brought a rewriting of history, to bring all past events into line with their present definition. If you ask them now, they will tell you that their orientation has not changed. They are, and always have been, militant. From the very beginning, their one interest has been to fight discrimination. That is why they were so quick to bring the NAACP into the case.

In spite of this, their change in self-conception has not been productive of other militant action. Although they may continue to think of themselves as "race men," and although they may behave like "race men" in any future situation in which they are directly refused service, they have given no evidence that they are likely to carry out the logical implications of the "race man" role and engage in a wider range of interracial activities on behalf of the Negro community. Stated otherwise, it would appear that an individual who uses a particular reference group in defining a particular type of situation will not necessarily use that reference group in defining other types of situations. This is perfectly consistent with the general observation that people do not necessarily behave consistently in different types of situations.

Summary

We have in this report endeavored to interpret the processes by which participants define unpatterned intergroup situations, and the processes by which definitions are in turn modified over the course of time. We recognize that the research has been conducted within a very limited range of institutional contexts; we further recognize that the social constraints operating within other contexts may be quite different. Nevertheless, we believe it likely that the present interpretation is applicable to situations arising in other social contexts; for that reason, we present this summary in the form of hypotheses amenable to testing in a broad range of institutional contexts.

UNPATTERNED SITUATIONS

Ambiguous or Confused Definitions. When an individual is constrained to act but feels that he cannot predict the consequences of his own or other participants' behavior, his response to the situation will be to seek cues from other participants' behavior that can be used as indices of their definition of the situation. Where he can turn to persons in formal leadership roles, he will do so; but where this is not possible, the behavior of *any* other participant will be utilized as an index of how "other participants" define the situation. Where there are no appropriate behavioral cues available, the confused participant will tend to perseverate in his confusion until new action intervenes to structure the situation.

Contradiction or Conflict of Definition. When an individual is constrained to act but feels that two or more distinct definitions (each with its appropriate behavioral imperatives) are applicable to the situation, he will first attempt to resolve the conflict by exemption, i.e., by assigning one definition a higher priority than that accorded to others. (This can be done either by exempting a particular type of event or a particular person from a more general definition.) Where this is not possible, he will attempt to achieve a compromise solution by which he can act in partial conformity to both (or all) definitions of the situation. When even this is not possible, he will seek to withdraw from the situation, unless otherwise constrained. If constrained, he will behave inconsistently, wavering between the two alternative definitions, until new action intervenes to structure the situation.

MODIFICATION OF DEFINITIONS

Direct, overt interpersonal conflict is not likely to change either party's definition of the situation; its principal effect is likely to be the reinforcement of each combatant's values. Major changes of definition are more likely to be the result of a series of minor redefinitions, each dependent upon one or more of the following:

Changed Referents. When an individual's experience in a situation (or in a series of situations) leads to the reinforcement of particular reference groups, or to the internalization of new reference groups, his ideas of how he should act in the situation will be modified to conform to his modified self-conception.

Expectations of Consequences. When an individual's experience in a situation (or in a series of situations) leads to modification of his expectations of the consequences of his behavior, his ideas of how he should act in the situation will be modified to meet his new expectations of these consequences.

Similarly, when an individual's experience in a situation (or in a series of situations) leads to the modification of his expectations of how other participants will behave, his ideas of how he should act in the situation will be modified to meet his new expectations of their behavior.

NOTES

1. We shall define a situation as a series of interactions, located in space and time, and perceived by the participants as an *event*: in this usage "situation" is a delimiting term, cutting out from the flow of experience a particular series of inter-personal actions which are seen by the participants as a describable event, separable from preceding and succeeding events, constraining the participants to act in particular ways, and having its own unique consequences.

2. "Although situations are in their very nature dynamic and unique, as soon as they become socialized—that is to say, built into the framework of society—they tend to become standardized to a certain extent. Thus we must distinguish between what is called patterned and unpatterned situations." [Karl Mannheim, *Man and Society in an Age of Reconstruction* (London: Kegan Paul, Trench, Trubner, and Co., 1940), p. 301.]

3. We are at the moment concerned only with situations where the individual participants are initially unable to achieve consistent workable definitions of the situation. Situations where two or more participants have *different* definitions of the situation will be considered later. In this latter case each participant has a consistent definition, and the problem is how definitions are *modified*, rather than how unstructured situations become defined.

4. Calling this behavior exemption does not necessarily mean that the bar-owner perceived his action as making an exception of these particular Negroes; he might have seen it simply as serving friends. Nevertheless the *effect* of his action is exemption, whether he consciously perceives it that way or not, because from the observer's point of view he is acting differently from the way he would act toward other Negroes.

5. Robert B. Johnson, a member of the Cornell research staff, attended these conferences in his role as a member of the NAACP executive committee. Johnson, and others of us who were involved in later situations, filled out detailed research reports after each period of observation.

6. On the basis of one case study, we certainly cannot generalize that this is always the process. One observation can, however, be made: in none of the situations studied (either in this series, or in the situations we initiated for our study of unpatterned situations) did direct and overt conflict bring about a change of definition. Wherever two participants with opposing definitions attempted to argue each other into changing their definitions, an impasse resulted. In fact, overt conflict served only to strengthen the participants' commitment to their original positions. Of course, a participant was on occasion forced to accede to another's demands; but this brought no lasting change in definition, merely resentful compliance.

7. For purposes of analysis and prediction, it is not necessary that the individual actor be aware of the role his referents play in defining the situation. "Reference group" may be used as an intervening variable in situational analysis if this provides a more adequate explanation of behavior than do alternative methods of analysis. (We may posit that an individual acts *as if* he used certain referents in defining the situation.) In the present research, however, this was not necessary: the plaintiffs came to be very much aware of the major role played by the NAACP leaders in their definitions of the situations.

THE EFFECTS OF SOUTHERN WHITE WORKERS ON RACE RELATIONS IN NORTHERN PLANTS

This analysis of the effects of southern white workers on race relations in northern industrial plants is part of a larger study of the adjustment of these migrants to northern, urban ways, as found in Chicago. The relationships of the southern whites to Negroes in the plants, and their effects on the policies of management, must be viewed in the context of the position of the so-called "hillbillies" themselves in the community and in industry.

Prior to the concentration of large numbers of migrants, both white and Negro, in defense centers during World War II, students of race relations evinced only a casual interest in the effects of southern white migration on race relations in other parts of the country. For example, Donald Young, in his *American Minority Peoples*, dismissed the movement of native white migrants as relatively unimportant, saying:

> The migrations of the old stock do not seriously concern us, except as their movement from the country to the city has brought intolerant provincials into contact with minorities whom they cannot understand.[1]

Erdmann D. Beynon, in a paper on "hillbilly labor" in Michigan, made only passing reference to the attitudes and behavior of the southern whites towards Negroes.[2] His brief comment exemplifies the assumption that the

From Lewis M. Killian, "The Effects of Southern White Workers on Race Relations in Northern Plants," in *American Sociological Review*, 17 (1952), pp. 327–331.

migrant reacts to contacts with Negroes in a new situation in the same manner that he did in the South:

Migration to northern industrial cities has brought the southern whites into new situations for which they have no cultural definition; therefore, their behavior has been determined largely by life in rural southern regions. For example, race prejudice towards Negroes persists and leads to conflict when they are compelled to work in the same gangs with Negroes.[3]

Little else but conflict could be expected if, indeed, southern white migrants defined interracial situations in the North solely in terms of southern mores and acted accordingly. Gunnar Myrdal made the assumption, based on "a common observation," that the transplanted southern white finds little necessity for accommodation to northern patterns but is more likely to change the situation to conform to his "southern prejudice."[4]

The Detroit race riot of 1943, occurring in a city with a large "hillbilly" element in its population, served to focus attention on the possible effect of southern white migrants on race relations in the North. While no systematic, intensive analysis of the role of the "hillbillies" in the Detroit riot has been reported, even by Humphrey and Lee,[5] the recent migration of large numbers of this group has been singled out repeatedly as one of the most important causes. Witness the dramatic statement of Thomas Sancton, made shortly after the riot:

During the 'thirties and especially after present armament expansion began, white southerners and other outlanders by the hundreds of thousands came to work in the plants. The old, subdued, muted murderous southern race war was transplanted into a high-speed industrial background.[6]

Thus it has been suggested that, because of the refusal of the southern white in the North to accept a "non-southern" definition of interracial situations, he is both an instigator of racial conflict and an agent for the diffusion of "southern" patterns of Negro-white relations. In the present study, the reactions of southern whites in Chicago to contact with Negroes in a specific situation—work—and their influence on the policies of management were analyzed.

The "Hillbillies" as a Group

The southern whites studied were members of many small "clusters" of migrants concentrated in an ethnically heterogeneous portion of the Near West Side of Chicago. The majority of them came from farms and small towns in the South Central States, especially western Tennessee. Although these people were known as "hillbillies" in Chicago, few of them came from mountainous areas and they regarded the name as a misnomer.

In this research, 150 southern white migrants were interviewed, and the actual behavior of these and many other southern whites was observed. Non-southerners and Negroes who were part of the social world of the migrants, including plant managers, foremen, policemen, teachers, bartenders, and other workers, were also interviewed.

Of most significance in the present context is the status of the "hillbillies" in the Near West Side. It was found that a vague, but recognizable, stereotype of the southern white migrant was held by many non-southerners, and that they were regarded as a distinct, cohesive ethnic group. While little hostility toward them was discovered, they were generally regarded by non-southern whites as a culturally inferior group. This was especially true in the case of some employers who consciously avoided hiring "hillbillies." In turn, the southern whites themselves exhibited definite group consciousness.

In Chicago, they found themselves only one group in a mosaic of diverse ethnic groups. The fact that they were white, native-born, and Protestant lost some of its prestige value in an area such as the Near West Side, with its large population of Italian-Americans. Negroes, while subject to many forms of discrimination in Chicago, still possessed far more freedom and power than they could enjoy in the rural South. Comparing their position with those of "foreigners" and Negroes in Chicago and in the South, the southern whites felt a relative loss of status which contributed to the development of a *defensive* group consciousness.

The impersonality and anonymity of many types of social relationships in the northern city stood in sharp contrast to the friendly intimacy of the small southern town. As a result, the "laissez-faire" attitude of the city folk was interpreted by the "hillbillies" as evidence of hostility. The term "hillbilly," even when used in jest, was often perceived as a derogatory group label. To the feeling that they, as southern whites, were a somewhat disadvantaged group was thus added the belief that they were a disliked group.

Their defensive group consciousness did not result in the development of in-group organization of a formal type. But the "hillbillies," preoccupied with "making a living," regarding the South as "home," and, suspicious of non-southerners, constituted a marginal and unstable element in the institutions and associations of the area in which they lived. It may be said that they felt themselves to be in, but not of, Chicago. Visits to the South were frequent, and many families periodically returned to their old homes to live for a year or two. This instability and mobility, more than anything else, caused the "hillbillies" to be regarded by employers as a marginal group of laborers, conveniently available when there was a shortage of other labor, but undesirable as members of a cadre of permanent workers.

Effect on Management Policies

The marginal position in industry of the southern whites themselves explains to a large extent the findings concerning their effect on race relations. The range of policies and practices regarding the hiring of Negroes in fourteen plants which employed southern white workers shows that the presence or absence of "hillbilly" workers had only an indirect and minor effect on the policy of management.

In four of these plants, Negroes were employed on jobs with white workers, and sometimes worked side by side with southern whites on machines or assembly lines. Three of these factories were small plants, employing 55, 110, and 225 workers respectively—the very type of plant in which some managers had said, "You can't have Negroes work with whites in such close quarters without trouble!" Not only did the southern whites in these plants work with the Negroes, but they shared the same rest rooms and dressing rooms. It is true that the proportion of "hillbillies" in these plants was not large. In the two with 225 and 55 workers respectively, the proportion was estimated at between 10 and 15 per cent, but had been higher during the War. The third plant, with 110 workers, had only one southern white because of a definite "anti-hillbilly" employment policy, but during the war the managers had employed both Negroes and a larger number of southern whites.

The fourth plant, which employed not only Negroes—about 15 per cent of the working force—but also southern whites, Mexicans, and a variety of workers of foreign extraction, was a larger establishment. Although the personnel manager regarded "hillbillies" as undesirable workers because of their mobility, the plant was still regarded as a good place to work by the southerners. It had 1,100 workers, slightly less than 10 per cent of them southern white. The personnel manager of this plant felt that the integration of Negroes into the plant had been accomplished without difficulty because of the firm stand taken by management. He stated:

Having southern white workers hasn't affected our policy at all. When they apply for a job we tell them, "We have Negro workers and they're good workers. If you don't want to work with them, you'd better not take the job." Very few decide that they won't take it. Occasionally we may have complaints about friction with the Negroes, but they may come from northern workers as well as from southern.

Francis J. Haas and G. James Fleming, in an article on "Personnel Practices and Wartime Changes," have said that one of the important steps to "fair employment" is "the taking of a firm position by management once it has decided to adopt the new policy."[7] In these plants, regardless of the presence of southern whites and other white workers who might be equally prejudiced, management had taken such a stand and found that "fair employment" practices could be adopted without difficulty. It may be that the relatively small proportion of southern whites employed in these plants was the result of an aversion by the "hillbillies" to working with Negroes. If so, this does not constitute discrimination in the form of segregation imposed on the Negro minority; instead, it is a form of voluntary self-segregation which hurts no one but the person who imposes it upon himself.

The policies of the ten plants which employed "hillbillies" but had few or no Negroes showed, however, that southern migrants who wished to enjoy such self-segregation could do so without having to spread "southern racist ideas." In all ten plants the policy of excluding Negroes existed before management became aware of the presence of the "hillbillies," and in only one plant was it even suggested that the presence of the southern whites was a deterrent to changes in the policy. Seven of these plants were small, with no more than 200 workers, and with no higher proportion of southern whites than were in some of the plants which did not exclude Negroes. The personnel managers of these plants did not give the fear of "trouble" from the southern whites as a reason for not hiring Negroes; instead, they gave very much the same reasons which Haas and Fleming reported to be "most common" as justification for nonemployment. These authors said:

The National Urban League in 1941–42 found the reasons given for nonemployment of Negroes to be of "infinite variety." Most common were the following: Negroes never applied; whites and blacks can't mix on the same job; haven't time or money to build separate toilets; no trained Negroes are available; they are racially unequipped for skilled work; the union won't have them; don't like Negroes and don't want them around; this is a rush job and we haven't time for experiments.[8]

The reasons given by these Chicago employers were very similar, as the following statements indicate:

This is a small plant and you couldn't mix Negroes with any whites, northern or southern. For one thing, we just don't have room for separate locker and washroom facilities.

Our policy about hiring Negroes is entirely independent of what the southern whites might think or do. We only hire them for a few "dirty" jobs.

The southerners don't enter into our policy towards hiring Negroes. We base our judgment on what we think the older workers would do, and they're mostly Italians. Anyhow, we don't have too many jobs Negroes could do.

We've just stayed away from hiring Negroes. We've never given what the southern whites might do any thought.

Regardless of the number of "hillbilly" workers being employed, inertia and unwillingness to experiment with a new group of workers, rather than the diffusion of "southern" prejudices, seem to have caused these managers to continue discriminatory policies.

On the other hand, it may be concluded that in the three larger plants with relatively large blocs of "hillbilly" workers—from 20 to 30 per cent of the working force—the presence of the southern whites, but not their actions, had an important indirect effect on the employment policies of the companies. These three plants had opened their doors to "hillbilly labor" during a period when the supply of local white labor was curtailed. The pool of southern white migrant laborers in the West Side constituted for them an alternative to Negro workers as replacements and additions to the working force. Had this alternative not been available, the pressure to hire Negroes would undoubtedly have been much greater. It is highly significant that one of these plants, although engaged in defense production and covered by the wartime Fair Employment Practices Order, hired no Negro workers during the entire period of the war. It was during this same period that the "hillbilly" workers, coming into the plant as replacements for Polish and Italian workers called into the service or attracted by more lucrative jobs, increased to over one quarter of the working force.

The management of this plant, as of the other two with large "hillbilly" blocs, had never hired Negro workers on an equal basis with whites. The standard explanations were given, such as, "We don't have the type of work Negroes can do!" In these three plants, and probably in some of the smaller ones, the southern whites did not cause a policy of discrimination in hiring to be instituted, but they made possible the continuation of an already existing policy.

On the basis of the policies and practices of management in these fourteen plants, it is evident that the presence of southern white workers did not cause an increase in discrimination against Negroes. In plants where management took a firm stand against discrimination, southerners not only failed to incite other white workers to voice protests against the policy, but at least some "hillbillies" accepted the policy themselves by taking employment. In other plants, already existing policies of nonemployment of Negroes, arrived at independently of the influence of southern whites, made it possible for the migrants to enjoy the dubious fruits of racial segregation in employment as fully as they might have in the South. The primary significance of the presence of the "hillbillies" was that their availability made possible the continuation of previously established discriminatory practices in spite of a shortage of local white labor.

The Reactions of the Migrants

Interviews with 140 "hillbillies" who had worked in Chicago plants corroborated this conclusion that the southern whites were able to make a peaceful accommodation to the norms of the new situation. Of these 140, 59 were working, or had worked, in plants that employed Negroes on the same jobs as whites. Of the 81 who had never worked with Negroes under such conditions, only twelve stated that they had deliberately avoided working in plants with a policy of nondiscrimination. The existence of an uneven pattern of race relations in employment in Chicago made it comparatively easy for the southern whites to retain this part of their racial ideology without making any accommodation in their behavior. As one young worker remarked:

> I guess I've just been lucky, but I ain't never worked in a place where they hired niggers. I would if the job was a good one, but I just never have.

On the other hand, of the 59 persons who had worked with Negroes without protest, all but four were "hillbillies" who expressed unqualified approval of "the way things are in the South." Some of the twelve who had deliberately avoided working with Negroes showed remarkable inconsistency in their actions. One man, who declared that he would "mess up the machine" of any Negro who was put to work in his plant, lived in the same block with Negroes; he also admitted that the first job he had in Chicago was as a waiter in a restaurant where he had to serve Negroes. The impression of those employers who believed, on the basis of their experience, that most of the "hillbillies" would work with Negroes if confronted by a firm policy was borne out by the actions of the southern whites themselves. In fact, some of the most violently anti-Negro southerners were among those who had worked with Negroes, such as a man who later returned to Tennessee because "he couldn't stand to send his children to school with Negroes," and a former member of the Ku Klux Klan.

To most of the "hillbillies," Chicago was not a place to live but merely a place to make a living. The South continued to be their principal reference group and they followed its practice of racial segregation and exclusion when it was conveniently possible. When confronted with situations in which these ways could not be adhered to without personal sacrifice, however, they tended to make the necessary behavioral adjustments even though changes in attitudes did not necessarily occur.

Conclusions

This study does not support the hypothesis that the southern white migrant, at least the working class migrant, is likely to change the northern interracial situation to conform to his "southern" prejudice. The southern whites studied here, a marginal group in industry themselves, were found to have little effect in deterring employers from hiring Negroes. Their principal effect in northern industry was to furnish an alternate pool of labor for employers who desired to continue an existing policy of exclusion. When confronted with a firm policy of non-discrimination, however, they tended to accept the situation as defined by management. Yet this did not indicate a radical change in the racial attitudes of the southern whites, but rather an accommodation to the exigencies of a specific situation. At the same time, the prevalence of policies of exclusion of Negroes in Chicago plants made such accommodation unnecessary for many of the "hillbillies."

NOTES

1. New York: Harper and Brothers, 1932, p. 41.
2. "The Southern White Laborer Migrates to Michigan," *American Sociological Review*, 3, No. 3 (June 1938), pp. 333–343.
3. *Ibid.*, p. 335.

4. Gunnar Myrdal, *An American Dilemma* (New York: Harper and Brothers, 1944), p. 79.

5. Alfred M. Lee and Norman D. Humphrey, *Race Riot* (New York: Dryden Press, 1943).

6. "The Race Riots," *New Republic*, 109 (1943), pp. 9–13.

7. *The Annals* of the American Academy of Political and Social Science, 244 (1946), p. 53.

8. *Ibid.*, p. 49.

NEGRO VISIBILITY

In the Fall of 1952 a research project dealing with racial factors and law enforcement was begun under the auspices of the Greenfield Center for Human Relations, University of Pennsylvania. An attempt was made to discover the extent to which Negroes were being integrated into urban police forces, and to this end employment data were collected from our 20 largest cities. Another phase of the project dealt with an investigation of the relationship between race of offender and race of arresting officer. Still another area involved assignment policies and efficiency patterns as they pertained to the interrelation of Negro and white police; for example, the extent to which Negroes and whites were being assigned as partners to the same patrol car, and the interaction between white patrolmen and Negro commanders. The latter two phases were conducted in the City of Philadelphia and entailed the gathering of district arrest figures by race, as well as an extensive interviewing program with police commanders, Negro policemen, Negro community leaders, and editors of the Negro press. In addition a printed questionnaire was distributed to the 2,101 white policemen assigned to district (precinct) duty; that is, those engaged in foot-beat or patrol car work. The present paper deals with some of the inter-item analyses of this questionnaire, and while space precludes the publication of the latter in its entirety some indication of its content is necessary.

The questionnaire was designed primarily to reveal something of the opinions held by white policemen regarding their occupational relationships with Negro policemen. Questionnaire items (in addition to the usual background factors) included single-answer, multiple-choice, and open-end questions, and were constructed largely on the basis of a preliminary series of interviews with both Negro and white policemen of all ranks. Included

From William M. Kephart, "Negro Visibility," in *American Sociological Review*, 19 (1954), pp. 462–467.

in the questionnaire were items inquiring whether the respondent objected to riding in a patrol car with a Negro partner, whether there was any objection to taking orders from Negro sergeants or captains, whether the respondent was satisfied with his present duty assignment, whether he would prefer to work in a white, Negro, or mixed neighborhood, whether he believed a white community objects to having a Negro policeman assigned to that area, whether he felt that Negro policemen should be assigned to Negro neighborhoods, and the like.

Preliminary interviews had disclosed a wide variation in response when the subject of Negro numbers was raised. Consequently two such items (non-contiguous) were included in the questionnaire: (a) About what percentage of arrests in your district involve Negro law violators? (b) About how many Negroes do you think there are on the police force? The inclusion of these two "visibility items" resulted in some rather pointed findings, and these in turn led to the formulation and testing of certain hypotheses relating to the perception or visibility of Negroes. For our purposes, visibility is defined as the extent to which Negroes are numerically overestimated, and in this sense will comprise the content-emphasis of the present paper.

The Philadelphia phase of the project was undertaken with the approval of the Commissioner of Police. Questionnaire distribution was carried out with the cooperation of the division inspectors and the help of the district captains. Of the 2,101 questionnaires given out to Philadelphia policemen, 1,081 (51.5 per cent) were returned.

Actual Negro Arrests

Examination of city-wide arrest figures indicated that some police districts show a high rate of Negro arrests and others a low rate.[1] It was decided, therefore, to test the relationship between the actual Negro arrest rate in a district and certain racial opinions held by the white policemen assigned to that district. Theoretically, of course, it is quite possible that white policemen assigned to a district with a high rate of Negro arrests would be more likely to resent working in a Negro area, riding with a Negro partner, taking orders from a Negro sergeant or captain, etc., than those policemen who are assigned to a district with a low Negro arrest rate. To answer questions of this kind, the districts were arranged in rank order of their Negro arrest rates. The districts were also arranged in rank order based on their *per-*

centage of positive responses to relevant items on the questionnaire; e.g., the district with the largest percentage of respondents who signified that they objected to riding with a Negro policeman was placed at the top, the district with the smallest percentage at the bottom, and so on. A rank-order correlation (rho) was then computed for each of the relevant questionnaire items.

Arbitrarily selecting correlations of .60 and higher as having some significance, the following profile emerges: The higher the Negro arrest rate in a district the more the white policemen in that district would "like another type of assignment, such as Traffic, Highway, Detectives, etc." (.60); the more they "believe a Negro policeman should be assigned to a Negro neighborhood" (.71); and the *less* they "would prefer not to have any Negroes assigned" to their district (−.67).

While the rate of Negro arrests in a given district seems to relate to some of the responses of the white policemen assigned to that district—apparently those relating to the matter of assignment—for the most part the correlations with questionnaire items are of a low order (21 out of 26 below .50). The opinions of white patrolmen on most of the itemized racial topics appear to be associated only slightly with the Negro arrest factor.

Estimated Negro Arrests

In terms of the visibility factor the relationship to be tested is that between racial opinions of white policemen and their *estimate* of Negro arrest rates, rather than the *actual* arrest figures. Inspection of the data indicated, however, that before turning to the relationship between the racial opinions of white policemen and their estimation of Negro arrests, it would be advisable to analyze (a) the general accuracy of the estimates, and (b) the variation in estimates among the several districts.

Accuracy of the Estimates

As has been mentioned, the information pertaining to estimated Negro arrests was derived from the question, "About what percentage of arrests in your district involve Negro law violators?" Since the actual percentages

William M. Kephart

had been obtained from Police Headquarters it was possible to compare the respondent's estimate for his district with the actual district figure. The results are as follows (N=915):[2]

Overestimated the percentage
of Negro arrests . . . . 75.0 per cent
Estimated correctly or
underestimated . . . . 11.2 per cent
No opinion . . . . 13.8 per cent

If the "No opinion" category is excluded, the results are:

Overestimated . . . . 86.9 per cent
Correct or under . . . . 13.1 per cent

It is clear that most of the white policemen tend to believe the percentage of Negro arrests in their own districts is higher than it actually is; as a matter of fact, they overestimate to a considerable degree, as the following figures indicate:

District[a]	Actual Percentage of Negro Arrests	Median Estimated Percentage of Negro Arrests
A	66.4	90
B	65.1	90
C	39.9	85
D	31.1	75
E	23.8	60
F	26.6	53
G	57.9	85
H	22.2	50
I	70.1	95
J	11.9	10
K	9.2	10
L	51.9	85
M	26.8	53
N	61.9	85
O	65.3	85
P	27.9	60
Q	14.8	20
R	31.7	30

[a]Letters do not correspond with the actual district numbers.

District Variation

While 86.9 per cent of these respondents overestimated the percentage of Negro arrests, and although this overestimation was manifest in all but two of the districts, the above table reveals that the degree of overestimation varies a good deal from district to district. In an attempt to account for the district variation, inspection of the individual district estimates led to the following hypothesis: *The higher the actual Negro arrest rate in a district, the greater the overestimation of that rate.* To test this hypothesis, districts were first arranged in order of the actual Negro arrest rate (see column "a" of the table below).

It must be realized that districts with a high Negro arrest rate have a potentially smaller margin for overestimation as compared to districts with a relatively low rate of Negro arrests. Therefore, before comparing the actual with the estimated Negro arrest rates, it was necessary to correct columns "b," "c," "d," "e" for the "ceiling effect." The figures shown in column "e" are the resultant corrections; i.e., they represent the ratios of

"a" (Actual Negro Arrest Rate)	"b" (Possible Over- estimation: 100-a)	"c" (Estimated Negro Arrest Rate)	"d" (Percentage of Over- estimation: c-a)	"e" $\left(\dfrac{d}{b}\right)$
70.1	29.9	95	24.9	.833
66.4	33.6	90	23.6	.702
65.3	34.7	85	19.7	.568
65.1	34.9	90	24.9	.713
61.9	38.1	85	23.1	.606
57.9	42.1	85	27.1	.644
51.9	48.1	85	33.1	.688
39.9	60.1	85	45.1	.750
31.7	68.3	30	*	*
31.1	68.9	75	43.9	.637
27.9	72.1	60	32.1	.445
26.8	73.2	53	25.7	.351
26.6	73.4	53	25.9	.353
23.8	76.2	60	36.2	.475
22.2	77.8	50	27.8	.357
14.8	85.2	20	5.2	.061
11.9	88.1	10	*	*
9.2	90.8	10	.8	.009

*Negative values.

overestimation to possible overestimation. The rank order correlation for the figures in column "e" is .78, thus supporting the hypothesis.

The fact that this hypothesis is supported by the data may have implications beyond the bounds of the present study. While it is hazardous to generalize on the basis of specialized groups (white policemen and Negro offenders) it is possible that the same progressive or possibly geometric form of increase in visibility would apply to more general groups (Negro-white ratios in schools, factories, or even cities). It may be that *as Negro numbers increase arithmetically, their visibility—perhaps up to a certain point—increases exponentially.* From our own data, plotted by a variety of graphical methods, it is not possible to demonstrate what this point is or whether, in fact, visibility is exponential. Nevertheless, a general hypothesis of this type, empirically tested within broader social or ecological groupings, might provide a contributory link in a generic theory of intergroup tensions.

Relationship to Opinions

While the large majority of white policemen overestimated the actual rate of Negro arrests in their district, the overestimation itself showed great variation, some respondents overestimating slightly, others by a wide margin. As a consequence, it was decided to test the following hypothesis: *The higher the estimated Negro arrest rate, the more likely it is that the white policeman making the estimate will have unfavorable opinions about Negro policemen.* For purposes of the study white policemen who signified that they object to riding with Negro policemen, or who believe there are too many Negroes on the force, or who object to taking orders from well-qualified Negro commanders, and so on, were assumed to have opinions unfavorable to Negro policemen.

To apply the necessary statistical test, individual estimates of Negro arrest rates were arranged in rank order within each district. Median estimates for each district were computed, and all the responses were then placed into three groups: those falling above the median-class of their district; those falling in the median-class; and those falling below the median-class. Data derived in this manner support the foregoing hypothesis. (Space precludes publication of the available tabular material. Table 18–1 is presented for illustrative purposes.)

TABLE 18-1

Relationship between Attitudes toward Riding with
Negro Patrolmen and Estimates of Negro Arrests

		"Would you have any objections to riding with a Negro patrolman?"			
		Per Cent Answering "Yes"	Per Cent Answering "No"	Per Cent with No Answer	Number of Cases
	Total	58.7	33.4	7.9	915
"About what per-	Above				
centage of	median class	71.3	20.7	8.0	310
arrests in your	Median class	66.7	29.7	3.6	138
district involve	Below				
Negro law	median class	46.7	44.9	8.4	343
violators?"	No opinion	51.7	37.1	11.2	124

Chi-square = 47.67, P less than .001. "No answer" or "No opinion" cells have been disregarded in chi-square calculations.

Estimates of Negro Policemen

The second facet of visibility explored in the present study is that relating to estimated numbers of Negro *policemen*. Unlike the percentage of Negro arrests, the proportion of Negro policemen assigned to the various districts showed little variation. One reason for this was the small number of Negroes on the force. According to personnel lists supplied by commanding officers, there were, at the time of the survey, 149 Negro personnel on the force, and some two thirds of the districts had no more than three Negro policemen assigned. Since it was not feasible to work with *district* figures the item referring to estimated number of Negro policemen was phrased, "About how many Negroes do you think there are on the police force?"

The following table shows the frequency distribution of the estimated numbers (N = 1,081):

Estimated Number of Negroes on the Force	Per Cent Responding
0-149	5.6
150-249	15.1
250-349	17.0
350-449	8.3
450-and over	16.6
No opinion	37.4

Excluding the "No opinion" category, the over-all percentages are:

Overestimated the number of
Negroes on the force 91.0
Estimated correctly or
underestimated 9.0

There is a marked tendency among the respondents to overestimate the number of Negro policemen on the force, just as there was in the case of Negro arrests. In both instances, estimates of Negro arrests and estimates of Negro policemen, the percentage of white policemen who overestimated was roughly the same—90 per cent. It would appear that to these respondents Negro visibility, at least in two areas, is high.

With regard to the visibility of Negro policemen, it can be seen from the above figures that the estimates are much higher among some respondents than others. Since a wide individual variation of this kind was also found in the estimates of Negro arrests, the possibility was strong that a concordance existed between the two sets of variations. The hypothesis to be tested was as follows: A *relationship exists between the white policeman's estimate of the Negro arrest rate and his estimate of the number of Negro policemen on the force.*

Comparative data are shown in Table 18–2, and the results lend no support to the hypothesis.

A number of other statistical relationships were explored, using the estimated number of Negro policemen as a variable, but results were negative.

The very fact of negative results, in this instance, is believed to be of im-

TABLE 18-2

*Relationship between Estimates of Negro Arrests
and Estimated Number of Negro Patrolmen* *

		"About what percentage of arrests in your district involve Negro law violators?"				
		Above Median Class	Median Class	Below Median Class	No Opinion	Number of Cases
	Total	33.8	15.1	37.5	13.6	915
"About how	0-149	33.3	11.9	42.9	11.9	42
many Negroes	150-249	32.8	17.2	43.2	6.8	134
do you think	250-349	34.3	16.6	42.7	6.4	157
there are on	350-449	38.6	18.7	40.0	2.7	75
the police force?"	450 and over	34.3	16.6	45.4	3.7	163
	No opinion	32.8	12.5	27.9	26.8	344

*No association.

217

portance, since the question that poses itself is, "Why is the visibility of the Negro offender a significant item; (i.e., why does it relate to unfavorable opinions) whereas visibility of the Negro policeman is a non-related item?" The answer might hinge on the fact that in the estimates of Negro police the "no opinion" percentage was quite large (37.4 as against a corresponding 13.8 per cent in the case of estimated Negro arrests). Or the answer might depend on the obvious difference between the two groups of Negroes —fellow workers on the one hand and law violators on the other.

The writer's explanation would take into account the fact that the percentage of Negro policemen is low while the percentage of Negro arrests is high. It has been suggested that as Negro numbers increase arithmetically their visibility increases exponentially. Since the number of Negro policemen in Philadelphia is not only small but (up to the time of the present study) has been *decreasing* in recent years, it may follow that their estimated numbers would not be expected to evidence any relationship to unfavorable opinions on the part of white policemen. Such a relationship might be expected only if the ratio of Negro policemen were large or increasing.

This interpretation, if true, would be applicable to groups other than policemen, and would lend itself, in terms of study design, to further testing. Attitudes toward Negroes could be compared with their estimated numbers in schools, businesses, or factories where the Negro ratio was small, as against the same comparison in similar organizations where the Negro proportion was large.

If interracial tensions are in any way a function of number, and if the manifestation of this function is demonstrably exponential in nature, the element of visibility emerges as a conceptually useful implement. If visibility is not exponential it would nevertheless be of pragmatic value in the general area of attitude measurement, and perhaps in the specific areas of scaling and projective techniques. Thus far, however, the concept of visibility has received little sociological recognition, and in view of this fact both theoretical and research considerations might prove rewarding.

Summary

On the basis of questionnaire returns from 1,081 white policemen assigned to the various Philadelphia police districts, it was found that about 90 per cent of the respondents overestimated the Negro arrest rate in their own districts. The higher the actual Negro arrest rate the greater was the over-estimation of that rate. It was suggested that as Negro numbers increase arithmetically, their mass visibility, perhaps up to a certain point, increases exponentially.

It was further hypothesized that the higher the estimated Negro arrest rate, the more likely it is that the white policemen making the estimate will have unfavorable opinions about Negro policemen. Statistical data adduced supported the latter hypothesis.

It was discovered that about 90 per cent of the respondents also overestimated the number of Negro policemen on the force. In both areas, Negro policemen and Negro arrests, a wide individual variation was found in the estimates. The hypothesis to be tested was that a relationship exists between the white policeman's estimate of the Negro arrest rate and his estimate of the number of Negro policemen on the force. Comparative data lent no support to the hypothesis.

Since the visibility of the Negro offender related to unfavorable opinions about Negro policemen, although visibility of the latter was a non-related item, the following explanation, based on the aforementioned exponential principle, was offered. Unlike the increasingly large Negro arrest rate, the number of Negro police in Philadelphia is not only small but has been decreasing in recent years, and it might follow that the latter's estimated number would not be expected to evidence any relationship to unfavorable opinions on the part of white policemen. Such a relationship might be expected only if the ratio of Negro policemen were large or increasing.

It was suggested, finally, that inasmuch as the concept of visibility had received scant sociological recognition, both theoretical and research considerations might prove rewarding.

NOTES

1. "Negro arrest rate" refers throughout to the number of Negro arrests per 100 total arrests.

2. Although the returned questionnaires numbered 1,081, which figure comprised the working N for the bulk of the statistical computations, one divisional clerk failed to separate the returns for the districts in his division. The 166 questionnaires collected from that division could not be used in the tabulations pertaining to district percentages, hence the N of 915 used in this set of data.

PART VI

The Demography and Ecology of Racism

Editor's Introduction

A characteristic of racist societies is that they keep racial statistics, the most exhaustive ones being found in the United States and South Africa. The availability of demographic data on race (however questionable their validity) has given rise to vast numbers of secondary analyses of the census, relating race to other variables or using race to construct new variables such as population ratios or segregation indices. A great many of these studies do not fall within the field of race relations as normally defined because they merely treat race as one of several independent variables affecting, say, fertility, mortality, or crime rates. Of the demographic studies more centrally focused on race, some have been primarily descriptive, e.g. have studied the demographic characteristics of non-whites or compared whites and non-whites on income, net reproduction rate, and the like. Others have related the racial composition to the spatial distribution of the population, a field somewhat pretentiously called ecology. (The propensity in American sociology to plot demographic characteristics on maps might better be called social cartography rather than ecology.) There is, for example, a sizable literature on segregation indices, a topic which made up in methodological controversy what it lacked in theoretical import. Finally, a number of studies (including those reproduced here) have simply made use of demographic data to solve theoretical or practical problems of more centrally sociological significance.

OCCUPATIONAL BENEFITS TO WHITES FROM THE SUBORDINATION OF NEGROES

That whites in the United States benefit to some extent from Negroes being kept low in the occupational structure may seem obvious. Given a constant occupational structure, keeping Negroes down will necessarily keep whites up. However, the assumption that the overall occupational structure is unaffected by the presence and subordination of Negroes may not be warranted. The effect of keeping Negroes down could be an increase in the number of low-level workers rather than upward pressure upon whites. Therefore, the belief that whites gain occupationally at all from the subordination of Negroes is an hypothesis only, and one which is investigated in this paper.

If the hypothesized occupational gains do accrue to whites, the extent of these gains depends upon two variables (again assuming constancy in the occupational structure). The first is the extent of discrimination. If all Negroes are kept below all whites the gain will be greater than if most Negroes are merely kept below most whites. Then, with any degree of discrimination, the gain to whites will vary directly with the percentage of the employed labor force which is Negro. For instance, whites will benefit little from the most extreme discrimination if only 1 or 2 per cent of the workers are Negro. But even moderate discrimination will aid whites appreciably where half of the workers are Negro.

From Norval D. Glenn, "Occupational Benefits to Whites from the Subordination of Negroes," in *American Sociological Review*, 28 (1963), pp. 443–448.

Therefore, if whites do benefit occupationally from discrimination against Negroes, one would expect the following specific hypotheses to be correct:

1. White occupational status generally is higher in those localities in which discrimination against Negroes is greater.
2. White occupational status generally is higher in those localities in which the relative size of the Negro population is greater.

The first of these hypotheses cannot be tested precisely because there is no really accurate measure of discrimination. One rough measure is the occupational status of Negroes, but this is influenced not only by the extent of discrimination but also by the relative size of the Negro labor force[1] and by a number of other factors. Furthermore, among the localities selected for this study Negro occupational status varied very little,[2] and therefore it is not a very useful independent variable for research purposes. However, the fact that hypothesis number *one* cannot be tested precisely may not be a great hindrance to attaining the goal of this study. It is likely that the relative size of the Negro population varies considerably more by locality than does discrimination; therefore, to assume discrimination to be a constant (for the purpose of testing hypothesis number *two*) is probably a justifiable simplification of reality. If whites anywhere benefit from the low status of Negroes, the status of Negroes everywhere in the United States undoubtedly is low enough to produce that benefit.[3] Furthermore, there is no reason to believe that discrimination and the relative number of Negroes are inversely related,[4] so there is little danger that the influence of one tends to mask the influence of the other. It seems, therefore, that a test of hypothesis number *two* provides a fairly good, although indirect, test of the more general hypothesis that whites benefit occupationally from discrimination against Negroes.

The localities used for testing this hypothesis were the 151 Standard Metropolitan Areas which had 100,000 or more people in 1950, and the workers included were only those in nonagricultural occupations, limiting the study to the metropolitan nonagricultural labor force very roughly controlled for several factors which influence white occupational status. For instance, the occupational status of whites in metropolitan areas is generally higher than the status of whites in smaller cities and is markedly higher than the status of rural whites. Therefore, if states or counties were used as units of analysis, differences in the distribution of whites among communities of different sizes would account for much if not most of the variation in whites' status.

Two techniques of analysis were used. First, the SMA's were divided into 14 classes according to the relative size of their Negro populations in 1950,[5] and the distributions of employed white male and female workers in each class among the nine nonagricultural occupational groups were compiled. To save space and make the pattern of variation more apparent, the 14 original classes were collapsed into four and the nine occupational groups were collapsed into five broad categories for presentation of the data here (see Table 19-1). Since the male and female patterns of variation were almost identical, only the male data are shown. An index of occupational status (abbreviated IOS) was computed separately for each sex for employed whites and employed Negroes, and the index values for males are shown in Table 19-1. The index is computed by assigning a value to each occupational group according to the median education of its workers as of

TABLE 19-1

Occupational Distribution of Employed White Males in Standard Metropolitan Areas with 100,000 or More People, by Percentage of the Population Negro, 1950

Occupation	Percentage Negro			
	0-2.9	3-9.9	10-24.9	25 and Up
Professional, technical, and kindred workers; and managers, officials, and proprietors, except farm	21.6	24.8	23.8	26.9
Clerical, sales and kindred workers	16.4	17.8	18.5	21.5
Craftsmen, foremen, and kindred workers	23.2	22.4	24.2	25.4
Operatives and kindred workers; and service workers (except private household)	31.0	28.1	27.8	22.7
Private household workers, and laborers (except farm and mine)	7.8	6.9	5.7	3.5
Total	100.0	100.0	100.0	100.0
White IOS	112	114	114	117
Negro IOS	94	96	94	94
Ratio of white to Negro IOS	1.19	1.19	1.21	1.24
Number of SMA's				
Southern	0	0	9	21
Border	2	8	14	0
Northern and Western	52	34	10	0
Total	54	43	33	21

1950 and their median income in 1949. The value is above 100 if both the education and income of experienced workers in the occupational group were above parity (defined as the median education and income of all experienced workers); and the value is below 100 if both education and income were below parity. Each worker is assigned the value of his occupational group, and the IOS for a number of workers is the average of their individual values. More specifically, the formula for the index is:

$$\text{IOS for an occupational group} = \frac{a/A + b/B \times 100}{2} \text{ when}$$

a = median income of experienced workers in the occupational group in 1949.
A = median income of all experienced workers in 1949.
b = median years of school completed by experienced workers in the occupational group as of 1950.
B = median years of school completed by all experienced workers as of 1950.

The male index values are computed from male income and education data, and the female values are computed from female data.[6]

Correlation analysis was the second technique used. IOS values were computed for white employed male workers in each of the 151 SMA's, and Pearsonian coefficients of correlation were computed between the IOS and the percentage of the population Negro separately for the Southern, the Border, and the Northern and Western SMA's.[7] These are given in Table 19-2. So many factors aside from the percentage of the population Negro are likely to influence white occupational status that any attempt to control for all of these would be futile. In fact, most of these are not measurable in any precise manner. However, one variable was controlled for, the total size of the populations of the SMA's. This variable is known to be positively associated with white occupational status, and there was reason to suspect that outside of the South population size might be commonly and highly enough associated with the two variables being investigated to produce a spurious correlation between them. The partial correlations with population size held constant are also given in Table 19-2.

A weakness of the IOS is that any variation in the distribution of workers among the detailed occupations within occupational groups is not reflected in variation in its values, and the detailed occupations within several of the groups vary considerably in their desirability. This would be a serious weakness if Negro and white IOS values were being compared, since Negroes are consistently less favorably distributed than whites within occupational groups. However, the distributions of metropolitan whites among the occupations within each group were roughly similar from one end to the other of the scale of relative size of the Negro population. Nevertheless, it

TABLE 19-2

Pearsonian Correlations, by Region

	Zero-Order	With Size of Total Population Held Constant
Between percentage of the population Negro and the white IOS		
South (N = 30)	+.441	+.464
Border (N = 24)	+.499	+.417
North and West (N = 97)	+.276	+.203
Between percentage of the population Negro and the median income of white persons		
South (N = 30)	+.315	+.367
Border (N = 24)	+.541	+.429
North and West (N = 97)	+.484	+.424

seemed worthwhile to supplement the occupational data with income data, since even the same detailed occupations might have been rewarded differently along the scale. Therefore, the 1949 average median income of white persons in the SMA's in each class was computed (Table 19–3) and cor-

TABLE 19-3

Average Median Income of White
Persons in Standard Metropolitan Areas
with 100,000 or More People, by
Percentage of the Population Negro, 1949

Percentage Negro	Average Median Income of White Persons
0- 2.9	$2,118
3- 9.9	2,278
10-24.9	2,232
25 and up	2,113

relation coefficients between percentage of the population Negro and the median income of white persons were computed by region (Table 19–3).

Findings

The white IOS both for males and females increased appreciably from the lower to the upper end of the scale of percentage of the population Negro, although the change was somewhat irregular. The most pronounced deviation from a linear association of the IOS with percentage Negro was in the interval of 20 through 24.9 per cent Negro, where the IOS was higher than in any other interval. However, the high IOS in that interval can be accounted for by the unusually favorable distribution of *all* workers in one SMA, Washington, D.C. Another deviation was a plateau in the lower-middle range of the scale of percentage Negro. In the range from 6 through 19.9 per cent, variation in the percentage of the population Negro was accompanied by little variation in the white occupational distribution. This plateau is explained by several large SMA's with unusually high total occupational distributions (e.g. New York and San Francisco-Oakland) being in the lower portion of the plateau. The difference between the white and Negro IOS values increased rather steadily from the lower to the upper portion of the range.

Except for this plateau, the percentage of white workers in seven of the nine occupational groups varied in an approximately linear fashion with the percentage of the population Negro. The percentage of whites who were craftsmen, foremen, and kindred workers remained almost constant, and professional and technical workers increased very slightly but not consistently up the scale. The percentages of whites in the other three more desirable occupational groups varied directly with the relative size of the Negro population, and the percentages in the four least desirable ones varied inversely. The failure of white professional workers to increase consistently up the scale can be attributed to Negroes' providing considerable professional service (such as teaching) for themselves and to a generally lower proportion of professional and technical workers in the Southern SMA's.

The percentage of the population Negro and the white IOS were positively correlated in each region, but the correlations were only moderate among the Southern and Border SMA's and small among the Northern and Western ones. Since the relative size of the Negro population is only one of many factors which influence white occupational status, it is not surprising that the correlations were not higher. In the North and West Negroes were numerous enough to affect white status appreciably only in a few SMA's, so a very large proportion of the variation in white status is accounted for by factors other than the relative size of the Negro population. Holding constant the size of the total populations of the SMA's affected the correlations little, but it did reduce somewhat the values for the Border and the Northern and Western SMA's.

The income of white persons did not vary in any consistent manner along the scale of relative size of the Negro population. The average median incomes near the top of the scale were about the same as those near the bottom. The failure of income to increase up the scale may have resulted partially from white workers being less favorably distributed within occupational groups in the Southern and Border SMA's. However, it probably resulted more from incomes within occupations being lower in the South. The lower incomes within occupations in the South in turn may have resulted to a large extent from the large numbers and the generally low status of Negroes. For instance, the low purchasing power of Southern Negroes tends to keep merchants less prosperous in the South than elsewhere. Discrimination may help the white worker in the South gain a higher occupational status, but it may also help keep his income lower than that of his occupational counterparts in other parts of the country.

However, one must not conclude that in 1949 no income gains accrued to whites from the low status of Negroes. The lower incomes of whites within occupations in the Southern and Border SMA's may have resulted largely from factors not directly related to the status and relative size of the Negro population. And within each region the relative size of the Negro population and the median income of whate persons were positively correlated.[8] Among the Border and the Northern and Western SMA's the correlations were higher than those between the relative size of the Negro population and the white IOS. The correlation in the North and West was surprisingly high, in view of the small correlation of percentage Negro with the white IOS, and one must be very cautious about attributing it to a causal relationship. The association could have resulted merely from larger numbers of Negroes being attracted during the 1940's to the more prosperous Northern and Western cities. Attraction of Negroes to the more prosperous cities could also partially account for the correlations among the Border and Southern SMA's.

In spite of the lack of strong evidence for income gains to whites from discrimination against Negroes, the occupational gains are important. The

Norval D. Glenn

rewards of higher occupational status are not merely monetary but include greater prestige, more pleasant working conditions, greater authority and independence, and other advantages. Furthermore, a given amount of money income was probably greater "real income" in those SMA's with the larger Negro populations. Data are not available which allow an accurate comparison of costs of living in the different SMA's in or around 1950.[9] However, domestic help undoubtedly cost less in the Southern SMA's, as probably did almost all services and goods produced by local labor. Whites in the Southern SMA's almost certainly enjoyed a more favorable style of life than did whites in the SMA's in which a smaller percentage of the people were Negroes.

Conclusions

The data presented here leave little doubt that in 1950 whites in American metropolitan areas which had large Negro populations were benefiting occupationally from the presence and low status of Negroes. These data suggest that American whites in general were and still are benefiting from anti-Negro discrimination.

The findings of this study lend credence to the view that discrimination and its supporting prejudice persist mainly because majority people gain from them. One should not go so far as to attribute the perpetuation of discrimination entirely to its functions to the majority, nor should the many known and possible dysfunctions of discrimination to the majority be overlooked. However, one should also avoid viewing discrimination as merely a self-perpetuating carry-over from a past era which will certainly and rapidly disappear once the Myrdalian "vicious circle" is broken. The tradition of discrimination against Negroes apparently receives continuous reinforcement from the present self-interests of the majority.

NOTES

1. For instance, with the most extreme discrimination, whereby all Negroes are kept below all whites, Negro occupational status will be the highest where the largest percentage of the workers are Negro, given a constant occupational structure.

2. See the Negro values of the index of occupational status in Table 19–1.

3. Again, see the Negro values of the index of occupational status in Table 19–1.

4. In fact, it is generally believed that the two are directly related. For relevant data and discussion see Hubert M. Blalock, Jr., "Economic Discrimination and Negro Increase," *American Sociological Review*, 21 (October 1956), pp. 584–588, and Hubert M. Blalock, Jr., "Per Cent Non-White and Discrimination in the South," *American Sociological Review*, 22 (December 1957), pp. 677–682.

5. Relative size of the total Negro population rather than of the Negro employed labor force was used because the data were originally tabulated for another study, for which the former variable was the more relevant. A partial replication of the present study with data on the relative size of the employed Negro labor force produced very nearly the same results reported here and revealed that a complete replication was not necessary.

6. The male index values for the 9 nonagricultural occupational groups are as follows: professional, technical, and kindred workers (157); managers, officials, and proprietors, except farm (140); clerical and kindred workers (122); sales workers (122); craftsmen, foremen, and kindred workers (108); operatives and kindred workers (95); private household workers (65); service workers, except private household (87); and laborers, except farm and mine (79).

7. All SMA's in Florida, Georgia, South Carolina, North Carolina, Virginia, Alabama, Mississippi, Louisiana, and Arkansas, plus Memphis, Tennessee, were classified as Southern. All SMA's in Oklahoma, Kentucky, West Virginia, Delaware, and Maryland, plus Washington, D.C., Springfield, Missouri, and Nashville, Knoxville, and Chattanooga, Tennessee, were considered Border. All SMA's in Texas were also considered Border, except El Paso, which was classified as Western.

8. In addition, it should be pointed out that in the South Negro-white income differences were more highly correlated than white income with percentage Negro. Heer found that in 1950 the ratio of Negro to white median income of males in the 43 SMA's of the former states of the Confederacy was inversely and rather highly correlated ($-.71$) with percentage of the population Negro (David M. Heer, "The Sentiment of White Supremacy: An Ecological Study," *American Journal of Sociology*, 64 [May 1959], p. 592). The greater disparity between Negro and white incomes may be experienced as a psychological benefit by whites in those localities with the largest Negro populations, even though their incomes are not appreciably higher than those of whites elsewhere.

9. The only Southern cities for which accurate data on prices are available for 1950 are Atlanta and Houston. The consumer price index for all items in 1950 was only slightly lower for Atlanta than for a total of 46 large cities. The index was higher for Houston than for all of the cities combined (Source: *Statistical Abstract of the United States: 1960*, p. 337). However, neither Houston nor Atlanta is typical of Southern cities. For instance, Houston (classified in this study as a Border SMA) had a much higher white median income in 1949 than any Southern SMA besides Baton Rouge. Atlanta whites also had a median income well above the average for the Southern SMA's.

NEGRO SUBORDINATION
AND WHITE GAINS

In his interesting article "Occupational Benefits to Whites from the Sub-ordination of Negroes" (*Review*, June 1963), Norval Glenn tested the hypothesis that a positive linear relationship exists between the percentage Negro in the population and the occupational status and income of the white labor force. Glenn's empirical data did not indicate whites have been substantially or systematically benefiting from the presence of Negroes. Using data on 151 SMA's with population 100,000 or more in 1950, he computed an index of occupational status for whites and Negroes based on the income and education of persons in five major occupational categories. This index was higher for whites than for Negroes, but the ratio of white to Negro scores did not appreciably increase as the percentage Negro in the SMA increased. Although a larger proportion of whites were in the higher occupational groups in SMA's with larger proportions of Negroes, the correlation between the white occupational-status index and the percentage Negro in the population was modest —. 44 in the South, .49 in Border SMA's and .27 in the North and West.

While these correlations are statistically significant, they do not indicate that whites have been gaining systematically from the presence of Negroes. Glenn also investigated the relation between white median income and percentage Negro, but these correlations were not much stronger, ranging from .35 in the South to .54 in Border SMA's. Finally, he found that white median income in four groups of SMA's does not rise as the proportion of Negroes increases. In spite of the lack of empirical confirmation of his

From Phillips Cutright, "Negro Subordination and White Gains," in *American Socio-logical Review*—Communications Section, 30 (1965), pp. 110–112.

hypothesis, however, Glenn concluded that whites have in fact benefited from the subordination of Negroes.

In an attempt to find empirical data to substantiate Glenn's intuitive assessment of the situation, I have re-analyzed the 1950 SMA data using different indices to measure white male occupational and income gains over Negroes. (An identical analysis of 1960 data produced virtually the same results and will not be reported here.) My occupational index measures occupational gains in terms of the proportion of the white male labor force occupying higher status jobs because Negro males are filling the lower-status positions. It is computed by first multiplying the number of jobs in seven major occupational groups by the percentage of the male labor force that is white. This yields an "expected" number of whites for each occupation. Then, the number of white "bonus jobs" (greater than proportional high-status jobs) was calculated for each SMA. The occupational index number for each SMA was defined as the ratio (expressed as a percentage) of the number of the white bonus jobs to the total white male labor force.

The 1950 SMA data reveal that when occupations are ranked by income, the upper-level occupations in all cities invariably have larger than proportional numbers of whites. For example, in Atlanta 77 per cent of the approximately 178,000 jobs for men were filled by whites. If whites were not benefiting from the presence of Negroes in the labor force, 77 per cent of the men in each occupational category would be white; but in fact, 97 per cent of managers and executives, about 95 per cent of clerical workers, and 94 per cent of professional and technical workers were white. Only 26 per cent of laborers and 33 per cent of nonhousehold service workers were white. Non-whites were clearly at the bottom of the occupational structure, while there were 16,700 more whites than proportional in bonus jobs. The total number of white bonus jobs equaled more than 12 per cent of the entire white male labor force and about 40 per cent of the male Negro workers. And Atlanta is far from being an extreme example: throughout the labor force represented by the 1950 SMA data, there were about two white bonus jobs for every five Negro workers, and in some cities the ratio reached one to two. How strongly is this index of white occupational gains related to the percentage Negro in the labor force?

My index of white occupational gains correlates .98 with the percentage of the labor force that was Negro in the 39 SMA's with 50,000 or more non-whites and .98 in the 93 SMA's with fewer than 50,000 non-whites. (Those with less than .5 per cent Negro were eliminated.) The correlation is .97 in Southern SMA's with 50,000 or more nonwhites and .98 in the 26

Southern SMA's with fewer than 50,000 non-whites; .87 in the 14 non-Southern SMA's with more than 50,000 non-whites, and .95 in the 67 non-Southern SMA's with fewer than 50,000 non-whites. Obviously this index of white occupational gains is closely related to the proportion Negro.

Glenn's conclusion that "the income of white persons did not vary in any consistent manner along the scale of relative size of the Negro population" (p. 447) was based on a correlation between median white income and the percentage Negro. This is obviously a spurious test of a Negro "effect" if Negroes migrate (as he indicated they might) toward high-income SMA's. The correlation between white and non-white income in the 132 SMA's with more than .5 per cent Negro is .63—above .70 in the non-Southern SMA's—indicating that such a migration may have occurred. A different test of white income gain seems appropriate.

If the median white male income were no higher than the median income of all males, then whites in general would not be benefiting from the occupational subordination of Negroes. The difference between white male median income and all male income is an appropriate measure of the dollar gain accruing to whites because Negroes are concentrated in low-paying occupations. For example, in 1949 the Atlanta male income was 2,308 dollars and the white male median was 2,801 dollars—a difference of about 500 dollars. The correlation between this indicator of white income gains and the percentage nonwhite in the population is .93 for all 132 SMA's and varied between .72 and .95 in the six regional categories indicated above. These correlations provide strong evidence that income gains do accrue to the white population because Negroes are present and tend disproportionately to occupy the low-paying jobs. It is also worth noting that correlations between white or Negro unemployment rates and the proportion Negro, −.33 and −.29 respectively in Southern and non-Southern SMA's, contradict the belief that large Negro populations push whites out of jobs because Negroes work for lower pay.

This research indicates that the white population, Northern and Southern, derives occupational and income gains that are directly associated with the proportion of Negroes in the labor force. Thus, not only may whites in Southern areas having had long experience with benefits from Negro subordination be expected to continue such patterns, but also whites in Northern cities with growing Negro populations may be expected to increase their resistance to equal employment opportunities.

PART VII

Responses to Oppression

Editor's Introduction

One of the battle cries of "radical" sociology is that we should stop studying the oppressed and start studying the oppressors. This statement fallaciously implies that we have been doing much of the former and little of the latter. In fact, in the area of race and ethnic relations, the reverse is true. There are many more attitude studies of white Americans, for example, than of black Americans. Furthermore, innumerable studies arbitrarily exclude blacks from samples on the rather flimsy ground that their presence would reduce the homogeneity of the sample, or introduce "contaminating" factors in whatever is being studied. (This subtle form of sociological racism is tantamount to saying that since blacks do not count in American society, or, in more pseudo-scientific language, since they are not "representative" of the population, they might as well be left out.)

In point of fact, sociology, and especially American sociology, has done a poor job of studying either oppressor or oppressed, the reason being that it has shied away altogether from the study of *oppression*. The sanguine strain in American functionalism, which dominated so much of sociology for so long, made it unfashionable to study the nasty aspects of social reality, especially power relationships. Or, if such unpleasant phenomena could not be altogether ignored, they became trivialized by relegation to a politically safer level of analysis. Thus, it is much safer to study the psychodynamics of racism rather than its economics, or to study the culture of poverty as distinguished from the politics of oppression.

All three of the articles in this section of the book are unusual in the literature, in that they deal, in a non-radical but "relevant" way, with responses to oppression. Each deals with an important racial minority in the United States, and the three groups are quite different from each other. Yet the common strain of racism in the dominant society gives a powerful underlying commonality to all three pieces. Broom's study gives us a glimpse from the receiving end of a concentration camp and constitutes a valuable contemporaneous documentation of one of the many infamous pages of American history. The other two pieces, on Afro-Americans and Spanish-Americans respectively, are case studies in the powerlessness of pariah groups and in adaptation to oppression.

FAMILIAL ADJUSTMENTS
OF JAPANESE-AMERICANS TO
RELOCATION: FIRST PHASE

There may never have been a problem which captured the attention of American sociologists more promptly, more completely, and more appropriately than the evacuation of the Japanese from the West Coast. In matters of topical interest there is always a danger that the necessities of empirical immediacy will blur equally pressing theoretical considerations, and this paper tries to steer between the Scylla of crass empiricism and the Charybdis of scholasticism.

The study is predicated on the assumption that methodologically the most suitable framework for the examination of Japanese adjustment is that of the family. Surely the family is the salient Japanese institutional form and the most pervasive system within the socio-cultural complex. Furthermore it is a crucial area of acculturation, inter-generational adjustment, and group solidarity.

Pragmatic considerations always condition the kind of research which is practicable (more so in sociology than in other sciences), and for that as well as for the reasons noted above the delimitation of the investigation to the field of the family was thought appropriate. This paper is to be regarded as the foundation and ground plan of a continuous study which will attempt to follow the Japanese-American familial adjustment through and beyond the war.[1] Thus the series of dramatic crises to which the people are being subjected will eventually appear in some perspective. Anything

From Leonard Broom, "Familial Adjustments of Japanese-Americans To Relocation: First Phase," in *American Sociological Review*, 8 (1943), pp. 551–560.

less than a thoroughgoing effort at describing the sequence patterns is inadmissible.

First there is presented a brief description of the background to the problem: the main features of the native Japanese family, an indication of the character of the acculturation which took place in Hawaii and on the West Coast, and a summary of the factors conditioning familial adjustment prior to the war. Secondly, there is a partial report of a comparative analysis of all Japanese marriages, 1,081 in number, occurring in Los Angeles County between May 1937 and December 1938, and between January 1941 and April 1942. Thirdly, there is offered a descriptive account of the adjustment to the evacuation of a sample of more than 100 Japanese-American families. The methods employed in gathering the last data are questionnaire, interview, and participant observation. The assistance of students of Japanese ancestry from this department was enlisted.

The hypothesis is offered for future rather than current testing that in terms of familial integration the adjustment will be found to be bi-polar in nature rather than modal.

The native Japanese family[2] of the latter part of the last century, which is taken as our point of departure, was characterized by a strong solidarity expressed in "mutual helpfulness." It was patriarchal in form and colored throughout by the notion of male superiority and the correlative desirability of male children. In discussing creation folklore Embree gives the following mythological support for masculine supremacy. "Performing a special marriage ceremony Izanagi and Izanami followed each other around a heavenly august pillar, and she greeted him, 'Ah, what a fair and lovely youth.' He greeted her in return and they were married. But their first children were 'not good' and by divination it was found that there had been an error in the wedding ceremony. The man, not the woman, should have spoken first, so the whole ceremony was repeated with Izanagi opening the conversation. Thus male superiority was assured for all time."[3] The father symbol (*koshu*) was an object of respect, even awe; the mother symbol was one to elicit warmth and affection, and maternal influence was dependent largely on affectional ties.

The individual, if it be appropriate to use the word, matured in a rôle system in which the dominant themes were filial piety, seniority (and more specifically respect for the aged), masculine superiority, and ancestor worship. The compulsive nature of deferential attitudes found linguistic expression in the use of honorifics (*keigo*) and in the emphasis placed upon verbal propriety in alluding to or addressing an elder.

Marriage was practically uniform and was effected by family action for purposes of familial continuity. Therefore, the rôle of the eldest male child was a prime concern of the family in terms of its organization as a primary group and of its ancestral ties. The actual marriage was usually arranged by a "go-between" (*nakaudo*), and there was small place for independent mate choice. In order to insure continuity, families without male children commonly practiced adoption. If there were a daughter, the adoptee might be the daughter's husband (*yōshi*), thus assuring both ancestor worship and retention of properties by the in-group. The adoption practices were capable of convenient variations such as the adoption of one's younger brother (*junyōshi*). Because the family's stake was so great, a careful scrutiny would be made of the lineage or "blood" of the prospective in-laws. Tuberculosis, leprosy, inferior social status, or a prison record were regarded as disabilities.

Patently in such a system the family would be the chief agency for social control, and the extension of family concepts and kin relationships into industrial and national spheres suggests its vigor. Miyamoto in his useful monograph points out the functioning significance of this theme as follows: "It is not so important that they speak of their community or nation as if it were a family; what is really significant is that they act towards it in many ways as if it were a family."[4]

Various familial principles and symbols ramify through the whole national life. The government of the Tokugawa feudal period stressed the ethical principles of filial piety and loyalty to one's superiors.[5] During school ceremonials there is read a charter of education from the throne which abjures "ye, our subjects be filial to your parents, affectionate to your brothers and sisters; as husbands and wives be harmonious."[6] Mrs. Ishimoto says of the Empress, "She was to them [school girls] a gracious mother, and indeed we called her 'The Mother of the Nation.' "[7] Prior to the death of the Meiji Emperor Mutsuhito, "Papers reported that many men committed suicide in the hope that their ancestors would accept the offering of a private life as a substitute for that of His Majesty. . . ."[8] Upon the Emperor's death a year of deep mourning occurred and even marriages were postponed until the year was over. (With utter irrelevancy the writer suggests from his meager insight that he does not concur in the reasoning behind the Doolittle policy of missing the Imperial Palace. The death of the Emperor would be an unparalleled blow to Japanese morale. Even a threat to his life might cause a cabinet crisis.)

Geisha may be adopted legally as daughters of the house. The mistress is termed mother, other geisha are called sisters and the strictures of filial duty operate as in the family. In the popular literature one of the standard themes is the struggle of the geisha against being prostituted by the foster mother.[9] The feudal form of familism has been a chief factor in the retardation of labor reforms in Japan. The inferiority of the bargaining position of the Japanese worker, especially women, depends in large part on the cultural practices deriving from filial patterns.

As in other populations which are denominated "minorities" the Japanese present a continuum of assimilation ranging from extreme traditionalism on the one hand, termed "Japanesey" by their own group, to the "haolified" or "Americanized" types on the other. Certain features, however, are worth reviewing. The period of Japanese immigration was brief and its termination abrupt. An examination of a population pyramid reveals a great preponderance of foreign-born males in the group over fifty years of age, a considerable preponderance of foreign-born females

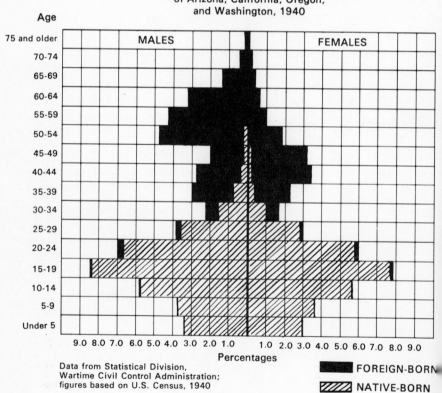

FIGURE 21-1
Age, Sex, and Nativity for Japanese-Americans
of Arizona, California, Oregon,
and Washington, 1940

Data from Statistical Division,
Wartime Civil Control Administration;
figures based on U.S. Census, 1940

FOREIGN-BORN

NATIVE-BORN

in the forty to fifty age groups, and an abrupt cleavage between the native- and foreign-born groups at the thirty to thirty-five level where the pyramid is quite narrow. This is suggestive, for it offers demographic support for culture conflict which would have the effect of canalizing along generational lines whatever struggle arose. It lends a concrete group-formed reality to the "problem of the second generation," to the cultural hybrid, and to marginality which in most minorities is much less clearly defined.

Miyamoto[10] periodizes the history of adjustment of the Japanese population in three intervals: The Frontier Period, The Settling Period, The Second Generation Period. The Frontier Period ended in 1907 with the Gentlemen's Agreement. During this time the immigrants nearly without exception planned to return to Japan. The Settling Period, from 1907 to 1924, saw ghetto formation, economic expansion, the leveling of sex ratios and family founding. The Second Generation Period beginning in 1924 found the people resigned to a life in America and orienting themselves to the rising *nisei*. To these must be added a fourth upon which we have just embarked. Perhaps it may be called the Period of Isolation, although a more dramatic term would be as suitable.

Table 21–1 shows the rapidity with which the native-born population came into numerical ascendancy. There should also be emphasized the very recent emergence of an adult native-born group to challenge the authority of the elders. Speaking of Seattle in the late thirties Miyamoto said: ". . . in the rising importance of the second generation we have the portent of a break from . . . ancient collectivistic traditions . . . the break will

TABLE 21-1
Japanese Population Characteristics*

Year	United States (Continental) Population	California Population	Sex Ratio (Males/100 Females)	Per Cent Native-born	Per Cent of Native-born Over 21 Years
1940	126,947	93,717	127.7	64.2	31.9
1930	138,834	97,456	137.6	50.3	7.1
1920	111,010	71,952	171.1	28.9	
1910	72,157	41,356	562.8	7.7	
1900	24,326	10,151	1735.6	1.4	

*From census data.

241

come suddenly."[12] How suddenly it came, and in what fashion! Not least important is the fact that the break coincided with the emergence of the *sansei*, the third generation.

It is my opinion, considering the wide cultural gap and the tendency to segregated residence, that the assimilation of the *nisei* has been notably great. Indeed a good case might be made for the proposition that there is a greater culture distance between the *issei* and the *nisei* than between the *nisei* and their caucasoid contemporaries. Besides the home, the chief institutional agency for culture conservation was the Japanese language school. Thirty per cent of our U.S. born cases failed to attend language school, and the mean was four years' attendance. The importance of such schooling might easily be overrated, for the quality of instruction was formal in character and varied with the training of the teacher.

Another conservative influence was the practice of visiting Japan. Because it is difficult just now to secure reliable information on this matter, I shall not essay any generalization beyond noting that the influence of such visits was mixed. Some youth, inept in Japanese and unused to old country ways, were pushed toward the American end of the culture continuum as they would not have been had they never visited Japan. What we need and what we do not have yet are data on age, duration, and frequency of the visits. The tendency to classify categorically as *kibei* all young people who have visited Japan is patently absurd. The term applies properly to persons who have been assimilated sufficiently to shift their cultural center of gravity to Japan, a process not accomplished in a few months.

In some instances the experiences of visitors to Japan were little less than traumatic and the *nisei* look back on their sojourn with resentment and a strong awareness of their identity with American culture. Here is an example: ". . . she explained that it was impossible for her to remain longer in Japan, although she had had every intention of doing so. She had found herself at a peculiar disadvantage there, because, though she looked like a Japanese, she was unable to speak the language; and besides, her dress, language, everything about her, in fact, betrayed her American origin. The anomaly struck the Japanese public as something scandalous, almost uncanny. When she appeared on the streets, crowds followed her."[13]

From the standpoint of family behavior, one focus of adjustment and conflict is linguistic habit. The use of honorifics is essential to familial interaction, and requires a linguistic facility not often achieved by *nisei*. In noting this Yamamoto says ". . . anything except the correct usage may make for either rudeness or absurdity."[14] Interpreting the language problem further she says, "There is a tendency for the first generation to think that their children are deliberately trying to forget the Japanese language. . . . The younger folks . . . shun contacts with the elders due to this Japanese language deficiency."[15] According to our findings the language pattern of the average Japanese-American home is fairly clear-cut. Parents speak Japanese to each other, the children English to each other and a kind of pidgin Japanese to their parents. Girls, associating more with their linguistically conservative mothers, have a higher degree of Japanese proficiency than do boys.

The in-group security of the Japanese population has not been altered by intermarriage to any considerable extent, but courtship practices have proved more susceptible to change. The use of the go-between has persisted in a large number of cases but in a formalistic rather than a functional sense. The *nakaudo* is likely to be secured after the fact, for the American ideology of independent mate choice has been accepted by the *nisei*. The dating complex and the notion of romantic love have also become part of the thoughtways of the young. Some aspects of the love pattern such as kissing, the public expression of emotion, free verbalization, social dancing, and the relatively high status of women are of course repugnant to the parental generation and provide areas of culture conflict.[16] In the intensive association of camp life the culture forms are not only divergent but visible, and the conflict tends to become overt.

On the other hand parents are no doubt more influential in determining mate choice than is customary among caucasoid Americans, and ancestral criteria of blood and status are significant. Many families undertake the traditional investigation of old-country backgrounds and before the war would send to Japan for a dossier on the suitor's family.

To turn to the particularities of intermarriage, Panunzio in his study for Los Angeles County covering the 1924–33 period found the Japanese intermarriage rate to be only 2.3 per cent.[17] Correct this figure for the evasions of the California law which forbids racial intermarriage with whites and our ignorance of out-of-state cases, and the real rate might well approach Adams' findings for Hawaii (1930–34) of 4.5 per cent.[18] Our 1941–42 data show six intermarriages, hardly more than one percent of the total. Although the number of cases is too small to warrant generalization, it is interesting that only one Chinese was involved whereas in Panunzio's cases seventeen of twenty-seven intermarriages were with Chinese, manifestly an expression of the penetration of global conflicts into the interstitial areas of Los Angeles.

In order to state objectively some of the effects of the war on Japanese adjustment, I should like to draw some data from a study to be published later of Japanese marriages contracted in Los Angeles County. The whole analysis covers the periods May 1937 through December 1938 and January 1941 through April 1942. For this discussion I shall use only the intervals May 1937 through April 1938 and May 1941 through April 1942. May through April was taken as the statistical year because the evacuation introduced a new situation. It will be inexpedient to offer the full statistical analysis here, but some generalizations may be made.

The dramatic increase in marriages in the second year over the first and in the war over the pre-war period may be explained only by the tensional system in which this minority operated. The latter figures are conservative in that the intervening period saw the introduction of a pre-marital medical examination requirement in California with the usual increase in out-of-state marriages. In turn, however, this factor is probably corrected by the age trend of the Japanese population.

Table 21–2 shows that in the first year there were 249 marriages; in the second there were 562. Of the latter 297 fell in the first four months of 1942.

TABLE 21-2
Number of Japanese Marriages in
Los Angeles County by Months

Month	1937-1938	1941-1942
May	19	30
June	21	54
July	17	24
August	16	30
September	31	29
October	24	30
November	25	40
December	17	28
January	11	42
February	25	67
March	24	103
April	19	85
Total	249	562

In the seven months before the outbreak of war we have a population responding, as did the rest of the nation, to the pressure of anxiety, fear, and excitement, and marrying because of it. December shows a sharp drop-off which I had interpreted as a catatonic phase of inactivity, but comparative study makes such a point of view doubtful. The high point was reached early in April when 44 marriages were solemnized in a single week.

It is further interesting to note that those in the upper age group were also affected by this trend. Fifty-four persons over 40 years of age were married between January and April of 1942 compared with fifteen in the 1937–38 period. There is a high degree of co-residence reported in this group, probably indicating a wish to formalize commonlaw or foreign marriages.

After Pearl Harbor ten venerable marriage licenses were used whose average age was 41 months, and only two of which had been secured within a year. It is clear even from brief analysis that the Japanese were hurriedly entrenching themselves within the familial institution, cementing and formalizing old relationships, and precipitating new ones.

In the weeks before evacuation courtships that saw marriage as months or years away matured and were consummated, and casual meetings became serious affairs. The only way to insure being evacuated together was to marry. Parents were bedeviled into granting consent long before they had time for seemly investigation. The go-between (*nakaudo*) was busy indeed, but in the haste compromises were made with ceremonial observances that otherwise would not have been allowed. Haste further meant that expensive and elaborate weddings were dispensed with, and couples who were postponing marriage for financial reasons found the obstacle removed. In the assembly centers affluence would not count for much. As an excuse the evacuation worked both ways.

Before proceeding a word must be said on the character of my sources of information. For the most part I have been dependent upon *nisei* trained in Western universities for direct information and for field assistance. My sampling is badly slanted wherever acculturational variables are paramount. The *nisei* who attended our universities were predominantly urban with a good deal of the cultural apparatus which that implies. They were more secure economically than the average Japanese-American. They were committed most thoroughly to the American way of life. Those who have collaborated as field assistants, *kibei* as well as *nisei*, were chosen because of their training in the social sciences, their facility in Japanese, or both. Later on it will be possible to make acknowledgment by name for their work and to assure them that if these studies make sense it is their fault.

If an enormously complicated set of relationships may be reduced to a few hunches, it is my opinion that the crises of war and evacuation resulted, at least temporarily, in an increase in familial interaction.

The policy of the Wartime Civil Control Administration of evacuating household groups as units reinforced the group stabilizing tendency, and family members who were not co-residents often returned home. There arose in a few minds the erroneous notion that evacuation by families was mandatory and so groups were re-formed that may have lost their functional character. If this notion seems improbable the reader must recall the flood of rumor in which the Japanese-Americans struggled at the time of evacuation, and indeed still do. The reëstablishment of family groups was by no means universal, however. Some were restored after evacuation, and some still wait upon administrative action. In a later report I hope to include information on the matter of post-evacuation residential changes.

With their facility in English the elder children had a large rôle in making decisions. However, when it became apparent that no distinction was to be made between the *nisei* and their Japanese-born parents and when loyalty tensions arose, the American citizens lost status. The culture conflicts did not resolve. Indeed the marginality of the *nisei* was thrown into high relief, but temporarily the social manifestations of strife were submerged by the necessity for collective action.

Another factor making for group stability was the practice of removing neighborhoods or organized groups together and housing them in the same areas in the assembly centers. Many of these groups had no previous existence but were organized to meet the emergency. Others were loosely integrated community groups which took on the special function and accepted outsiders.

The general circumstances surrounding the evacuation are well enough known so that they need not be recited here. The cumulative and confusing pressures may be appreciated from the following chronology:

January 29, 1942. First Attorney-General's order establishing prohibited restricted zones on West Coast and regulating movement of enemy aliens. Subsequent orders on January 31, February 2, 4, 5, and 7.

February 13. Letter to the President from Pacific Coast Congressional Delegation recommending evacuation from strategic areas of all persons of Japanese ancestry.

February 19. Executive order authorizing designation of military areas from which any person might be excluded. Beginning of voluntary evacuation.

February 21. Tolan Committee begins Pacific Coast hearings on enemy aliens and Japanese-Americans.

March 2. Proclamation by General DeWitt designating Military Areas No. 1 (western half of the coastal states and southern Arizona) and No. 2 (remainder of four states).

March 14. Wartime Civil Control Administration established under Western Defense Command to supervise evacuation.

March 16. Work started on assembly center at Manzanar.

March 18. War Relocation Authority created to relocate evacuated persons.

March 19. Fourteen Western governors oppose settlement of Japanese evacuees in their states.

March 23. One thousand voluntary evacuees from Los Angeles leave to prepare Manzanar center. All persons of Japanese ancestry ordered to evacuate Bainbridge Island near Seattle by March 30.

March 27. Curfew for all persons of Japanese ancestry in Military Area No. 1, requiring them to be at home between 8:00 P.M. and 6:00 A.M., forbidding certain possessions, and restricting travel without permit to five miles from home.

March 29. Further voluntary evacuation from Military Area No. 1 prohibited.

March 30. Three thousand persons of Japanese ancestry ordered to evacuate Terminal Island in Los Angeles Harbor to Santa Anita Assembly Center by April 5.

June 2. Persons of Japanese ancestry forbidden to leave California part of Military Area No. 2 (eastern half of state) anticipatory to evacuation of this area.

June 3. Evacuation of 100,000 persons of Japanese ancestry from Military Area No. 1 completed.[19]

Here are the questions that were being asked: Would there be an evacuation? Would an exception be made of citizens? When would the evacuation come? What areas would be included? How much time would be allowed between notice and evacuation? What property might be taken? What property should be disposed of and how? Should an attempt be made to move inland before the curfew was established? (Eight thousand did move inland, of which more than half remained outside the centers.[20]) For most of the population the questions were answered in a period in of less than two weeks between the notice of the evacuation date for their area and their actual removal.

Another factor that increased the stress of family adjustment was the detention of more than 4,700 persons.[21] Most of these were *issei* males, the most responsible segment of the community and those most practiced in making overt societal adjustments. Furthermore they comprised a disproportionately large number of family heads. The significance of the figure 4,700 becomes clear upon noting that there were over 23,000 family heads among the Japanese-Americans in the four Western states (Arizona, California, Oregon, and Washington). The capacity to adjust of any family would be damaged by the loss of its responsible head; the effect on the Japanese-American family with its heritage of patriarchal responsibility was often shattering. The statistical support for this statement lies in the fact that 45.6 per cent of all *issei* in the four Western states were listed as family heads by the 1940 census, whereas 6.0 per cent of *nisei* were so listed.

It is important to note that the condition was not merely a temporary one. By January 1943 about 1,400 detained persons had been placed in relocation centers with their families, 2,000 had been sent to internment camps where aliens defined as disloyal are incarcerated, and the remainder were still in detention camps awaiting hearing.[22]

Although the residence plan in the relocation centers presumed the preservation of the family unit, the limitations of space required compromises with the plan. Detached individuals were housed with small family groups. The average size living quarters for a family of five is a single room 20 by 25 feet; for smaller families less space is allowed. Auditory privacy for individual or family is absent even when housed in separate units, for the necessarily flimsy construction keeps out no noises. The construction provided is known in military parlance as "theatre of operations" type of tar-paper covered barracks and is designed to last for five years. The *nisei* who had not the background of adjustment to the rather alfresco type of native Japanese residence are the most disturbed by living conditions.

The whole problem of the inability of the primary group to isolate itself was and is one of the commonest complaints. To the concern of their elders, children and adolescents became sexually sophisticated and voyeuristically oriented. Lovers became inhibited or defiant or both. The problem is a cultural as well as a personal one when one recalls Japanese conservatism about public demonstrations of affection. Here is an extract from a letter which states the confusion of a young newlywed. "Married life is no lark in camp when you're in love and don't mind if people know it. You want them to know it, but, of course, social pressure prevents. Seeing the same Japanese neighbors day in and day out while you pass by those gossiping groups of men and women makes you freeze up. In my own vicinity I rarely hold hands . . . but my conscience doesn't bother me when I'm away from home where I don't know the old people. I guess we can't blame the oldsters for making meaningless comments about those passing by, but pretty soon they become rumors, etc. All of this conservative behavior only because our parents didn't experience the same type of sex behavior during their prime. In fact, my parents have never seen us kissing except once at our wedding ceremony."

The most important influence on family integration was the loss of function and the absence of need for any kind of collective action. After the intensive collaboration of planning for removal, which knit the group so tightly together for a brief span, there suddenly were no decisions to be made, little work to do, and no household routine. The house-organizing plans were translated into barrack existence with community dining halls, laundries, and toilet facilities. No longer were there any common purposes or activities to provide functional ties and group meanings. The father's authority as head of the household lost much of its functional character, the age-hierarchy was all but destroyed, and group purposes disappeared. Nothing further from the Japanese plan of family organization could have been contrived.

Each member became a free agent, and small children detached themselves from parental supervision, returning to the home barracks perhaps only to sleep. Especially in the assembly centers the age group promptly became the organizing principle, and the clique became a predominant form of organization. Community activities such as religious observances, supervised recreation, education and work were arranged on age lines, thereby reinforcing the tendency. In the relocation centers the system of organized education was the most effective time-filling device.

Almost all observers report that the elders are concerned about the decay in manners of the children. Perhaps the general tensions plus the frictions of barracks existence were responsible for the population becoming verbally less inhibited and more aggressive.

There has been a tendency a priori to interpret the breakup of the Japanese colonies in our cities as assimilative in character. In the very long run this may be true, but the immediate results have been quite the opposite. *Nisei* who never would have acquired any facility in Japanese are learning it. After the first adjustments of relocation, the cultural reënforcement that the *issei* received from each other made for reacculturation both of themselves and their children.

Because there are no horizons to the life space, and because there can be none, group-forming decisions are postponed. Having children, for an example, is regarded as extremely undesirable. There is a great deal of doubt as to the wisdom of contracting new marriages. It will be interesting to discover if this doubt is expressed in a low marriage rate.

In retrospect it is difficult to conceive how the population could have met the crisis as well as it did without its strongly integrating primary group forms. Initially at least the emergency yielded a further cohesion. At the end of 1942 two general sets of forces were observable. First a tendency of the *nisei* to withdraw from the familial group with its conservative Japanese cultural attributes, as evidenced by age group formations. The opportunity to move from the centers which has been afforded some persons, mostly *nisei*, reënforces and gives reality to the withdrawal. Second there are those who have tended increasingly to identify themselves with their parents and the parental culture (by no means necessarily with Japan). Partly this may be traced to the frustrations of camp life and the war effort.

Partly it is due to their intensive association in small living quarters and their loss of status as a culturally emergent group. If policies and politics permit, the tendency to withdraw promises to be ascendant.

We are pursuing the investigation in the following ways: (1) As nearly as possible family histories are being kept up to date. It is planned to attempt to maintain such contacts beyond the war so that we shall have a set of adjustmental histories as complete as possible. Because our collaborators are assimilated and clearly loyal persons they are being relocated out of the centers and our task increases in difficulty. (2) Pre-evacuation and post-evacuation marriages are being studied from the comparative standpoint. (3) Mixed marriages are being investigated inasmuch as they illuminate such features as group definition, isolation, and the like. (4) An attempt is being made to secure full histories of divorces. The divorce rate promises to be very high.

This paper has outlined the first steps in the analysis of a set of problems which in some respects are as close as sociological data ever get to being experimental. It has presented a brief summary of the backgrounds of Japanese-American families and their first adjustment to a situation unique in American history. In the most modest fashion it offers itself as an acknowledgment of a salient obligation of social scientists, the documentation of the present.

NOTES

1. A brief preliminary statement "Familial Problems and the Japanese Removal" appears in Proceedings of the Pacific Sociological Society 1942, *Research Studies*, State College of Washington, 11 (1943), pp. 21–26.

2. Generalizations on the native Japanese family are from various sources. Especially useful were: John F. Embree, *Suye Mura* (University of Chicago, 1939), *The Japanese* (Washington: Smithsonian Institution War Background Studies, 1943); Shidzué Ishimoto, *Facing Two Ways* (New York: Farrar and Rinehart, 1935); Etsu I. Sugimoto, *A Daughter of the Samurai* (New York: Doubleday, Doran, 1925). For extended bibliography see the following: Hugh Borton, Serge Elisséeff, and Edwin O. Reischauer, *A Selected List of Books and Articles on Japan in English, French, and German* (Washington: American Council of Learned Societies, 1940); *Catalogue of the K. B. S. Library* (Tokyo: Kokusai Bunka Shinkokai, 1937).

3. Embree, *The Japanese*, p. 2.

4. Shotaro Frank Miyamoto, "Social Solidarity among the Japanese in Seattle," *University of Washington Publications in the Social Sciences*, 11, no. 2 (December 1939) p. 84.

5. Embree, *op. cit.*, p. 9.

6. Ishimoto, *op. cit.*, p. 71.

7. *Ibid.*, p. 63.

8. *Ibid.*, p. 68.

9. *Ibid.*, pp. 286 f.

10. *Op. cit.*, pp. 64–66 *et passim*.

11. *Op. cit.*, p. 69.

12. Quoted from Robert E. Park, *The Survey*, May 1, 1926, p. 136, in E. Stonequist, *The Marginal Man* (New York: Scribner's Sons, 1937), p. 104.

13. Misako Yamamoto in *Social Process in Hawaii*, IV (Sociology Club, University of Hawaii, 1938) p. 47.

14. *Ibid.*

15. Cf. R. H. Ross and E. H. Bogardus, "Four Types of Nisei Marriage Patterns," *Sociology and Social Research*, 25 (1940), pp. 63–65; and R. H. Ross and E. H. Bogardus, "Second-generation Race Relations Cycle: A Study in Issei-Nisei Relationships," *Sociology and Social Research*, 24 (1940), pp. 357–363.

16. Constantine Panunzio, "Intermarriage in Los Angeles, 1924–33," *American Journal of Sociology*, 47, 5 (1942), pp. 693–695.

17. Romanzo Adams, *Racial Intermarriage in Hawaii* (New York: Macmillan, 1937), p. 344.

18. Abridged and adapted from War Relocation Authority, *First Quarterly Report* (March 18 to June 30, 1942), pp. 1–5.

19. Hearings before a Subcommittee of the Committee on Military Affairs, U.S. Senate, Seventy-Eighth Congress, First Session, on S. 444 (Washington: 1943), pp. 2–3.

20. *Ibid.*, p. 39.

21. *Loc cit.*

POWER STRUCTURE AND THE
NEGRO SUB-COMMUNITY

Recently Bernard Barber noted that "a hard look at contemporary social science will show that there is very little consensus on a theory of influence and that there is also very little sound empirical research on which such a theory might be based."[1] Also, Roucek has commented that "there has been a definite disinclination to view the field of minority-majority relations as another aspect of human power relations.[2]

This paper reports findings from a study of influence and power as these phenomena operate within the context of the Negro sub-community of a large Northwestern city. The project was designed to replicate Floyd Hunter's work in the sub-community of "Regional City."[3] Hunter presents one of the few exceptions to Roucek's criticism noted above. Such studies represent a major step in the direction of bringing the field of minority relations out of the special value context within which it has long been encompassed and placing it within the framework of general sociology.

A comparison of the findings reported in this paper with Hunter's permits the study of functional relationships between the structure of the influence system and other dimensions of community structure. Such case studies offer a valuable, if partial, approach to the comparative study of communities. For example, Pellegrin and Coates have investigated the relationship between absentee ownership of the major industries of a middle-sized Southern city and the structure of power relations within that community.[4] In a study of the structures of power in an American and a British community, Miller reports differences in the occupational distribution of power leaders in the two contexts, which are related to the differences in the value

From Ernest A. T. Barth and Baha Abu-Laban, "Power Structure and the Negro Sub-Community," in *American Sociological Review*, 24 (1959), pp. 69–76.

systems of the two nations reflected in different prestige rankings associated with similar occupations.[5] These researches demonstrate the fruitfulness of attempts to develop a typology of power structures within the framework of comparative community theory. In addition, they further the understanding of community process and structure.

The Negro Community in Pacific City

As Hunter's "Regional City" dominates the economic and political organization of the Southeast, so the "Pacific City" of this study dominates in the Northwest. The two communities are quite similar in total population and economic structure.[6] Stimulated mainly by the expansion of job opportunities during and following World War II, the Negro community of Pacific City has greatly increased in population within the past seventeen years. Federal Census data show that from a total of 3,789 in 1940, the Negro population of Pacific City expanded to 15,666 in 1950, an increase of 313.5 per cent for the decade. It is estimated that at present the population is in excess of 25,000. The pattern of residential location is similar to that of most major American cities: Negroes are generally centrally located and highly concentrated in "black belt" areas. Although the city prides itself on its "liberal" policies concerning race relations, the index of residential segregation is high in relation to other comparable cities.[7] Early in the 1940s Negro migrants to the city were characteristically young, male, unskilled workers. Available evidence indicates, however, that since 1950 the stream of migration has included an increasing proportion of more highly educated, married men engaging in professional activities.

There are some important differences between the Negro communities of Pacific City and Regional City. The 1950 Census data show that Pacific City's Negro population comprised a relatively small proportion of the total population (approximately 3.4 per cent), whereas in Regional City approximately a third of the population was Negro. As noted above, the Negro population in Pacific City more than tripled in the decade 1940 to 1950. The corresponding rate for Regional City during that period was about 16 per cent. The former dramatic increase has had a disturbing influence on the relatively stable pre-war Negro community of Pacific City. The incoming stream of migration has brought with it a large number of professionally trained Negroes of high occupational status; their leadership now appears to overshadow most of the "old time" community leaders. At the same time, many of the in-migrants came from Southern states, carrying the cultural characteristics of Negroes in that region, which, in many ways, were inconsistent with those of the Pacific City sub-community, resulting in some social disorganization.

The Negroes of Pacific City occupy somewhat more prestigeful and better paid jobs than those of Regional City. In 1950, a larger proportion of them were concentrated in service occupations, especially government jobs, as compared with the concentration of workers in the unskilled labor category in Regional City. These occupational differences are reflected in the income figures for the two communities. The Federal Census data show that in 1949 the median income for whites in Pacific City was 2,356 dollars as compared with 2,218 dollars in Regional City, while Pacific City's Negroes earned an average of 1,709 dollars in that year as compared with 1,045 dollars for Negroes in Regional City.

One index of the differences in the over-all patterns of interracial relations characteristic of the two cities may be seen in the legal structure of the two states. In Regional City the official policy of segregation in schools and other public facilities has long been supported by the law, while in Pacific City a state F.E.P. law has been in effect since 1949 as well as a longstanding "public accommodations" law. The state legislature recently passed an "Omnibus Civil Rights Bill" almost unanimously, with provisions for the protection of minority rights in housing as well as in public accommodations and employment. The schools of the community are officially non-segregated although the pattern of residential concentration has had its usual results: a high proportion of Negro children in relatively few schools.

Study Design and Methodology

Since this study was intended to replicate Hunter's work in Regional City, his research design was followed in so far as possible.[8] Therefore, during the initial stage of the project, in order to locate individuals characterized as influential within the Negro sub-community, lists of names of people who had held office in the major organizations of the sub-community, plus additional names gotten from interviews with Negro informants known to the authors, were obtained. The names of sub-community organizations through which influence might be channeled were taken from a list prepared by the Chamber of Commerce, supplemented by other organizations mentioned by Negro informants. Also, a list of "important issues for the sub-community" suggested by the informants was compiled. In addition, the local Negro newspaper provided other names of leaders, organizations, and issues. From these sources 154 potential influentials, 84 organizations, and about 12 issues were obtained.

Two questionnaires were constructed, one containing the names of the potential leaders and the other the organizations. A panel of ten Negro respondents, representative of the various institutional areas of the sub-community, was selected. In a personal interview each respondent reported how well he knew each potential influential and added names of others whom he believed to have been omitted. He then selected from the list the names of ten people he would choose "to help in a major project requiring a decision by a group of sub-community leaders." The interviewee also rated each of the organizations as "most influential," "influential," or "less influential" in initiating or supporting actions of importance to the Negroes in the city.

With information from the first ten interviews, the list of leaders was reduced to 33 names, each of which had received three or more choices from the ten previous respondents. The list of organizations was similarly reduced to a total of 27. These modified lists were submitted to six other Negro informants who, in turn, were asked to rate the leaders and organizations and to add the names which they believed to have been omitted. The resulting final lists consisted of 36 probable influentials and 27 organizations.[9]

A second phase of the field work involved interviewing the 36 probable influentials.[10] Each respondent was asked to fill out a questionnaire seeking information about his background and activities in the community.[11] The respondent was asked to indicate how well he knew each of the other influentials and to estimate his average monthly number of social and committee contacts with each; and, again, the respondents were invited to add the names of any leaders they felt had been omitted from the list. Each was asked: "If you were responsible for a *major* project which was before the community that required *decision* by a group of leaders—leaders that nearly everyone would accept—which ten on this list would you choose, regardless of whether they are known personally to you or not?"

Each influential also was asked to rate the 27 organizations on the three-point scale of influence, adding such other groups that he believed had been omitted. Finally, each was asked to name two issues or projects which he considered to be "most crucial" to the sub-community. The respondent indicated whether or not anyone had contacted him about each issue, whether he had contacted others, and what media of communications were used in these contacts.

The Findings

SUB-COMMUNITY LEADERS

This study is primarily concerned with the 36 probable leaders whose names received three or more mentions by the panel of 16 judges. The names of these leaders, their occupations, the number of votes each received as a "top leader," and the number of mutual choices each received, are listed in Table 22–1.

Sixteen (or 44 per cent) of the leaders are women. This tends to confirm the popular belief, expressed by several of the leaders themselves, that women hold high positions in the leadership structure of the sub-community. Although two of the individuals high on the list in terms of number of votes are women, for the total group of 36 leaders women received an average of 6.1 votes compared with an average of 13.9 for men. This generally lower position of women in the leadership structure is probably due to the nature of their participation in the organizational activities of the community. Although, on the average, female leaders belong to about as many organizations as do men (8.42 memberships for men and 8.25 for women), women far exceed the men in fraternal and "social" activities. In this respect, we find many more women participating in the leadership activities of the sub-community than did Hunter. Male leaders concentrate their organizational activities in civic and professional organizations.

The findings concerning the age distribution of the leaders differ from those of Hunter. The mean age of the 36 Negro leaders was 44.8 years; Hunter's comparable figure is 54.3 years.

About 52 per cent of the leaders in the Pacific City sub-community were self-employed, averaging about three employees under their supervision. Two leaders supervised more than ten employees: a nursing home operator supervised 18 employees, and an insurance executive supervised 16 workers. (No non-leaders employed a sizeable number of workers.) Again these findings differ markedly from those of Regional City, where Hunter found that the "top leader" supervised 1800 workers and that eleven others supervised 25 or more workers. The much smaller figures for Pacific City

TABLE 22-1

Sub-Community Leaders Ranked by Number of Votes
Received from Other Leaders in Leadership Poll

Leader	Number of Votes	Number of Mutual Choices	Occupation
1. Walters	31	9	Social Worker
2. Taylor	27	7	Lawyer
3. Bassett	25	6	Small business (druggist)
4. Troy	25	8	Minister
5. Barner	24	9	Architect
6. Baldwin	22	6	Lawyer
7. Smith*	20	10	Housewife
8. Treat*	17	4	Social Worker
9. Moster	16	6	Minister
10. Willard	15	4	Retired
11. Williams	13	4	Small business (bail bond)
12. Stephens	12	2	Social Worker
13. Worth	12	2	Small business (real estate)
14. Hardy*	10	3	Social Worker
15. Fallsworth	9	1	Small business (photographer)
16. Dunham	9	2	Physician
17. Young*	9	3	Office Secretary
18. Parks*	7	4	School Teacher
19. Main*	6	4	Personnel Clerk
20. Barrier*	6	1	Housewife
21. Olaf*	6	2	Sales (insurance)
22. Ford	5	3	Small business (insurance)
23. Stone*	5	3	Unknown
24. Homer	4	1	Lawyer
25. Planter	4	2	Small business (nursing home)
26. McNeil	3	0	Dentist
27. Spear*	3	2	Small business (beauty school)
28. Masters*	3	1	School Teacher
29. Horne*	3	2	Unknown
30. Roberts	3	1	Physician
31. Moore*	2	0	Social Worker
32. Miller*	2	1	Sales (real estate)
33. Stewart	2	0	Lawyer (Pros. Office)
34. Taylor*	2	1	School Teacher
35. Sullivan	1	0	Small business (dry cleaning)
36. Gold*	1	1	Service Worker

*Denotes female leader.

reflect the positions held by the top leaders in the occupational structure of the community. Eight of the 36 leaders were engaged in small business activities, including insurance and real estate brokerages, a drug store owner, a beauty school, and a photography shop, while most of the leaders were professionals: five social workers, four lawyers, three physicians, three public school teachers, two ministers, and one architect. If power within the community derives in part from high positions in its economic or political structure, it is clear that none of these leaders in Pacific City's Negro sub-community possessed such power.

Only four of the 36 leaders were locally born (within the state). On the other hand, 60 per cent of them came originally from the South. These figures reflect the impact of migration on the leadership structure of the community. Although the leaders had been in Pacific City for 16.5 years on the average, only 80 per cent of them owned their homes. The leaders had also achieved a fairly high educational status, having completed about 16 years of school on the average.

THE "TOP SEVEN LEADERS"

In an attempt to determine whether or not there was any "leadership clique" among the Negroes of Pacific City a special analysis was made of the seven persons who had been mentioned as "top leaders" by one half or more of the 36 people interviewed. These seven "elitists" were distinguished from the other leaders by superior educational attainment, *shorter* length of residence in the community, and by their sex, all but one being men. All of the top seven owned their homes and four of them were self-employed.

Hunter demonstrates that the "top leadership group in the Negro sub-community tends toward closure" in two ways. First, almost all of the leaders were known to each other ("Ninety per cent of the leaders know each other 'well' or 'socially'") and, second, his sociometric data show a correlation between the number of votes received as a top leader and the number of mutual choices.[12]

Acquaintanceship among the 36 leaders in this study was also very high, with 93 per cent of the leaders reporting knowing each other "well" or "slightly." Among the seven top leaders, all reported that they knew each of the others well. In addition, with the exception of "Smith-Baldwin," all of the top seven reported having both "committee and social contacts with each other regularly." These findings tend to confirm those of Hunter on this point.

258

Ernest A. T. Barth and Baha Abu-Laban

Table 22–1 lists the names of the leaders, the number of votes they received, and the number of mutual choices they achieved. The well known correlation between sociometric leadership standing and the number of reciprocated choices achieved as a leader holds for our top seven, for they received an average of 7.9 such choices whereas the remaining leaders averaged 2.0. A further indication of the formation of a "closed" top leadership group is the relationship between the actual number of mutual choices and the total possible number of mutual choices. Within the top seven, of the 21 possible mutual choices,[13] 13 (or 62 per cent) were actually made and in only one case was there a reciprocal nonchoice.

These top seven were only slightly better known to the wider leadership group than were the others. Use of an "acquaintanceship score," with a range from zero (not known to any of the other leaders in the group of 36) to 105 (known well by all other members of the leadership group),[14] gave these seven an average score of 95.6 as compared with 90.9 for the remainder of the group.

One major differentiating characteristic of the top seven leaders is the degree to which they participated with others in organizational committee activities. There participation average with the other leaders was 16.7 as compared with 10.6 such contacts for the remaining 29. This supports the contention of several of the respondents that "the top leaders in this community got there because they were very active in organizational work." The belief was expressed that if such activity ceased the top leadership position would quickly be lost.

The top seven shared one other characteristic: each had taken part, at one time or another, in interracial activities in an "equal status" context in which he (or she) acted as a spokesman for the Negro community. Here, perhaps, is a case of "prestige drainage," with Negro leaders draining prestige from the white leaders with whom they were in contact.

ISSUES CONFRONTING THE SUB-COMMUNITY

If the nature of the power process in the local community is to be fully understood the types of issues that are most crucial to those who exercise this power must be analyzed. Each of the 36 leaders was asked: "What, in your opinion, are two of the major issues before the Negro community— either immediately past or current?" Table 22–2 lists the issues mentioned and the frequency of their mention.

From Table 22–2 it is apparent that the issues of concern to the leaders identified in this study were those associated with problems of interracial

TABLE 22-2

Issues Before the Negro Sub-Community Listed by
Frequency of Mention by 36 Sub-Community Leaders

Type of Issue	Number of Times Mentioned
Minority Housing	33
Civil Rights Legislation	17
Concentration of Minority Children in the Schools	11
Parks and Recreational Facilities in Minority Residential Areas	4
Discrimination in Employment and Career Counseling for Children	4
Police Brutality	1
Unity in Action within the Sub-Community	1
No issues mentioned	1

relations and the effects of minority group status, and more specifically, with attempts to change the existing social structure of the community. In spite of the presence of at least one organization of Negro business men and the fact that several of the leaders were themselves business men, their major concerns did not directly involve business problems (or most political programs). In their position as *leaders in the Negro sub-community*, they were preoccupied with problems of the "Negro protest." In some measure, perhaps, this interest reflects the attitude that, lacking the needed power, their influence on major decisions concerning general economic and political policy in the community is minimal.

COMMUNITY ORGANIZATIONS AND
THE STRUCTURE OF POWER

The formal organizations and administrative agencies, as well as the less formal but relatively stable cliques, offer mechanisms through which community decision-making activities may be channeled. In Regional City, Hunter reports that, although the "top" and six other leaders in the sub-community did not generally work through formal policy committees, the majority did so.[15]

In an attempt to identify the organizations in Pacific City through which policy decisions flow, a list of the major organizations in the sub-community was drawn up.[16] Each of the 36 leaders was asked to rate each organization on a three-point scale as (1) most influential, (2) influential, and (3) less influential. These organizations are listed in Table 22–3 in order of the numbers of "most influential" votes.

In two respects this list is comparable to that reported in Hunter's study.[17] Although 8 of the 27 organizations listed are of the Greek letter variety, none of these received more than two mentions as "most influential," indicating that at best they play a relatively minor role in the decision-making activities of the sub-community. And, again as in the case of Hunter's list, the organizations considered "most influential" (including the local Urban League, although its major function is community organization and case work) have a pronounced political content in their programs. With one minor exception, the churches, perhaps the most fully segregated

TABLE 22-3

Sub-Community Organizations Rated by 36 Sub-Community Leaders, Ranked According to Number of "Most Influential" Ratings Received

Organization	Number of "Most Influential" Ratings
Urban League	33
N.A.A.C.P.	29
Jackson Street Community Council	17
Christian Friends for Racial Equality	17
Association of Colored Women	16
Eastside Y.W.C.A.	16
East Madison Street Commercial Club	16
Cosmopolitan Century Club	9
Eastside Y.M.C.A.	8
Prince Hall Masons	6
The People's Institutional Baptist Church	4
The Brotherhood of Sleeping Car Porters	4
Philorati Club	4
Mary Mahoney Registered Nurses	3
Fraternal Organization	2
Veteran's Organization	2
Fraternal Organization	2
Fraternal Organization	2
Fraternal Organization	1
Sorority	1
Fraternal Organization	1
Fir State Golf Club	1
Fraternal Organization	1
Church Club	1
The Elks	1

of all sub-community organizations, were not mentioned—an interesting finding, especially in view of the fact that two of the top ten leaders are ministers.

Three further observations concerning these organizations are in point here. First, six of the top seven groups are directly concerned with inter-racial relations and "race betterment." Second, only one of the organizations on the entire list (ranking seventh) has as its principal interest the business organization of the sub-community. Finally, although union membership among Pacific City's Negroes is fairly widespread, only one union was mentioned, one that rated low in influence. This finding is consistent with the fact that, although there are several professional Negro union leaders in the community, none of them was cited as a "top leader." It appears that the major concern of the Negro sub-community, as well as of its leaders, lies with issues centering around minority status and group protest.

It may be noted that no "luncheon clubs," "supper clubs," or other informally organized groups appear on the list of the influential organizations. Early in the field work, an attempt was made to discover any such groups, but only one, the "Sunday Night Supper Club," was mentioned. One informant, a recent migrant to the community and a highly trained educator, in citing this club, noted that several top leaders whose names appear in Table 22–1 were active members. However, the club was only recently organized and appears to be primarily a recreational group.

Summary and Conclusions

According to Mills, Hunter, Miller, and others, the structure of power in American society and in American communities is derived in large part from the institutional structure of the society. The majority of the leaders identified by Hunter and Miller in their field studies were occupants of high positions in the economic organization of their communities. Mills argues that power resides principally in the realms of economic, political, and military organization, and suggests further, that the structure of the "power elite" is related to the rate and nature of social change in a society at any given time. The fruitfulness of a comparative approach to the study of power is suggested by these views. Such an approach would aim at specifying the conditions relevant to the type of power structure and processes in a community or society and would require a typology of community power structures.

Although the findings of this study do not, of course, make it possible to develop a systematic theory of power, the following conclusions are relevant to this purpose. First, it is evident that, although there is an identifiable structure of leadership in the sub-community of Pacific City at the present time, the leaders themselves are not "power wielders" or "decision makers" in the sense in which the terms are used by Hunter and Mills: they hold positions of little importance to the community's institutional structures; their decisions have no serious ramifications for the larger community.

In Pacific City there is an ecologically indentifiable "Negro community"—why is there no genuine power structure of the type found in Regional City? This lack can be attributed in part to the relatively small Negro population, insufficient to support large-scale separate institutions; in part to the rapid expansion of the population in the sub-community (evidence from interviews indicates that the old-leadership structure [prior to 1940] was disrupted and almost wholly destroyed by the impact of the incoming migrants); and in part to the attitudes of the leading figures in the minority community, who have worked hard for liberal legislation, better education for Negroes, and better housing on an open market. In this work they have been remarkably successful, and prefer not to risk these gains by supporting segregated institutions.

Several of the respondents insisted that it is incorrect to speak of a "Negro community" in Pacific City, maintaining that most Negroes are not conscious of being members of a racial community as they are in many other cities. Perhaps this helps to explain why the Negro leaders are those who are active in "protest" organizations—for these may be about all that remain of a Negro sub-community.

In any event, the sub-communities of Regional City and Pacific City represent quite different types. The well organized, stable structure of power in Regional City is missing in Pacific City. Although leadership groups have certain similar characteristics, those in Regional City wield power *within* the sub-community and those in Pacific City do not. Leaders in Regional City are motivated, at least in some measure, to maintain their segregated sub-community, while in Pacific City the leaders seek opposite goals. These findings emphasize the importance of the general community context in the study of power relations.

NOTES

1. Bernard Barber, *Social Stratification: A Comparative Analysis of Structure and Process* (New York: Harcourt, Brace, 1957), p. 234.

2. Joseph S. Roucek, "Minority-Majority Relations in Their Power Aspects," *Phylon*, 17 (First Quarter, 1956), pp. 25–26.

3. Floyd Hunter, *Community Power Structure: A Study of Decision Makers* (Chapel Hill: The University of North Carolina Press), 1954.

4. Roland J. Pellegrin and Charles H. Coates, "Absentee Owned Corporations and Community Power Structure," *American Journal of Sociology*, 61 (March 1956), pp. 413–419.

5. Delbert C. Miller, "Industry and Community Power Structure: A Comparative Study of an American and an English City," *American Sociological Review*, 23 (February 1958), pp. 9–15.

6. *Ibid*.

7. Donald O. Cowgill and Mary S. Cowgill, "An Index of Segregation Based on Block Statistics," *American Sociological Review*, 16 (December 1951), p. 825.

8. Hunter, *op. cit.*, "Appendix: Methods of Study," pp. 262–271.

9. Cf. Robert O. Schulze and Leonard U. Blumberg, "The Determination of Local Power Elites," *American Journal of Sociology*, 63 (November 1957), pp. 290–296.

10. All of the interviews were conducted by Baha Abu-Laban, a former resident of the Middle East, whose swarthy appearance stimulated short friendly chats with the respondents and comments concerning his ethnic identity. The interviews were characterized by a high level of rapport in our judgment.

11. Twenty-nine of the 36 respondents returned these questionnaires.

12. Hunter, *op. cit.*, pp. 119 ff.

13. A "mutual choice" was defined as the instance in which there was a reciprocal selection as a top leader.

14. Each respondent was asked to indicate "how well he felt he knew" each of the other members of the leadership group on a four-point scale ("Don't know," "Heard of," "Know slightly," "Know well"), with each response assigned a weight from 0 to 3.

15. Hunter, *op. cit.*, p. 125.

16. The technique of obtaining this list of organizations is discussed above.

17. Hunter, *op. cit.*, pp. 125–126.

SUBORDINATE LEADERSHIP IN A BICULTURAL COMMUNITY: AN ANALYSIS

It is held in the present paper that the ability of a subordinate group to generate effective leadership in its relations with a dominant alien people is a critical aspect of dominant-subordinate group relationships. The subordinate group in question here is the Spanish of the Southwest. We wish to see Spanish leadership in its autonomous setting, to see it in relation to the intercultural system which is emerging between Spanish and Anglo-Americans, and to consider leadership and some of its acculturational consequences.

Regional Background of the Case

The Spanish-speaking people are one of the largest United States ethnic minorities, and are concentrated principally in the southwestern part of the nation. Those whose forefathers were in the area in 1848 when the United States acquired the territory are also among the oldest ethnic groups, although many others have entered the region from Mexico over the intervening years. The Spanish-speaking are not powerful politically, a fact closely related to the perennial lack of leadership among them. They are seen by some authorities as surprisingly undifferentiated, compared to other large American ethnic groups, in schooling, in occupation, in income,

From James B. Watson and Julian Samora, "Subordinate Leadership in a Bicultural Community: An Analysis," in *American Sociological Review*, 19 (1954), pp. 413–421.

and in degree of acculturation.[1] Perhaps the most outstanding fact about the Spanish, besides their lack of leadership, is their low rate of acculturation. The special historical status of the Spanish may have a bearing upon the two facts, and the broad historical context suggests linkages between the leadership question and that of low assimilation.

The Southwestern Spanish[2] were a separate society when they came into contact with, and in a sense were conquered by Anglo-Americans, or "Anglos." Speaking a separate language and practicing separate customs, they were highly visible culturally. They represented nevertheless a modified branch of European civilization, unlike the Indians from whom they had received many influences, and unlike African slaves. In contrast to many Europeans who migrated to the United States, however, they had not voluntarily elected to adopt the lifeways of the dominant group. Moreover, they were more "native" and ecologically more adapted to their habitat in the Southwest than the dominant group. In these two respects they were more like Indians than immigrants. In the growing similarity of their goals with those of the dominant group, the Spanish are comparable to the present United States Negro, though their cultural similarity to Anglos is much less. In the sense of being a "conquered people" enslaved by their conquerors, the Spanish are somewhat like colonial people but more strictly comparable to the French of Canada. They differ from the French, however, in having smaller numerical strength relative to the dominant group, and they did not occupy the beachhead and focal areas of the Anglo-American culture and society. Their relative isolation (1650–1900) from the parent culture as well as from the Anglo culture is also an important factor with respect to assimilation.

Hence, historically having less motivation toward assimilation and deeper environmental and traditional roots than most U.S. immigrants, less commitment to and a less exclusive need for identification with the dominant cultural system than U.S. Negroes, but smaller numerical strength and less strategic position than the Canadian French, the Spanish as a group might be expected, more than others, to sense ambivalences about assimilation. Again, beside the fact of an increasing struggle for status in the Anglo system, one must place the opposing fact—peculiar to the Southwestern Spanish—that they have at their backs an effective reservoir of Spanish language and national Mexican culture to help reinforce and stabilize any tendency toward cultural separatism.

All of these broad, contradictory factors probably play their part in the default of Spanish leadership, as well as the more specific factors discussed below. In the larger Southwestern setting ambivalence about nativism *vs.*

assimilation would obscure the direction Spanish leadership should take and thus hamstring the development of effective leadership.

Turning to the present, there is singularly little controversy concerning whether Spanish leadership is weak, regardless of the point of view of different commentators. Agreement is all but unanimous among scientific investigators,[3] among social workers and public and private agencies interested in the Spanish-speaking people, among Anglo politicians, and among the people themselves. The Spanish of "Mountain Town," the subject of the present paper, are no exception.

The Community Studied

In the summers of 1949 and 1950, students from the Department of Sociology and Anthropology of Washington University, under James B. Watson's direction, carried out part of an intended long-range study of a small Anglo-Spanish community. Samora further pursued field work in the community, relating particularly to the question of Spanish-speaking leadership and organization, in the spring and summer of 1952.[4] It is largely with the findings from this bi-ethnic community that we propose to explore the question of weak leadership, but with the general background of the region always in mind.

Mountain Town, as we have called the community, is located in a high mountain valley of southern Colorado. It is at about 7000 feet above sea level, in an area of mixed truck farming and cattle and sheep ranching. Its 1950 population was close to 2500, comprising approximately 58 per cent Spanish-speaking and 42 per cent Anglos. (Hence the Spanish-speaking are not numerically a "minority" in the community itself, and will not be so called.) Founded around 1870, Mountain Town developed as a community of Anglo miners, storekeepers, and homesteaders. There were at the time but few "Old Spanish" families in the area, and they did not precede the Anglos by more than a decade or two. Mountain Town, hence, developed differently from the older established Spanish communities to the south which Anglos have come to dominate. The difference may have a bearing in the discussion which follows.

Descendents of original Spanish settlers still live in or near Mountain Town. It is probable that at least some of them could have been classed as *Patrón* families. Two or three are still landowners. However, the vast majority of Spanish-speaking families in Mountain Town came at a later date, many possibly around 1920. Much of this migration was from the Spanish villages of northern New Mexico, and kinsmen can often still be traced to or from that area. Practically none of these people are land-owners, except for house plots; nor are they often proprietors in any other sense. The largest number are still seasonal wage workers, unskilled or semi-skilled "stoop labor." Some of the women work as domestics, but many more work in the fields or produce-packing sheds. As a group, the Spanish-speaking depend for employment on the prosperity of local agricul-ture.

While the foregoing generalizations stand, some Spanish are now mak-ing their way slowly up the socioeconomic ladder as store clerks, garage or filling station employees, a few as operators of small groceries or oil sta-tions, and several as salaried clerical personnel. There has been a gradual increase over the last 25 years in the number of Spanish-speaking who have eighth grade schooling, and gradually more go on or complete high school.[5] The war industries of the Pacific Coast attracted a number from Mountain Town and materially raised their economic level, and service in the armed forces broadened the ethnic outlook of not only Spanish but also of some Mountain Town Anglos. There is no question of palpable Spanish ac-culturation. Bilingualism, to mention an important facet, now prevails among a majority of the Spanish and increasingly one finds older people the only strict monolinguals.

Many older Anglo residents of Mountain Town feel that they have seen a definite change in the social and economic status of the Spanish-speaking, but there is no denying that traditional attitudes and traditional ethnic rela-tionships still generally prevail. The Anglo and Spanish-speaking groups are sharply distinguishable as to religion, economic status, occupational status, language, surnames, residence, and usually physical appearance. Ethnic distinctions along these lines are made by nearly all members of both groups. The Spanish are nearly all nominally Catholic and the Anglos are nearly all nominally Protestant. Political and economic control of the community is in the hands of the Anglos. There is not the slightest ques-tion of their superordinate position in relation to the Spanish as a whole, though certain individuals of Spanish background clearly receive personal respect and prestige well above that of many Anglos.

The Anglo-Spanish relationship has some of the properties of a caste system. Spanish and Anglo are practically endogamous. Religious participa-tion is mostly along ethnic lines, and many Anglo Protestants would not want the conversion of non-Protestants at the expense of any sizeable Spanish attendance in their churches. Although somewhat ill defined, there is residential distinctness in Mountain Town, and distress is felt by some Anglos at having close "Mexican" neighbors. The Spanish are excluded almost completely from Anglo social and civic organizations (*e.g.*, lodges, Volunteer Firemen, Chamber of Commerce, Junior C of C, Rotary), except to some extent, the P.T.A. and a veterans' group. In the cases of many of these organizations, the vast majority do not qualify for membership (*e.g.*, in Rotary), but the lack of qualifications appears to be largely incidental. Parties, dancing, picnics, and visiting are uniformly intra-ethnic, as are bridge, sewing circles, teas, and bazaars. As in a true caste system, obviously the sharp differentiation of interaction is not simply the will and doing of one group by itself. The Anglos, for example, find out, when they decide to broaden the membership of the Parent-Teachers Association, that it is not easy to enlist Spanish parents or to have them assume office.

Spanish Disunity

The disunity among the Spanish group is quite evident in Mountain Town. Disunity does not mean the existence of factionalism, it refers, rather, to the lack of common action and to limited group cohesion. When an issue of import to the members of the group comes up, few people will do anything about it. This has been proved many times in such things as politics, school segregation, employment, arrests, welfare aid, and in general discrimination.

Considering the distinctness of sociocultural boundaries, the disunity of the Spanish group is striking, for the rigid exclusiveness of the Anglos might theoretically be a strong factor in their cohesion. Nor can Spanish disunity find its explanation in any wide socioeconomic disparity within the group. Nevertheless, Spanish cohesion seldom transcends such verbalizations as *nosotros* ("we") or *la raza* ("our people"), a generalized resentment of Anglo dominance and discrimination, and a readiness to perceive injustice in Spanish-Anglo dealings.

Disunity is a large factor in the lack of political power of the Spanish. In Mountain Town numbers do not explain the failure of the subordinate group—a majority—to put people they trust into critical offices. The Spanish are not wholly indifferent about certain elective offices, the sheriff, for example, who, if prejudiced, may enforce the laws quite one-sidedly. The school board offices are also thought to be ethnically critical or sensitive because of constant fear of segregation. But the election of an avow-edly pro-Spanish candidate is rare indeed. Perhaps few Anglo politicians have understood the basic disunity of the Spanish, but a good many have at least recognized it. Occasionally, however, a direct appeal is made to the Spanish as Spanish. The results in Mountain Town bear out the cynical who feel it is better to ignore the ethnic issue. "They will not even vote for their own people" is commonly asserted, and this is bitterly conceded by most Spanish.

The failure of unity and leadership in politics is not the only type of weakness of the Spanish group. There is, of course, a more informal type of leadership in interethnic relations. The spokesman, as he is often called, is a leader to whom politicians or others may turn for advice and commit-ments on matters seen as affecting the interests of the ethnic group. There are two or three Spanish individuals in Mountain Town—one in particular —whom most Anglos consider to be spokesmen. The same individuals were cited by the majority of the Spanish when asked by Samora who were the leaders of their group. Yet these individuals usually make com-mitments for their group only at great risk. Actually, they generally refuse to do more than express an opinion or give very general advice. Investiga-tion failed to show that any individual among the Spanish, including those most mentioned as leaders by Spanish and by Anglos, was willing to assume the responsibilities of a real spokesman for the group. There was no reason to believe that any of the persons mentioned could actually keep significant commitments if he made them.

But if a distinction is made between the inter-ethnic leadership described above and intra-ethnic leadership,[6] is the picture of the latter more favor-able? Investigation was made by the junior author and his wife of 16 *sociedades* and *mutualistas*, lodges and mutual benefit organizations, which exist in Mountain Town with exclusively Spanish membership and objec-tives, as well as of lay societies ancillary to the Roman Catholic Church. The findings, reported in detail elsewhere, were rather uniform.[7] On the whole, the non-church associations were characterized by ineffectual leader-ship, very poor attendance, irregularity of procedure and schedule, lack of decisive action—even in inducing new members—and often a precarious existence. Careful comparison of the church-sponsored sodalities (*e.g.*, Altar Society, Family Society) revealed the priest as central to their direc-tion and probably instrumental in their better showing compared to the secular groups. Even when the priest tried to play a less prominent role, circumstances, if not his own inclinations, tended to thrust him into a position more beside than behind the figure in the chair. Lay leadership, by the priest's admission, from observation of the members, and by their testimony, was not considered adequate.

The facts about the Mountain Town Spanish suggest deficiency, then, both as to leadership in inter-ethnic relations and as to leadership of purely ethnic organizations, except those ancillary to the Church. Yet strong factors for cohesion unmistakably exist—Anglo exclusiveness, a relatively undifferentiated Spanish group, a common ethnic tongue, Spanish group concepts, recognition of group-wide grievances, their majority voting position, and even some Anglo political attempts to unify the Spanish vote. In the light of such factors, we may ask why leadership is so ineffectual among the Spanish.

The Hypothesis of Leadership Deficiency

It is the contention of this paper that four principal conditions account for the inadequacy of Spanish leadership in Mountain Town and probably to some extent among the Spanish of the larger Southwest:

1. Traditional forms (patterns) of leadership, which functioned well enough in pre-Anglo-Spanish culture, have been unadaptable and possibly a handicap to the development of adequate patterns of group leadership in the contact situation.

2. Increasingly, the status goals of the Spanish group as a whole lie in the direction of Anglo culture; for the achievement of such goals, hence, leaders relatively well adapted to the Anglo system are increasingly indicated.

3. General ambivalence and suspicion are accorded individuals of Spanish background who are "successful" since the terms of success are now largely Anglo terms (viz. (2) above), and it is widely assumed that success is bought by cooperation with the outgroup and betrayal of one's own.

4. Although caste-like enough to give sharp definition to the two groups, Anglo structure is relatively open to competent Spanish and thus permits the siphoning off of potential Spanish leadership, individuals relatively well adapted to the Anglo system.

The net result of these conditions is that, in the lack of adaptable traditional types, the only potential leaders who might be qualified to provide the kind of leadership indicated today are by virtue of their very qualifications absorbed into the larger body politic and are disqualified in the minds of their own fellows.

Discussion

1. The conclusion is widespread that what can be said about traditions of authority in Mexico, and even Latin America, applies on the whole to the Spanish of the Southwest. If so, the pre-Anglo-Spanish picture was one of strong authoritarian roles, the padre, the *patrón*, and the *jefe de familia*.[8] The *caudillo* is of course a classic Latin American type. In fact, a suggestive interpretation can be made of these roles in Spanish culture as variations on the same fundamental theme, strong and decisive authority, and F. R. Kluckhohn has commented that the Spanish-American is quite systematically trained for dependence upon such authority.[9] Such a pattern would scarcely appear by itself to be an impediment to the existence of effective Spanish leadership in inter-ethnic relations.

But the traditional pattern of local, secular authority among the Spanish is of the wrong kind. First, in many places, the *patrón* pattern was simply unable to survive the innovations of Anglo contact. In Mountain Town the *patrón-peón* relationship has no strong personal relevance for the majority of Spanish. They probably still possess some cultural adjustments to the pattern, but many lack deep roots in the community and hence lack any long-standing familial connection with local *patrón* lineages. Moreover, there is relatively little tenant or even employee relationship nowadays except with Anglo landlords or employers. Crew bosses and labor middlemen exist, to be sure, but these intercultural agents are usually themselves committed to Anglo employers.

Yet there are two *patrón*-like figures in Mountain Town, and these were the ones most often mentioned as leaders by the Spanish Samora interviewed. There was some ambivalence about them, however. Many who named these "leaders," apparently in default of anyone else, declared that they could not be counted on in a pinch or that they would not do all that they could for the Spanish people.[10] Investigation showed that these pseudo-*patrones*, when called upon, usually served their fellow Spanish in limited and personal ways. They might give an individual help in the form of advice or instructions. They sometimes helped him fill in an official form or make out an application. They might, though rarely, intercede, using their personal influence with some governmental (*i.e.*, Anglo) agency, typically the County Welfare bureau. Intercession in these cases would almost never be insistent; in fact, it is ordinarily reluctant. The pseudo-*patrones* were not reported by anyone as ever attempting to organize their people for some lasting and broadly based social action.

Interestingly enough, leadership in approximately these limited terms matches fairly well the authors' understanding of the older *patrón* pattern. The *patrón* did not form committees, found organizations, or often refer formally to his followers for common assent to social decisions. He bound them to him on a personalistic basis, with advice and counsel and by providing assistance to those lacking other resources. Such paternalistic leadership could function in the status system of colonial Mexican culture; it cannot function very extensively where the *patrón* cannot assure his followers of security in reward for their loyalty—they work for Anglos—and where even the status of the *patrón* himself is guaranteed by no *latifundium* manned with loyal retainers. Too often his status depends—even more than that of successful Anglos, he feels—upon the sufferance and approval of those in dominant positions. In such a situation erstwhile leader and follower can do little for each other in the traditional terms which were the very core of the *patrón-peón* relationship.

It may be relevant to add that the *patrón* himself was usually identified with the same general social class as those who held most of the important formal offices in the government. Ties of kinship were traditionally common between *patrón* and official. It is probably not going too far to suggest that the *patrón* himself tended in many instances to act informally as an agent of government in relation to the *peones*—"His word was law." To the extent that *patrón* status was adjusted to fit such an identification with and informal extension of governmental authority, it would likely not be an adaptable form of leadership when kinship and status identification with the dominant group were made ambivalent or impossible through their replacement by aliens.

It will be recalled that the church-sponsored societies in Mountain Town are generally the most effective ones among the Spanish. The lack of inter-ethnic leadership by the church certainly cannot be blamed, like that of the *patrón*, on any local restriction of the church's ability to function, nor probably on any intrinsic maladaptation of church leadership. Rather, the reason is probably that the Roman Church in the United States is only indirectly political and that not all its communicants are Spanish. In any event the church does not attempt to provide local leadership for the Spanish as a group in their common struggle for status. A special factor in Mountain Town is the national origin of the priests, who come from Spain. This factor may be of no consequence, however, as Southwestern Spanish parishes with American-born priests may have no greater church leadership than Mountain Town in inter-ethnic relations.

2. No attempt will be made to argue that traditional Spanish culture everywhere in the Southwest approximates that of Anglos in all its basic values. The case to the contrary has been effectively presented elsewhere, *e.g.*, concerning time orientation and the value attached to formal schooling.[11] Even with only superficial observation it is clear that "go-getter" tendencies are much less typical of Spanish than of Anglos, and there may be some basis in fact for other traits ascribed to the Spanish in the Anglo stereotype, as well as *vice-versa*.

Nevertheless, it is possible to carry the emphasis of Spanish-Anglo cultural differences to the point where certain obvious and growing similarities of goal and value are overlooked or omitted. Generalizing, necessarily, the Spanish in Mountain Town are interested in better jobs, better pay, and more material things, such as automobiles, housing, and appliances. There is increasingly a concern for having children complete at least grammar schooling and learn at least moderately fluent English. Measures taken by the school system, which either are, or are interpreted by the Spanish to be, attempts at segregation (such as a special first grade for English-deficient children), are strongly resented, as is discrimination in hiring and firing in employment, and alleged inequality in the administration of Old Age Pensions. The Spanish in Mountain Town, however, as we are emphasizing, are not very effective in changing conditions as they would.

It may be that the Mountain Town Spanish differ somewhat as to goals from those in some other parts of the Southwest. They are almost entirely landless, and are predominantly low-paid agricultural labor, a kind of rural proletariat. Yet they are resident, not essentially a migratory group. However, we are not convinced that Mountain Town is markedly unrepresentative of Spanish elsewhere in the Southwest.

The Spanish goals sketched lie in the direction of Anglo goals and for their realization a mastery of Anglo techniques and behavior patterns is necessary. Insofar as advancement toward such goals involves group-wide status, Spanish leader qualifications must necessarily include such skills as literacy, relatively high control of the English language, and knowledge of social, political, and legal usages primarily based on the dominant culture. Few Spanish in Mountain Town possess such thorough adjustment to and broad familiarity with Anglo culture, dependent as it largely is upon extensive schooling.

James B. Watson and Julian Samora

3. Only a handful of eight Spanish individuals in Mountain Town possess the necessary qualifications in markedly higher degree than their fellows. As a matter of fact, it is essentially individuals with proven ability in Anglo culture who are singled out for mention as "leaders" in the survey conducted by Samora. What, then, if anything, keeps these persons from exercising the leadership functions so generally desired by the Spanish? As was mentioned, a good deal of ambivalence exists concerning these people (almost all men) in the minds of most Spanish questioned. It is often stated that these "leaders" will not really accept an active part in directing a struggle for Spanish equality; they will only do such things for their fellow Spanish as they think will not antagonize the Anglos. They are even frequently accused of working for the Anglos and not for *la raza*. And not a few feel that such leaders could only have achieved their—usually modest—socioeconomic position at the expense of "selling out to the Anglo" or "by climbing over their own people." They are referred to as "proud" (*orgullosos*). Another adjective has been coined in Spanish especially to describe such relatively successful members of the Spanish community. Samora found that they are called *"agringados"*—"gringoized."

Here, then, is the dilemma: that the very traits which would qualify an individual to provide the sort of leadership called for are such as to cast suspicion upon his loyalty in the eyes of many he would lead. Is it that the qualified "leaders" make little effort to lead effectively because they feel—perhaps correctly—that they would have difficulty in getting an effective followership? Or is it that they get no effective following largely because of their own reluctance to exert leadership? No simple answer to the question will do, of course, particularly as leadership and followership are reciprocal roles and the lack of either precludes the other. It may be hard to say if there is a causal priority in Mountain Town between the two factors, but something more like a vicious circle is suggested by the frequent testimony of Mountain Town Spanish: many agree, on the one hand, that the relatively assimilated "leaders" are "proud" (*orgullosos*) but admit, on the other, that the people are "envious" (*envidiosos*) and are themselves unable to "follow" (*seguir*) anyone. It appears to be the case both that the hypothetical leaders are unwilling to lead and that the hypothetical followers are unable to accept followership.

4. The factors so far suggested for the default of Spanish leadership clearly have their intercultural aspects, though they appear in some respects intrinsic to the Spanish culture. The fourth factor is more completely extrinsic to the Spanish side of the picture. It is that the ranks of the Anglo social structure are not completely closed to the exceptional Spanish

individual who achieves appreciable mastery of Anglo culture. There is obviously no question about discrimination against individuals of Spanish background for equally competent Spanish and Anglos do not have an equal probability of success. But Anglo discrimination is paradoxically not rigid enough, in a sense, for the "good" of the Spanish as a group. That is, those able to deal with Anglos on their own terms frequently have a chance to do so—as individuals. Hence, they are not completely frustrated, embittered, or thrust back into their own group where they must either quit the struggle altogether or turn their energies and skills to leading their people in competition with the Anglos. Instead, although against greater obstacles than an Anglo, the unusual person frequently achieves a degree of success to some extent commensurate with his abilities relative to those of his fellows.

From the standpoint of leadership the Spanish situation is not helped by Anglo mythology. The Anglo social myth recognizes two racial types among the Spanish-speaking. One is the "Real Spanish," with higher intelligence, industry, and dependability, while the other is the "Mexican," a term frequently preceded by opprobrious adjectives according to the context. The latter type, according to the Anglo, lack ambition, and generally possess just the qualities which lodge them where they are found in the social order.

The Spanish themselves make no distinction between "Real Spanish" and "Mexicans." When referring to themselves in Spanish they use the term "*mejicanos*"; when referring to themselves in English they use the term "Spanish." When the Anglos refer to them, the Spanish prefer that they use the term "Spanish" rather than "Mexican," because of the derogatory connotation of the latter term.

There is greater social acceptance of the "Real Spanish" by Anglos, particularly when they show mastery of Anglo culture—which tends to corroborate the myth. This divisive effect of Anglo mythology on the Spanish group, although difficult to assess, is nonetheless real.

The net result of these characteristics of the Anglo system is to lower the motivation of qualified persons to lead, and perhaps to contaminate the successful individual in the view of his group. His partial acceptance by the Anglo gives seeming verification to Spanish suspicions of disloyalty. The intercultural source of this effect on subordinate leadership is dramatically underscored by the Mountain Town evidence.

The three most overtly successful Spanish individuals in Mountain Town confirm in every major respect mentioned what has been said above. They are much more competent and successful in the Anglo system than most Anglos; they are given a social acceptance by the Anglo group which, although far from unqualified, sets them markedly apart from the great majority of the Spanish; they are predominantly regarded by Anglos as "spokesmen" for the Spanish group, although by no means are they themselves willing to play the role intensively; they are mentioned with the highest frequency by the Spanish interviewed as "leaders" and the only people of their own to whom one could turn for certain kinds of assistance; but they are complained against as *orgullosos*, as being unwilling to do as much for the *raza* as they easily might, and as being subservient to the Anglo and unwilling to risk offending him. These individuals are, then, leaders largely by default and would not otherwise be mentioned as leaders. Although almost uniquely qualified in some respects to lead, they do not. In a situation where adequate inter-ethnic leadership would call for the exercise of organizing skill and close indentification of the destinies of leader and follower, these individuals largely limit themselves to personalistic functions roughly comparable to those of the *patrón* of yore, and a social distance tends to be kept which is in some respects as great as between *patrón* and *peón*. Though the comparison with traditional patterns is suggestive, we need not, as has been discussed, hark back to the *patrón* system to explain everything in the situation found today. Intercultural factors in the Spanish relationship with Anglos are of strategic importance in explaining leadership deficiency.

NOTES

1. Leonard Broom and Eshref Shevky, "Mexicans in the United States: A Problem in Social Differentiation," *Sociology and Social Research*, 36 (January 1952), pp. 150–158.

2. The term "Spanish," used throughout the paper, refers to "the Spanish-speaking people."

3. Cf. Robert C. Jones, "Mexican Youth in the United States," *The American Teacher*, 28 (March 1944), pp. 11–15; Olen Leonard and C. P. Loomis, *Culture of a Contemporary Rural Community, El Cerrito, New Mexico* (Washington: USDA, BAE, 1940); R. W. Roskelley and C. R. Clark, *When Different Cultures Meet* (Denver: Rocky Mountain Council on Inter-American Affairs, 1949); George I. Sanchez, "The Default of Leadership," in *Summarized Proceedings IV*, Southwest Council on the Education of the Spanish-Speaking People, Fourth Regional Conference (Albuquerque, New Mexico, January 23–25, 1950); Ozzie G. Simmons, *Anglo Americans and Mexican Americans in South Texas, A Study in Dominant-Subordinate Group Relations* (Ph.D. Thesis, Harvard University, 1952); Ruth D. Tuck, *Not With The Fist: Mexican-Americans in a Southwest City* (New York: Harcourt, Brace and Company), 1949.

4. Julian Samora, *Minority Leadership in a Bi-Cultural Community* (Ph.D. Thesis, Washington University, St. Louis, 1953).

5. James B. Watson, *Preliminary Observations Based on the Community of Mountain Town* (Unpublished manuscript, Washington University, St. Louis, n.d.).

6. Julian Samora, *op. cit.*, p. 52.

7. *Ibid.*, pp. 13–51.

8. O. Leonard and C. P. Loomis, *op. cit.*, p. 15.

9. F. R. Kluckhohn, "Dominant and Variant Value Orientations," in C. Kluckhohn and H. A. Murray, *Personality in Nature, Society, and Culture*, 2nd ed. rev. (New York: Knopf, 1953).

10. Julian Samora, *op. cit.*, pp. 74–76.

11. Cf. F. R. Kluckholn, *op. cit.*, pp. 352–354; R. L. Beals *op. cit.*, pp. 5–13; Arthur Campa, "Mañana is Today," in T. M. Pearce and A. P. Thomason, *Southwesterners Write* (Albuquerque: University of New Mexico Press), 1947.

PART VIII

The Culture of Racism

Editor's Introduction

One of the more fruitful traditions of sociological research that has fallen into disuse or even mild disrepute in recent years, was in fact a kind of cultural anthropology of North America. Based on techniques of field work and participant observation, it was a hallmark of the "Chicago school" under Park and some of his colleagues and disciples, such as Doyle, Stonequist, and Wirth. Among its salient qualities were sensitivity to the minutiae of symbolic behavior (such as etiquette), normative relativism, a *verstehende* approach, and empathetic understanding of the world view of underdogs. The four older pieces reprinted in this section share that general orientation. The first two, besides making for most enjoyable reading, tap a highly significant and yet neglected aspect of intergroup relations. As a source of sociological evidence, the folklore of interethnic or interracial humor is of paramount importance in understanding the more subtle, elusive and qualitative aspects of group relations, in revealing the prevailing stereotypy, and, generally, in eliciting the depth data which no questionnaire or formal interview can ever disclose. The importance of oral literature as a source of historical and sociological data is now being rediscovered in the field of African scholarship where it was originally seen as a substitute for scanty or non-existent written sources; but clearly the significance of folklore and oral literature is not limited to non-literate societies. Who can claim, for example, to understand in depth the black protest movements or indeed other radical forces such as the New Left or Women's Liberation without an empathetic grasp of their rhetoric, life style, indeed of their entire sub-culture?

Slotkin's historical ethnography of jazz and of its diffusion in American society is also of a type that sociologists have unfortunately let anthropologists pre-empt at considerable cost to the quality of their data. Not only is much of what is accepted as sociological theory unwitting North American ethnography, limited in applicability to the United States or, at best, Western industrial societies, but it is often not very good ethnography. Seeman's piece on a particularly invidious aspect of racism among brown and black Americans, while hopefully rendered obsolete through the development of black pride, remains, however, of considerable historical significance. Indeed, the very development of the "black-is-beautiful" movement as a reaction against the self-deprecation inflicted by white racism is itself creating new identity problems for the millions of Americans who do not come anywhere close to being either "white" or "black."

HUMOR AS A TECHNIQUE
IN RACE CONFLICT

The type of group behavior we call race relations contains many aspects which must be classified as conflict patterns of behavior. In conflict, the involved parties make use of a variety of techniques to gain ascendancy or temporary advantage. Since subtle barbs often strike more telling blows than gratuitous insult or rational argument, not infrequently these techniques include humor, satire, irony, and wit.[1]

Humor lends itself particularly well to use as a conflict device because of its almost boundless limits in subject matter, and because its nature is such that it often contains more or less well concealed malice. Jowett has said that every amusing story must of necessity be unkind, untrue, or immoral. Thomas Hobbes believed that humor arises from a conception of superiority in ourselves by comparison with the inferiority of others. Crothers has called it the "frank enjoyment of the imperfect," and more recently James L. Ford has said that humor "is founded on the deathless principle of seeing someone get the worst of it."[2] It is not surprising that humor frequently is used as a conflict technique.

Throughout the history of minority-majority group relations in this country the set of techniques which we may denominate by the general term humor has played a definite role in interpersonal and intergroup relationships. Apparently all minority groups suffer derogation in this manner, and apparently all use the same weapon in return. In the United States, this has been particularly true with reference to Negroes and Jews, but quite noticeable also in connection with Catholics, Mormons, Quakers, Italians, Greeks, Germans, Irish, Chinese, Japanese, Indians, Mexicans, and others.

From John H. Burma, "Humor as a Technique in Race Conflict," in *American Sociological Review*, 11 (1946), pp. 710–715.

Such use of humor may be considered as a universal phenomenon. Valid studies can be made of humor as a conflict technique in connection with any American minority group, but for purposes of cohesion and integration a single minority group, the Negro, will be discussed here.

An obvious division of "race-conscious" humor into four categories immediately presents itself. That is, the joke may be (1) by Negroes and pro-Negroes, (2) by Negroes and anti-white, (3) by whites and pro-white, or (4) by whites and anti-Negro. Types two and four are by all odds the most common and particularly fit the present discussion.

In any conflict it is most gratifying to cause one's adversary to appear ludicrous in his own eyes. Where this is not possible, very considerable satisfaction can be secured by making your opponent appear ludicrous in your eyes. It is exactly this which humor does. It is difficult to the point of impossibility to assign malice a specific role in "race" humor. One person may relate a humorous situation somewhat derogatory to a minority group and do it in all good will; possibly in his own mind taking into account only the situation itself and attaching it to a minority group only because he himself heard it told that way. He may think of himself as a liberal and as having nothing but good will for the minority involved. In other cases the same situation may be related by a different person. To him the real humor is in the discomfiture of the butt of the joke. He would see nothing of humor in the situation if the butt were of his own group. It should be pointed out further that a given joke may not appear derogatory to the majority who circulate it, but may be deemed scurrilous by the more sensitive minority who are more or less unintentionally involved.

In many instances the bit of humor is in itself merely a tool, and thus may be manipulated as any user sees fit. Thus there are many maliciously humorous situations which are related by whites with the Negro as the butt of the humor and related by Negroes with the white as the recipient of the barb. Many jokes become "race conscious" or "racially humorous" merely by the addition of color to the persons involved. For example, when a *colored* boy could not do his geometry, his *white* teacher says he should be ashamed, for when George Washington was his age he was a surveyor. To which the Negro youth replies, "Yes, and when he was your age he was President." With the simple addition of color, the barb of the humor no longer particularly strikes at teachers (pupil-teacher conflict and "teacher" stereotypes), but now becomes symbolic of the Negro-white conflict and draws its humor from the discomfiture of the stereotyped superior white.

In any event, most Negro-white wit makes one race or the other appear as the butt of the humor. In the case of jokes by whites about Negroes, it is typical that some stereotyped characteristic or supposed characteristic is the point of the humor. Stories about Negroes and chickens, chicken houses, and chicken stealing depend for part or most of their humor on the stereotyped insatiable appetite of the Negro for chicken. To a person who does not have a comparable stereotype, they hold little or no humor.[3] Very much like the above and also very common are stories centering in the thickness and hardness of the Negro's skull and the blackness of his skin.

A high percentage of humor of any type centers in the various aspects of sex, and this is true of jokes by whites about Negroes.[4] Given the not uncommon stereotyped conception of the Negro as a sexually uninhibited person, it is not surprising that a myriad of jokes exist which relate to the sexual exploits or delinquencies of the Negro, particularly Negro girls. Some depend upon sex, and some depend almost entirely upon the above mentioned stereotype.[5] A typical example of the latter is the rather lengthy story concerning the Negro man being charged with rape by a Negro girl. He explains his side of the story and concludes by telling the white jurors, "and you know as well as I do that there ain't never been *no* nigger gal raped." This convulses the jury, who immediately free him. Needless to say, without the proper stereotype, such stories are completely humorless.

Another favorite type of humor by whites about Negroes lampoons the pomposity, avarice, ignorance, and emotionalism of the stereotyped "nigger preacher" and his congregation. A large proportion of these situations might be humorous regardless of the racial angle, as is true of many other types of "Negro" jokes. Such, for example, is the case in which the visiting Negro minister catches the chief Deacon abstracting 50¢ from the collection; he remonstrates, and the Deacon replies, "Bless you, Brother, I been leadin' off with that same 50¢ piece for nearly eight years." So, too, the case of the Negro minister raising funds who tells his congregation, "The church has been walking (loud amens); but it ought to run (loud amens); it ought to do more, it ought to fly (loud amens); but to fly it needs money;" (dead silence, then one voice, "Let her walk, Brother, let her walk"). Such humor does not depend wholly on its racial connotations, but the possession of the proper stereotype adds considerably to the enjoyment of the listener.

To most Caucasians the notion of jokes by Negroes lampooning whites comes somewhat as a surprise. Yet as an actuality such humor may out-date its white counterpart. For many decades Negroes were usually in a position in which their conflict and defense techniques against the whites had to be covert rather than overt. This favored the growth of the more subtle type of humor as a weapon of both offense and defense.[6] Some modern stories still retain this subtlety of derogation; as for example the two Negro maids who were comparing notes:

"At my place I have a terrible time; all day it's 'Yes, Ma'am,' 'Yes, Ma'am,' 'Yes, Ma'am.'"

"Me, too," says the other, "but with me it's 'No, Sir,' 'No, Sir,' No, Sir.'"

It must be noted especially in this connection that humor lies primarily in the individual's reaction to a situation, not in the situation itself. Nothing in the whole field of humor is more common than the observation that a situation which is uproariously funny to one person will serve only to amuse someone else mildly, and will leave a third party blank and uncomprehending. An incident concerning a deaf man may be quite humorous to those who hear well, but completely devoid of humor for those who are hard of hearing. Thus it is typical that whites see little if anything of humor in many jokes by Negroes concerning whites, and vice versa. This holds true regardless of whether malice is intended or not. It is to be expected, for example, that the jokes here used as illustrations of anti-white humor will seldom appear humorous to white readers, and vice versa. So marked is the influence of one's viewpoint that an occasional story is told by both Negroes and whites, each thinking it is a joke on the other party. One such example concerns the new Negro foreign language professor who attempts to vote in the southern town in which his college is located. He must pass a literacy test. He is given a newspaper and asked what it says. He reads from it. He is given in succession Spanish, French, and German papers, from which he reads. Then he is given a Chinese paper and triumphantly asked what it says. Unable to read Chinese, he throws it down saying, "It says Negroes can't vote in——!"

It is unfortunate that many of the most illustrative jokes against whites, like those against Negroes are too crude and obscene for the printed word. In them the real power of the pent-up animosity of the Negro appear most clearly and starkly. These bits of humor very commonly involve "the retort discourteous" by a Negro girl[7] to a white woman or to a white man. Less frequently is a Negro man involved; seldom is the alleged conversation between a Negro man and white woman, except in the case of stories transmitted solely by oral methods. One of the rare exceptions to this is the story of the white woman who enters a street car; a white soldier surrenders his seat which is next to a Negro civilian. She says "I won't sit next to that 4F nigger."

The Negro calmly asks, "Have you a son in the service?"

"I have two, both overseas."

"Good," says the Negro, "tell them to look for the right arm I left over there."

The lady got off at the next stop.

To the Negro any joke is particularly humorous if it shows Jim-Crow "back-firing" on a southerner. Rather common is the situation in which a Negro is treated as a "darky" and then is discovered to be the superior of the white in distinction, education, or rank. Typical is the situation during the late war in which a southern officer stationed in England was seated next to a Negro at an official dinner. He completely ignores the Negro until the end of the meal, when he condescends to remark, "Rastus, Ah reckon you-all miss yo' watermelon." It soon develops that the Negro is the guest-of-honor, a renowned Oxford scholar, and a high colonial official who makes a brilliant speech. Naturally the officer figits very uncomfortably and when the Negro sits down he says sarcastically to the officer, "Yes, Rastus sho' do miss his watermelon."

A back-firing Jim Crow story now going the rounds reputedly concerns a high officer in the National Urban League. This Negro wishes to purchase a car in Atlanta. The white salesman greets him warmly, but constantly refers to him as "boy." All is arranged, but the "boy" says he wishes to wait a day to make the final decision. When he returns he is greeted with "Glad to see you, boy. You'll be proud of this car; not another boy in Atlanta will have a better one."

"Sorry," the Negro replies, "but the deal is off. I read the law last night and it says minors in Georgia cannot purchase cars; and since I am a boy, as you have so frequently reminded me, it would be illegal to buy a car from you." With which he exits.

As often as not the stories of the back-fire of Jim-Crow attitudes contain a sort of double bitterness toward the restrictions and toward the attitudes of the whites who impose such restrictions.[8] When such attitudes and such restrictions both react against the white, the story is doubly appreciated. For example, in an Eastern college city a torrid romance between a light-skinned colored boy and a white girl was interrupted by the draft. A year later he was back on furlough; to his surprise she had become a mother.

"Why didn't you write me you were married?"

"I'm not; and this is your child."

"Why didn't you tell me; I would have come home and married you."

"I know, but I talked it over with my family and they decided they'd rather have an illegitimate child in the family than a nigger."

As a matter of fact, colored people very commonly laugh at the absurdity of Jim-Crow incidents or the variegated nuances of the color line. They could hardly accept the white world's daily boorishness in any other way and retain their mental equilibrium.[9] This may account for the following story told the author by Negroes in three different areas; in each case it was recounted as an actual incident.

"I went into the store at —————— to get some tobacco. I asked for 'Prince Albert' and the clerk said 'See the man on that can? He's white. Say "Mister Prince Albert." I thought for a minute and then said 'No thank you, sir; I believe I'll just take Bull Durham; I don't have to "mister" him.' "

Negroes as a whole recognize that some whites are more their foes than are others. Thus Rankin, Bilbo, Dies, Talmadge, Eastland, G. L. K. Smith, the K.K.K., D.A.R., and "southern crackers" receive more than their share of barbed sallies. So do the poll tax, share cropping, segregated schools, southern politics, segregation in the army, and the like.

Not infrequently "race" humor has a grim and even macabre quality. Such is the famous cartoon which appeared first in the *People's Voice* of New York after the Detroit riots. It portrayed two small white boys looking at hunting trophies hanging on the wall of father's den. Among them is the mounted head of a Negro. One small boy says proudly, "Dad got that one in Detroit last week." To many whites the idea is devoid of humor; yet, many Negroes thought it unusually funny and it was reprinted a number of times.

Langston Hughes attributes another such story to a late college president.[10] In its essentials the incident is that the president was descending the train steps at Atlanta when he heard a scream behind him. A white woman had caught her heel and was falling head first down the steps. The Negro raised his arms to catch her and then quickly dropped them to his sides and let her fall. At this point his Negro audiences usually were swept by gales of laughter, for that was the end of the joke. To them it was funny, for they well knew that in Atlanta something very serious was likely to happen to any Negro who for any reason put his arms around a white woman. She was hurt badly, but it was a good joke on Jim-Crow. Much the same technique was used by Jay Jackson when the Negro hero of his comic strip "Bungleton Green" is unable to make whites believe saboteurs are about to blow up the local war plant. He deliberately trips a white girl and then catches her in his arms. Pursued by the angry lynch-bent mob, he leads them direct to the saboteurs and then explains the necessity for his dangerous action. It is this same hero and his girl friend whose well chosen, sonorous phrases, clear enunciation, and philosophical speeches are constantly contrasted with the poorly enunciated, ungrammatical and illogical speech of the white southerners.

A refinement of this technique is frequently used by one of the largest Negro magazines. Its page, "The African Way," contains numerous jokes in which the untutored African savage makes a fool of the white man or ridicules satirically the white man's beliefs, actions, or culture. Also, during the war many jokes circulated by Negroes had a double flavor, for the whites involved were designated as German Nazis or Italian Fascists. This enabled the humorist to "kill two birds with one stone," so that such jokes were frequently particularly malicious and especially successful.

It must not be inferred that most jokes told by Negroes are "race conscious" jokes. This is no more true than to infer that all jokes told by whites are for purposes of minority group defamation. What is true is that from the huge welter of humor, wit, and satire which is current today, both written and oral, it is possible to isolate and examine a not inconsequential amount of humor which has as its primary purpose the continuation of race conflict.[11] Even more common is the borderline type; its chief purpose is humor, but it has secondary aspects which definitely can be related to racial competition and conflict and the social and cultural patterns which have arisen from them.

It might be argued that "race conscious" humor is not actually a conflict technique, since much of it is humorous even if not racially applied, and that racial connotations are chiefly fortuitous. This may be true for a given bit of wit, but not for the totality. Any persons or groups who are the butt of jokes thereby suffer discriminatory treatment and are indirectly being relegated to an inferior status. This is, in turn, typical of conflict in general and gives additional support to the fact that humor is one of the mechanisms rather frequently pressed into use in the racial conflicts of America.

NOTES

1. "Wit is a Weapon," (unsigned editorial), Nation, 939 (November 28, 1934), p. 609.

2. All quoted in Milton Wright, What's Funny—and Why (New York: McGraw-Hill, 1939), pp. 6–8.

3. Cf. David L. Cohen, "White Folks are Easy to Please," Saturday Review of Literature, 27 (November 25, 1944), p. 12.

4. Cf. Gunnar Myrdal, An American Dilemma (New York: Harpers, 1944), p. 38.

5. For a more detailed discussion of Negro-white sexual stereotypes see John Dollard, *Caste and Class in a Southern Town* (New Haven: Yale University Press, 1937), Chap. 7 and pp. 394–398.

6. For a discussion of covert types of Negro aggression see Dollard, *op. cit.*, Chap. 14, passim, and W. E. B. DuBois, *The Souls of Black Folk* (Chicago: McClurg & Co., 1903), pp. 204–205.

7. For a discussion of different standards of caste behavior for Negro men and women, see Dollard, *op. cit.*, pp. 288–289.

8. B. F. Doyle, *The Etiquette of Race Relations in the South* (University of Chicago Press, 1937), p. 163.

9. See Myrdal, *op. cit.*, pp. 38–39, and Dollard, *op. cit.*, Chap. 14, passim.

10. *The Best of Negro Humor* (Chicago: Negro Digest Publications, 1945), p. 96.

11. Cf. Myrdal, *op. cit.*, p. 38.

A CONTENT ANALYSIS
OF INTERGROUP HUMOR

A curious "step-child" in sociological research is humor. This may be the result of an implicit and dubious assumption among sociologists that jokes are, by their very nature, frivolous and frivolity in human relations does not merit their attention. Psychologists, on the other hand, have given the subject much of their time and efforts,[1] and philosophers continue to probe its elusive nature today,[2] continuing a line of interest which dates back to Aristotle.[3]

The questions which these psychologists, philosophers and others[4] have sought to answer have been few. Why do people laugh? What is the nature of humor? What are the techniques of humor? Yet there is virtually no agreement among them in answer to the first two questions.[5]

For the few interested sociologists, the function of humor—especially intergroup humor—has been the center of attention.[6] They are agreed on a fairly obvious point that humor is a special product as well as a medium with social functions.[7] But they disagree among themselves and with others who are not sociologists in defining a theory of the function of humor. Obrdlik and Burma, for example, propose that humor functions as an effective weapon of social conflict and control. Witness its use of irony, invective and sarcasm. It enhances and reenforces the morale of those who use it and deflates the victims against whom it is directed. Specifically in minority-majority group relations, humor is one of many conflict devices used by each group in its interaction with others in order to attain or retain ascendancy in status and morale.[8]

Others take issue with exclusive devotion to the conflict-control theory

From Milton L. Barron, "A Content Analysis of Intergroup Humor," in *American Sociological Review*, 15 (1950), pp. 88–94.

of humor. Myers[9] points out that laughter is not always malicious; it is often colored by annoyance with the object, but frequently it is accompanied by liking, respect, and even reverence for the object. Dollard recognizes the aggressive orientation of some jokes, but he cautions that joking may serve purposes other than the expression of hostility.[10] Eastman claims that although many of the most popular jokes release our suppressed impulse to "take a crack" at somebody,[11] one needs to refer to Piaget's position that a laughing baby cannot possibly have attitudes of derision toward and superiority over others. This is because of a baby's incomplete consciousness of self and others.[12] Furthermore, men may enjoy more fully the jokes on women, and women on men, but men do laugh at jokes on men, and women at jokes on women.[13] Myrdal's adherence to the conflict-control theory is also qualified, for he finds other functions for intergroup humor within the framework of his general theory of the *American Dilemma.* He maintains that "when people are up against great inconsistencies in their creed and behavior which they cannot, or do not want to, account for rationally, humor is a way out. It gives a symbolic excuse for imperfections, a point to what would otherwise be ambiguous. It gives also a compensation to the sufferer. The 'understanding laugh' is an intuitive absolution between sinners and sometimes also between the sinner and his victim. The main 'function' of the joke is thus to create a collective surreptitious approbation for something which cannot be approved explicitly because of moral inhibitions."[14] Lastly, there is Freud's support of Myers, Dollard, Myrdal and Eastman with special reference to jokes directed against Jews. He maintains that a number of such jokes do not conform to the conflict-control theory of humor because they were invented by Jews themselves engaging in self-criticism.[15]

It is futile to anticipate a resolution of this and other controversies among philosophers, psychologists and sociologists of humor until an empirical body of descriptive, systematic and classified data on jokes is made available. Intergroup humor may well be a convenient point of departure in gathering such data, for sociologists have already demonstrated special interest in it. The raw material may be sought in the several published anthologies of humor. However, censorship does preclude a claim for perfect representativeness. That is, many jokes concerning intergroup relations as well as other social phenomena are characterized by obscenity in oral communication but censored in script by revision or deletion.[16]

Aims and Methodology

No attempt will be made in this paper to formulate a new theory of inter-group humor. Rather, its aims are to initiate the empirical and systematic classification of descriptive data necessary for a subsequent formulation of such a theory, and to pose some questions which the theory must answer.

For purposes of this paper, three American ethnic groups, Negroes, Jews, and Irish were selected and jokes about them were sought in three anthologies.[17] A thorough cross-check of the anthologies was made for duplicated jokes. Their elimination led to a work-field of 300 Negro, 160 Jewish, and 274 Irish jokes, a total of 734 for the three groups combined. The next step was to analyze and classify each group's jokes under the following six categories: (1) dialect, (2) theme, (3) proper names, (4) sex composition, (5) occupations, and (6) intergroup or intragroup composition.

Findings

The pervasiveness of stereotypes in intergroup jokes thus became evident.

DIALECT

Consider, for example, the use of dialect. As the accompanying table shows, in all but 2.6 per cent of the Negro jokes, at least one Negro participant speaks in "Negro" dialect, whereas in each of 66.8 per cent of the Jewish and 79.5 per cent of the Irish jokes there is at least one Jew or Irish speaking in the respective dialects. Even the rare professional Negro in jokes uses dialect, and it is not unusual for a Jewish child to do likewise.

In what social patterns does dialect appear? Jokes in which two members of the same ethnic group are participants, one of whom speaks in dialect and the other does not, account for only 2.3 per cent of the Negro, 2.5 per cent of the Jewish and 2.9 per cent of the Irish jokes. Those in which a Negro, Jew or Irishman engages in conversation with a member of an outgroup, neither of the participants using dialect, account for only 1 per cent of the Negro, 2.5 per cent of the Jewish and 1.4 per cent of the

Percentage of Jokes in Dialect

	Negro	Jewish	Irish
Use dialect	97.3	66.8	79.5
Intragroup—one only	2.3	2.5	2.9
Intergroup—neither	1.0	2.5	1.4
Intergroup—both	0.0	1.8	1.1
Intergroup—minority no outgroup yes	0.0	0.0	0.0

Irish jokes. In other jokes involving outgroup participants, no case may be found in which the Negro and white both use dialect, whereas only 1.8 per cent of the comparable Jewish jokes and 1.1 per cent of the comparable Irish jokes have dialect-speaking Gentiles and non-Irishmen respectively. Again, there are no cases of either Negroes, Jews or Irish refraining from dialect in the presence of outgroup affiliates who do. The only alternative pattern of dialect usage in jokes containing outgroup participants is the one most widely used: *the Negro, Jew or Irishman speaks in dialect; the white, Gentile, or non-Irishman does not.*

THEMES

Many of the individual jokes about the three minority groups have two or more themes. Recording each theme as a separate unit and calculating its absolute frequency, a comparative order-rank emerges for the respective groups as shown in the table on page 293.

A clear-cut deduction is that Jewish joke-themes are most readily stereotyped among all three groups, followed in order by Negro and Irish themes. There is relatively little variation in depicting Jewish traits and activities in jokes. But some stereotypes are not so exclusively "Jewish" that transposal to another group is impossible, a procedure known to take place between Negro and white jokes.[18] For example:

ABERDEEN

"Katz, a traveling salesman, was held up in the West by a storm and flood. He telegraphed his boss, Klein, in New York: 'Marooned by storm. Wire instructions.' Klein wired back: 'Start summer vacation as of yesterday.' "[19]

"A traveling salesman, with headquarters in this old city so celebrated for its parsimonious natives, was held up in the Shetland Islands by a severe wintry gale. He telegraphed his office: 'Marooned by storm. Wire instructions.' The reply: 'Commence summer vacation as of yesterday.' "[20]

Order-Rank	Negroes	Jews	Irish
1	"Deviant" behavior (91)*	Commercial and financial skills and obsessions (116)	Paradox (53)
2	Verbal difficulty and mental inferiority (86)	Verbal blunders (23)	Verbal difficulty and mental inferiority (38)
3	Religious fervor and participation (52)	Obnoxious personality traits (21)	Cleverness (34)
4	Poverty (43)	Peculiar names and concealment (8)	Alcoholism (25)
5	Marital conflict and sexual disorganization (41)	Food taboos (4)	Belligerence (19)
6	Subjection to ridicule and exploitation (18)	Unclassified (3)	Improvidence (15)
7	Maladjustment (11)		Trials and imprisonment (14)
8	Fear (11)		Religious devotion (12)
9	Color value system (11)		Xenophobia (11)
10	Eating (9)		Falls from elevation (9)
11	Animals (7)		Funerals and wakes (9)
12	Cleverness (5)		Ethnocentrism (6)
13	Prestige search (5)		Marital conflict (6)
14	Lodge benefits (4)		Derogation of others (5)
15	Other (than color) physical traits (4)		Something for nothing (5)
16	Money (2)		Antagonism to M.D.'s (5)
17	Railroad (2)		Theft (4)
18	Unclassified (4)		Prolific fertility (4)
			Laziness (4)
			Marriages and weddings (4)
			Deflation (3)
			Physical traits (3)
			Leg-pulling (3)
			Self-evidence (3)
			Philosophical outlook (3)
			Self-negation (3)
			Reversal of meaning (3)
			Lying (2)
			Name confusion (2)
			Preference for lower class (2)
			Carelessness (2)
			Literal vs. derived meaning (2)
			Noise (2)
			Unclassified (27)

*Bracketed numbers in this and subsequent classifications refer to the absolute frequency of the specified item.

Order-Rank	Negroes	Jews	Irish
1	Rastus (41)	Cohen (27)	Pat (Patrick) (90)
2	Sam (18)	Abie (Abraham) (21)	Mike (Michael) (48)
3	Sambo (17)	Ikey (Ike) (21)	Murphy (16)
4	Mose (17)	Levy (Levi) (14)	Casey (14)
5	Mandy (16)	Izzy (7)	Bridget (11)
6	(E)liza (11)	Moe (7)	Dennis (7)
7	Brown (7)	Isaac (5)	(O')Sullivan (5)
8	Johnson (7)	Isidore (4)	Hogan (4)
9	Jones (6)	Rachel (4)	Kelly (4)
10	Ephraim (4)	Katz (4)	McGinnis (4)
11	Jim (4)	Dave (David) (3)	(O')Grady (3)
12	Dinah (4)	Goldberg (3)	Rafferty (3)
13	Lijah (4)	Silverstein (3)	Dooley (3)
14	Jackson (4)	Sol (Solomon) (2)	(O')Ryan (3)
15	Remus (3)	Klein (2)	Riley (O'Reilly) (3)
16	Zeke (3)	Finklestein (2)	O'Brien (3)
17	Henry (3)	Jake (Jakey) (2)	(O')Halloran (2)
18	Ike (2)	Rifka (2)	Hooley (2)
19	Pompey (2)	Rubinstein (2)	(O')Brannigan (2)
20	Amos (2)	Isaacstein (2)	Peter (2)

Stereotypes in Negro joke-themes have been analyzed and interpreted in general terms elsewhere.[21] Comparison of Negro and Jewish joke-themes reveals an interesting paradox. That is, for Negroes, allegedly a "racial" group, religious themes occupy third place in order-rank. On the other hand, for Jews, allegedly a "religious" group, virtually no such joke-themes are found. In a comparison of Negro, Jewish, and Irish joke-themes, one finds verbal difficulty or blunder the second in rank for all three groups. Mental deficiency and poverty are prominent with reference to Negroes and Irish but negligible in the case of Jews.

Of special interest in Irish joke-themes is the first order-rank given to the paradox or "Irish Bull." This is especially significant because of its apparent inconsistency with the conflict-control theory of humor. Here the object of the joke is its creator too. In Irish jokes "it often happens that the humor is unintentional. Of this kind the 'Irish Bull' is the outstanding example. This ludicrous blunder in speech—the *Taurus Hibernicus*—is an amusing juxtaposition of opposite meanings and mixed metaphors, and is said to derive its name from one Obadiah Bull, an Irish lawyer practicing at the English Bar about the middle of the eighteenth century who became famous for his blunders in speaking. . . ."[22]

PROPER NAMES

Although Negro dialect and Jewish joke-themes are more clearly stereo-typed than their counterparts in the comparable minority groups, Irish names surpass Negro and Jewish names in clarity of stereotype. Pat and Mike, as the accompanying classification of the twenty leading names in each group demonstrates, make absolute as well as proportionate appearances far beyond those of any given Negro or Jewish names. Another differential lies in the greater use of first names for Negro participants as contrasted with the preponderance of surnames in the cases of Jews and Irish.

SEX COMPOSITION

Sex composition in intergroup jokes may take any one of at least ten alternative patterns. It is self-evident that these alternatives in turn fall into two general divisions: (1) the intrasexual and (2) the intersexual. Their distribution in Negro, Jewish, and Irish jokes is shown in the table on page 296.

Males are participants in intergroup jokes much more frequently than females. Furthermore, most jokes about Negroes, Jews, and Irishmen are intrasexual, and within that framework, the outstanding patterns are (1) two minority males, (2) two intergroup males, and (3) one minority male. Within the other framework, that of intersexual jokes, all three groups share one outstanding pattern—that of minority male and minority female. The remaining intersexual patterns which, of course, have intergroup participants, distribute themselves differently in Negro and Irish jokes on the one hand and Jewish jokes on the other. That is, the former more frequently have a minority female and an outgroup male, whereas in the latter the reverse is true: one finds more often a minority male and an outgroup female.[23]

It may be significant that both of the last mentioned intersexual patterns usually have caste characteristics. Accompanying the patterns, one usually finds explicit indications of occupational stratification re-enforced by age differentiation or spatial distance. For example, those jokes which involve a Negro female and a white male describe the relationship as that of maid-patient, client-lawyer, patient-doctor, cook-master, student-school official, or wash-woman-conductor. Those involving a Negro male and a white female describe impersonal interactions by phone, or concern student-teacher and handyman-housewife. In comparable Jewish jokes, the Jewish

Sex Patterns in Intergroup Jokes

	Negroes		Jews		Irish	
	No. of Jokes	Per-centage	No. of Jokes	Per-centage	No. of Jokes	Per-centage
I. *Intrasexual*						
a) two minority males	80	26.7	44	27.5	53	19.34
b) two minority females	5	1.7	1	0.6	6	2.18
c) two intergroup males	101	33.7	38	23.8	62	22.62
d) two intergroup females	19	6.3	0	—	5	1.82
e) one minority male	35	11.9	38	23.8	101	36.86
f) one minority female	7	2.4	0	—	5	1.82
II. *Intersexual*						
a) minority male and female	26	8.7	14	8.8	14	5.10
b) minority male and outgroup female	6	2.0	12	7.5	4	1.45
c) minority male and outgroup male	12	4.0	2	1.2	8	2.90
d) minority male—female outgroup male	—	—	—	—	2	0.725
Unclassified cases	9	3.0	11	6.8	14	5.10
Totals	300	100.0	160	100.0	274	100.0

male and Gentile female engage in phone conversations, or are markedly stratified as salesman-housewife, student-teacher, and furrier-customer. The few Jewish jokes whose pattern involves a Jewish female and a Gentile male take the form of passenger in relationship to conductor or ticket agent. In jokes whose participants are Irish male and non-Irish female, a gardener or carpenter confronts a housewife. When an Irish female and non-Irish male are the participants, the relationship is that of maid-master, plaintiff-lawyer, tenant-landlord, patient-doctor, or janitress-artist.

OCCUPATIONS

There are two significant and related characteristics in the occupational affiliation of Negro joke participants. Whenever there is a white participant in a Negro joke, his or her occupation is *always* revealed, but in the all-Negro jokes, one frequently does not learn each participant's occupation. Secondly, the white's occupation, with one exception,[24] is obviously superior to that of the Negro who participates in the same joke with him.

As the following classification of the twelve leading Negro-white, Jewish and Irish joke-occupations reveals, white occupations are far superior on the whole to those of Negroes. If one removes the religious occupations of minister and deacon, the Negro's work is decidedly menial. Aside from the

Joke-Occupations by Race and Ethnicity

Order-Rank	Negroes	Whites	Jews	Irish
1	Minister (39)	Judge (20)	Clothier (15)	Laborer (20)
2	Maid (10)	Housewife (12)	Unspecified Businessman (12)	Priest (19)
3	Deacon (8)	Doctor (10)	Student (7)	Defendant-Prisoner (9)
4	Laundress (7)	Lawyer (8)	Passenger (4)	Housewife (8)
5	Porter (5)	Minister (6)	Patient (3)	Soldier (7)
6	Soldier (4)	Employer (4)	Furrier (3)	Maid-Servant (6)
7	Laborer (4)	Farmer (3)	Salesman (3)	Construction Worker (5)
8	Student (3)	Boss (3)	Tailor (3)	Job Applicant-Unemployed (4)
9	Waiter (3)	Planter (2)	Storeowner (2)	Driver-Coachman (4)
10	Handyman (3)	Passenger (2)	Lawyer (2)	Juror (3)
11	Barber (2)	Foreman (2)	Peddler (2)	Witness (3)
12	Farmer (2)	Traveler (2)	Pawnbroker (2)	Seaman (3)

Negro-white contrast, one is struck by the greater similarity between Negro and Irish occupations than between either group and the Jews.

INTER-INTRAGROUP COMPOSITION

The classification below shows there is the least uncertainty about intra- or intergroup composition in the case of Negro jokes. In addition, Negro jokes have a slight predominance of intergroup participants, whereas Jewish and Irish jokes relate Jew to Jew and Irish to Irish more often than they relate Jew to Gentile or Irish to non-Irish. In those Jewish jokes in which the specific outgroup identity of the Gentile participants is given, the Irish appear most frequently, followed by the Scotch, English, Catholics, and Protestants. In comparable Irish jokes, the English are outstanding participants, followed by the Scotch, Jews, Swedes, Negroes, Americans, and Dutch.

Percentage of Jokes by Group Composition

	Intra	Inter	No Indication or Uncertainty
Negro	49.0	50.33	0.67
Jewish	46.8	41.2	12.0
Irish	45.2	35.7	19.1

Conclusions

How does this content analysis relate itself to the conflict-control theory of intergroup humor? Among other things, it poses the following questions which an adequate theory must cover:

1. Why are there differentials in the stereotypes of comparable minorities? Specifically, why are Negro dialect, Jewish themes, and Irish names more intensively stereotyped than their counterparts in the minority triumvirate?

2. Why does the male more frequently appear in intergroup jokes than the female?

3. Who invent and orally communicate these jokes? Until this question is answered, the conflict-control theorists may be said to operate on a tenuous assumption that the ingroup only supports the ingroup and attacks the outgroup whenever it engages in intergroup joke verbalization.

4. What basis is there to the suspicion[25] that minority "victims" may in some cases invent as well as communicate such jokes about themselves?

5. Should the aforementioned suspicion be well-founded, to what extent is self-hatred involved? To what extent is antagonism between subdivisions of a minority group involved?

Evidently, answers to the last three questions must be sought by empirical research in the field of *oral* communication.

NOTES

1. Of major significance is the work of Sigmund Freud. See A. A. Brill, ed., *The Basic Writings of Sigmund Freud* (New York: Random House), 1938, Book IV, pp. 633–803. Less pretentious psychological studies are represented by Herbert Barry, "The Role of Subject Matter in Individual Differences in Humor," *Journal of Genetic Psychology*, 35 (March 1928), pp. 112–128; Norman R. F. Maier, "A Gestalt Theory of Humor," *British Journal of Psychology*, 23 (July 1932), pp. 69–74; H. A. Wolff and C. E. Smith, "The Psychology of Humor," *Journal of Abnormal and Social Psychology*, 28 (January-March 1934), pp. 341–365; Donald Hayworth, "The Social Origin and Function of Laughter," *Psychological Review*, 35 (September 1928), pp. 367–384.

2. See, for example, Arthur Koestler, *Insight and Outlook* (New York: Macmillan, 1949), Part I, pp. 3–110.

3. See Freud's acknowledgments in Brill, *op. cit.*, pp. 633–803.

4. Miscellaneous lay analysts of humor include David L. Cohn, "White Folks Are Easy to Please," *Saturday Review of Literature*, 27 (November 25, 1944), pp. 12–13; Langston Hughes, *The Best of Negro Humor* (Chicago: Negro Digest Publications, 1945); Milton Wright, *What's Funny and Why* (New York: McGraw-Hill, 1939).

5. Stanley Walker, "What is Humor?" *North American Review*, 243 (March 1937), pp. 176–184.

6. An exception is Antonin J. Obrdlik, " 'Gallows Humor'—A Sociological Phenomenon," *American Journal of Sociology*, 47 (March 1942), pp. 709–716.

7. *Ibid.*, p. 709.

8. *Ibid.*, pp. 715–716; John H. Burma, "Humor as a Technique in Race Conflict," *American Sociological Review*, 11 (December 1946), pp. 710–711. Consistent with this theory is Burma's four-fold classification of Negro-white humor. That is, jokes may be (1) by Negroes and pro-Negro, (2) by Negroes and anti-white, (3) by white and pro-white, (4) or by whites and anti-Negro.

9. Henry Alonzo Myers, "The Analysis of Laughter," *The Sewanee Review*, 43 (October-December 1935), p. 5.

10. John Dollard, *Caste and Class in a Southern Town* (New Haven: Yale University Press, 1937), p. 309.

11. Max Eastman, "What We Laugh At—and Why," *Reader's Digest* 42 (April 1943), pp. 66–68.

12. Max Eastman, *Enjoyment of Laughter* (New York: Simon and Schuster, 1936), pp. 30–31.

13. *Ibid.*, p. 59.

14. Gunnar Myrdal, *An American Dilemma* (New York: Harper and Brothers, 1944), pp. 38–39.

15. Brill, *op. cit.*, p. 705.

16. Cf. Max Eastman, "Wit and Nonsense: Freud's Mistake," *Yale Review*, 26 (September 1936), p. 71; Burma, *op. cit.*, pp. 712–713.

17. Lewis and Faye Copeland, eds., *10,000 Jokes, Toasts and Stories* (New York: Garden City Publishing Company, 1946); Lewis Copeland, ed., *The World's Best Jokes* (New York: Halcyon House, 1948); Moulton Powers, ed., *Best Jokes For All Occasions* (New York: Permabooks, 1948).

18. Cohn, *op. cit.*, pp. 12–13; Burma, *op. cit.*, p. 711.

19. Powers, *op. cit.*, p. 186.

20. *The New York Times Magazine Section* (February 6 ,1949), p. 2.

21. Cohn, *op. cit.*, pp. 12–13; Burma, *op. cit.*, pp. 711–712; Dollard, *op. cit.*, pp. 136–137, 160, 162, 168–170.

22. P. A. Sillard, "Some Irish Bulls," *Catholic World*, 145 (September 1937), pp. 696–697.

23. For the implications this may have in comparative aspects of American caste systems, see Milton L. Barron, *People Who Intermarry* (Syracuse: Syracuse University Press, 1946), pp. 179–180.

24. "A white man during reconstruction times was arraigned before a colored justice of the peace for killing a man and stealing his mule. It was in Arkansas, near the Texas border, and there was some rivalry between the states, but the colored justice tried to preserve an impartial frame of mind.

" 'We's got two kinds of law in dis yer co't,' he said: 'Texas law an' Arkansas law. Which will you hab?'

"The prisoner thought a minute and then guessed that he would take the Arkansas law.

" 'Den I discharge you fo' stealin' de mule, an' hang you fo' killin' de man.'

" 'Hold on a minute judge,' said the prisoner. 'Better make that Texas law.'

" 'All right. Den I fin' you fo' killin' de man an' hang you fo' stealin' de mule.' " Copeland and Copeland, eds., *op. cit.*, p. 657.

25. The "Irish Bull," for example, is one source of suspicion.

JAZZ AND ITS FORERUNNERS
AS AN EXAMPLE
OF ACCULTURATION

An interesting illustration of R. E. Park's thesis that continued contact between two groups leads to eventual assimilation, is to be found in the development of jazz, which reflects the increasing contact between Negroes and whites in the United States. With this contact one characteristic after another of Negro music has been gradually adopted by popular white music. First, a stereotype of Negro music which had little relation to the real thing was developed in the coon song of the minstrel show; then the simpler aspects of Negro musical rhythm were taken over in ragtime, followed by the diffusion of Negro harmonies to produce the blues. Finally, as a result of more intimate contact, most of the features of Negro music were taken over through the medium of hot jazz, which in turn has now been modified by white music.

American Negro Music

Too little is known about African and early American white music to be able to determine the relative influence of each upon the development of American Negro music. At any rate, the introduction of the Negro to

From J. S. Slotkin, "Jazz and Its Forerunners as an Example of Acculturation," in *American Sociological Review*, 8 (1943), pp. 570–575.

the Americas produced a musical fusion, of which the best early description is the following:

The voices of the colored people have a peculiar quality that nothing can imitate; and the intonations and delicate variations of even one singer cannot be reproduced on paper. . . . There is no singing in *parts*, as we understand it, and yet no two appear to be singing the same thing—the leading singer starts the words of each verse, often improvising, and the others, who "base" him, as it is called, strike in with the refrain, or even join in the solo when the words are familiar. When the "base" begins, the leader often stops, leaving the rest of the words to be guessed at, or it may be they are taken up by one of the other singers. And the "basers" themselves seem to follow their own whims, beginning when they please and leaving off when they please, striking an octave above or below (in case they have pitched the tune too high), or hitting some other note that chords, so as to produce the effect of a marvellous complication and variety and yet with the most perfect time and rarely with any discord.[1]

This American Negro music has influenced white American popular music, and it is the purpose of the present paper to sketch that influence.

Coon Songs, 1830–1890[2]

In the period of the coon song the majority of white people had little or no contact with Negroes, so that a stereotype of Negro music developed which had scant relation to the real thing.

During the period of slavery, there were musically gifted Negroes on many plantations.

Every plantation had its talented band that could crack Negro jokes, and sing and dance to the accompaniment of the banjo and the bones—the bones being the actual ribs of a sheep or some other small animal, cut the proper length and scraped clean and bleached in the sun. When the wealthy plantation-owner wished to entertain and amuse his guest, he needed only to call for his troupe of black minstrels. There is a record of at least one of these bands that became semi-professional and travelled round from plantation to plantation giving performances.[3]

These Negroes were heard by white entertainers who imitated them; there is a record of a white impersonator of Negroes in New York City as early as 1769.[4] But the founder of the classical minstrel tradition was Thomas D. Rice, who in 1830, as "Jim Crow," imitated the mannerisms, costume, song, and dance of a Negro whom he came across while one day strolling along the river front of Cincinnati.[5] At first actual Negro music and songs were used, but with the development of the minstrel show by white men who had no first-hand acquaintance with Negro life and music a stereotype was established, according to which the Negro was predominantly interested in fried chicken, watermelon, dice, cutting people with a razor, and singing sentimental songs about the South.[6] The songs of Stephen Foster represent the best of this tradition. When Negroes finally began to participate in minstrel shows, the stereotypes were so fixed that they imitated their white impersonators and did not go back to the authentic Negro traditions. The only real Negro characteristic of minstrel music was intermittent syncopation. To the banjo, castanet bones, and the jawbone of a calf or mule struck with a shin bone, a violin and tambourine would usually be added from the collection of European instruments.[7]

Ragtime, 1891–1914

The first distinctive characteristic taken over by the whites from Negro music was its syncopated rhythm; it had been used intermittently in minstrel music, but the regular use of the simpler syncopations produced ragtime.

With the advent of Negro entertainers on Broadway who freed themselves from the conventional trammels of the minstrel show, white people for the first time had an adequate opportunity to discover the nature of Negro music. The startling effects of Negro musical rhythm first came to the attention of the white world through Negro musical comedies produced in the early 1890's. The first of these was the *Creole Show,* in which the minstrel tradition was broken by a group of colored ex-minstrels, chorus, and dance team. Negro rhythms thus introduced were then taken up by Tin Pan Alley and swept the country. Ragtime reached its peak in 1910.

The ragtime era had its orchestral arrangers, but interest was so intensely concentrated upon purely rhythmical effects, and so orthodox was the constitution of the ragtime band, that little progress was made in tone-color contrapuntal humor and the other devices characteristic of jazz.

The ragtime band, indeed, especially as it was known to the whites of the middle Nineties, was the same band that played in the orthodox ball rooms of the day.[8]

Blues, 1914–1917[9]

The second characteristic of American Negro music to be adopted by whites was its harmonies; in particular, the modified pentatonic scale, especially the interpolated minor third and the flatted seventh. This was done in the age of the blues.

Blues were popular among the Negroes of the lower Mississippi River, but remained a local phenomenon until a Negro appeared who had received some academic musical training and could write down the music; this was W. C. Handy, the composer of *St. Louis Blues*. The incident which brought the blues to the attention of whites is characteristic.

In 1909 the fight for the Memphis mayoralty was three cornered, the corners being Messrs. Williams, Talbert, and E. H. Crump. There were also three leading Negro bands: Eckford's, Bynum's, and Handy's. As a matter of course the services of these three were engaged for the duration to demonstrate to the public the executive ability of their respective employers; through Jim Mucahy, a ward leader before whose saloon the Handy forces had often serenaded, his candidate turned out to be Mr. Crump. . . . His band opened fire at the corner of Main and Madison with a piece [in the blues style] (named, of course, "Mr. Crump"), of such vivacity that it caused dancing in the streets and an outbreak of public whistling. With such a song, and with none like it forthcoming from Eckford's or Bynum's, the popular choice (Crump and Handy) was a foregone conclusion; the one became the mayor and the other locally famous. . . . In 1912 he [i.e., Handy] . . . brought out a first edition of a thousand copies [of the song], wordless and renamed *Memphis Blues*.[10]

Jazz, 1917[11]

At the turn of the century an urban music, hot jazz, developed among the Negroes of New Orleans. This music was played in the brothels and saloons of the red light district frequented by whites. This intimate contact—both figurative and literal—between Negroes and whites was the first opportunity for the latter to come into contact with the full flavor of Negro music on a large scale.

In New Orleans after the Civil War, Negroes began to use more and more the usual wind and string instruments of the whites. . . . Soon Negro groups, having learned to play by ear, were engaged to play for dances and by 1880 were found on some of the packets on the Mississippi River. On the boats the Negroes worked as porters, barbers, and waiters during the day and entertained the passengers with music at night.[12]

Because of the social isolation of Negroes in the United States, they had little or no opportunity to learn much about West European music or instrumental technique. As Louis Armstrong says:

Not knowing much classical music, and not many of them having proper education in reading music of any kind, they just went ahead and made up their own music. Before long, and without really knowing it themselves, they had created a brand new music, they created swing. They made a music for themselves which truly expressed what they felt. They were composers *and* players, all in one, and they composed as they played and held what they had done only in their musical memory. . . . Now I think that there are two kinds of men chiefly who *can* break loose [from tradition] like that. One is the kind of man who learns everything about his art and what has been done before him so he can go beyond it, and the other is the kind who doesn't know anything about it—who is just plain ignorant, but has a great deal of feeling he's got to express in some way, and has to find that way for himself. Swing came mostly from the last kind of men. That is why, during those early years, people noticed two things about it, that it was very strong and vital, and also that it was crude and not "finished."[13]

Boys learned to play an instrument, not by taking lessons, but by practicing on it until they achieved sufficient technical dexterity to express what they wanted to say. Thus Bunk Johnson says of his boyhood.

Now me and my old cornet, when my mother got it, night and day I puffed on it and when I did get the slite of it, Oh boy, I really went.[14]

After a boy had a certain amount of technique at his command, he tried to get lessons from his favorite instrumentalist so as to improve his playing. For example, Armstrong states,

I was constantly hanging around after "King" Oliver. I looked towards him as though he were some kind of a god, or something similar. Between the years of 1914 . . . and 1917, I never missed hearing him play his music. He was my inspiration. . . . He took such a liking to me he started giving me lessons and answered anything I wanted to know. He taught me the modern way of phrasing on the cornet and trumpet.[15]

Because of social isolation, American Negro urban instrumental music did not adopt the white forms or technique, but rather developed as an instrumental version of the already existing Negro vocal music; the one with which the musicians were most familiar. Consequently, hot jazz has the following characteristics:[16]

304

1. Negro musicians employ their instruments differently from white musicians trained in the orthodox style.

a. They use their own technique in playing, and particularly as a result of the use of vibratos, glissandos, and such mechanical tone modifiers as mutes and plungers, achieve new tonal effects with their instruments. Consequently when European musicians first heard jazz music, says Jim Europe, they "felt sure that my band had used special instruments. Indeed, some of them, after attending one of my rehearsals, did not believe what I had said until after they had examined the instruments used by my men."[17]

b. They achieve a virtuosity which is unparallelled. The technical demands of hot jazz are greater than those of most Western music.

c. They emphasize wind and percussion instruments in their bands, rather than the strings as in West European orchestras. A jazz band has two parts, a rhythmic section which produces rhythm and background harmonies, and a melodic section, which supplies the melodic designs. The rhythmic section consists of a piano, banjo or guitar, percussions, and strong bass or tuba. The melodic section consists of woodwinds, usually alto and tenor saxophones and clarinet, and brass, i.e., trumpets and trombones.

2. Negro musicians took over the old American Negro style of improvisation; in hot jazz "it's the originality that counts."[18]

The spirit of improvisation has been well expressed by Armstrong:

I do know that a musician who plays in "sweet" orchestras must be like a writer who writes stories for some popular magazines. He has to follow along the same kind of line all the time, and write what he thinks the readers want just because they're used to it. That keeps him writing the same kind of thing year after year. But a real swing musician never does that. He just plays, feels as he goes, and swings as he feels.[19]

In large jazz bands collective improvisation is virtually impossible because of the difficulty of integrating more than a few instruments, and therefore arrangements are resorted to; however, an attempt is made to keep the arrangement as spontaneous in feeling as is compatible with the requirements of a large group of musicians.

There are two aspects of improvisation:

a. Improvision usually occurs in the form of breaks and choruses. In breaks, the musician improvises during a pause between phrases; choruses are variations on a theme which may or may not be stated in its original form.

b. There are two types of improvisation, either solo improvisation against a rhythmic background, or collective improvisation to produce counterpoint.

The following are but a couple of examples of the jazz musician's dexterity in improvisation.

305

I once heard Count Basie and his band play *The Jersey Bounce* with a contrapuntal complexity beyond anything I have heard in Western classical music. Amazed, I had Basie play the piece every night for a week during his stay, but it was played in a relatively simple fashion, though differently each time. When I asked why his men didn't play it the way they had the first time, he replied, "I guess the boys were feeling good then."

To illustrate a lecture on jazz I gave to my students Basie and some of his men came to play. I refused to tell them in advance what I expected of them, so that they would play impromptu. After each point in my lecture I merely turned to the musicians and said, "please play something illustrating this point." After about 15 seconds preliminary musical introduction, and without any conversation between the men they would go into a piece which exemplified the discussion.

3. Old American Negro styles of harmony and counterpoint have been taken over.

4. The syncopation common in the old songs has been adopted. Beside the displacement of accent (through accenting the off-beat) which had been used previously in ragtime, jazz uses polyrhythm (i.e., superimposed accent different from the fundamental beat). Modifications of the original rhythm result in a swinging quality which is typical of hot jazz.

5. Jazz developed in the dives and brothels of New Orleans; jazz lyrics were therefore sophisticated and urban in character, rather than of the folk quality found in Negro spirituals and sinful songs from rural areas. Most often they consisted of a cynical treatment of sex; the title of a famous song by Tony Jackson, the featured pianist and entertainer at one of the largest brothels in New Orleans at the turn of the century, is typical: *I've Got Elgin Movements in My Hips with a Twenty Year Guarantee.*

Hot jazz became known to white musicians who played in the red light district of New Orleans, and they began to imitate the Negro music as best they could. However, because the Negro and white musical traditions were so dissimilar, the latter's version of jazz was different from the real thing.[20] It was a band of white musicians who first acquainted the whole United States with jazz, for the Original Dixieland Band left New Orleans to play first in Chicago from 1914 to 1916, and then in New York during the rest of 1916. While in the latter city they made some phonograph recordings which started the jazz craze.

With the migration of Negroes to the North in 1917, many jazz players left New Orleans, and in the period from 1918 to 1929 Chicago was the center for the development of jazz. White musicians such as Bix Beiderbecke and Muggsy Spanier heard Negro players in various speakeasies, and consciously attempted to learn their techniques; as a result they were called "white niggers." But many of these white musicians had received formal training in their instruments, and were acquainted with orthodox musical theory; they therefore modified hot jazz to include these elements. As Armstrong says,

It is very true that the swing music we have today is far more refined and subtle and more highly developed as an art because the swing men who learned to read and understand classical music have brought classical influences into it. I think that may be said to be the real difference between the original New Orleans "jazz" and the swing music of today.[21]

However, even in the twenties hot jazz remained unknown to the wider white groups, an index of the degree of isolation of hot jazz musicians, and the difference between their music and that of orthodox players, is to be found in the elaborate special vocabulary which they developed.[22]

About 1930 the jazz center shifted to New York, and hot jazz fully assimilated both Negro and white influences. Typical of the present trend are the compositions and style of playing of Duke Ellington and his band, concerning which has been said, "Ellington's works are no more examples of African folk song than James Weldon Johnson's poems are examples of the Dahomy dialect; they both represent the application of the Negro temperament to an alien tradition and an acquired language."[23]

So far only hot jazz has been considered. However, the adaptation of jazz to white tastes has also occurred. Early in the history of jazz, white musicians appeared who took over some of the elements of hot jazz—its rhythms and harmonies in particular—and modified them to fit Western musical theory and instrumental techniques. This gave birth to straight or sweet jazz, first developed by Art Hickman and his St. Francis Hotel Orchestra of San Francisco, in 1914; Paul Whiteman is perhaps its best known exponent, and his "symphonic jazz" is characteristic of this type of music.

Intermediate between hot and sweet jazz is Benny Goodman, for example, and in his orchestra's rendition of works by Raymond Scott such as *Powerhouse*, the fugue *Dodging a Divorcee*, or *In an Eighteenth Century Drawing Room* (after a Mozart minuet), are to be found illustrations of a type of music that begins to shade into Western European orchestral compositions influenced by the American Negro musical idiom.

To sum up: In the nineteenth century white musicians took over a few characteristics of Negro music which they adapted to the tastes of the whites, but in the post-World War I period, not only had whites developed an understanding of Negro popular music which they adopted, but conversely, the Negro idiom has been affected by West European music through the influence of white jazz musicians.

NOTES

1. W. F. Allen, *et al.*, *Slave Songs of the United States* (New York, 1867), pp. iv–v.
2. On minstrel music, *vide* D. Paskman & S. Spaeth, *"Gentlemen, Be Seated!"* (New York, 1935); C. Wittke, *Tambo and Bones* (Durham, N.C., 1932.)
3. J. W. Johnson, *Black Manhattan* (New York, 1930), p. 87; *cf.* Wittke, *op. cit.*, pp. 6–7.
4. Wittke, *op. cit.*, pp. 9–19.
5. *Ibid.*, pp. 20–32.
6. *Ibid.*, pp. 174–209; also Paskman & Spaeth, *op. cit.*
7. I. Goldberg, *Tin Pan Alley* (New York, 1930), p. 53; Wittke, *op. cit.*, pp. 136, 142.
8. Goldberg, *op. cit.*, p. 164.
9. On the blues, *vide* W. C. Handy & A. Niles, *Blues* (New York, 1926).
10. *Ibid.*, pp. 13–14.
11. On the history of jazz, *vide* A. Niles, "Jazz," *Encyclopaedia Britannica* 14th ed., 12 (New York, 1929), pp. 982–984; C. E. Smith, "Jazz" *Symposium*, I (1930), pp. 502–517; R. Y. Giles, "Jazz Comes of Age," *Scholastic*, 27, No. 5 (1935), pp. 7–8; C. E. Smith, "Swing," *New Republic*, 94 (1938), pp. 39–41; P. E. Miller, *Down Beat's Yearbook of Swing* (Chicago, 1939); F. Ramsey & C. E. Smith, eds., *Jazzmen* (New York, 1939).
12. Ramsey and Smith, *op. cit.*, p. 9.
13. *Swing That Music* (New York, 1936), pp. 72–74.
14. Ramsey & Smith, *op. cit.*, p. 24.
15. *Op. cit.*, pp. 25–26.
16. For technical analyses of jazz, *vide* G. Seldes, "Toujours jazz," *Dial*, 75 (1923), pp. 151–166; V. Thompson, "Jazz" *American Mercury*, 2 (1924), pp. 465–467; D. Milhaud, "The jazz band and Negro music," *Living Age*, 323 (1924), pp. 169–173; D. Knowlton, "The anatomy of jazz," *Harper*, 152 (1925–26), pp. 578–585; E. Combe, "Jazz and guitar," *Living Age*, 228 (1926), pp. 326–330; G. Antheil, "Jazz is music," *Forum*, 80 (1928), pp. 64–67, 957–958; G. W. Howgate, "Jazz," *Forum*, 80 (1928), pp. 636–637; H. Panassié, *Le jazz hot* (Paris, 1934), trans. L & E. Dowling (New York, 1936); R. Dickerson, "Hot music," *Harper*, 172 (1935–36), pp. 567–574; W. Sargeant, *Jazz, Hot and Hybrid* (New York, 1938); *idem*, "Jazz," *International Cyclopedia of Music and Musicians* (New York, 1939), pp. 896–900; W. Hobson, *American Jazz Music* (New York, 1939).
17. *Literary Digest*, 56 (April 26, 1919), p. 28.
18. King Oliver, quot. Ramsey & Smith, *op. cit.*, p. 78.
19. *Op cit.*, pp. 29–30.
20. "All the Original Dixieland Jazz Band's interpretations were handled the same way: there were no solos, except for a few short breaks, and the musicians simply played together first the verse and then the chorus of the different pieces, with little subtlety, always in the same key. It was a continuous collective improvisation of only relative interest, for the musicians either did not elaborate very much, or else they always elaborated on the same phrase. Even when one of the performers would play solo for a

few short breaks, he would often play the same break over and over." Panassié, *op. cit.*, p. 222.

21. *Op. cit.*, pp. 74–75.

22. "There are more than four hundred words used among swing musicians that no one else would understand. They have a language of their own, and I don't think anything could show better how closely they have worked together and how much they feel that they are apart from 'regular' musicians and have a world of their own that they believe in and that most people have not understood." Armstrong, *op. cit.*, 77–78; *vide* C. L. Cons, "The jargon of jazz," *American Mercury*, 38, no. 149 (1936), p. x; H. B. Webb, "The slang of jazz," *American Speech*, 12 (1937), pp. 179–184; " 'Swing' notes," *ibid.*, 12 (1938), p. 158; Miller, *op cit.*, pp. 172–176.

23. C. Lambert, *Music Ho!*, 2nd ed. (London, 1937), p. 203; for an interesting criticism of Ellington, *vide ibid.*, pp. 213–215.

SKIN COLOR VALUES
IN THREE ALL-NEGRO
SCHOOL CLASSES

Recent studies of the American Negro have stressed the significance of the value pattern in which lightness of skin is a desideratum. The widespread and penetrating character of the color influence is suggested by Myrdal's comment that "cliques, clubs and social life in general seem to be permeated by this color preference."[1]

The majority of these studies, however, have been done with adolescents or adults, and we thus get only a *recall* of the meaning of skin color in earlier childhood, a recall overlaid, no doubt, with the rationalizations and frustrations of the intervening years. The work reported here focuses upon skin color discriminations as they operate in exclusively Negro child groupings. It presents direct evidence regarding the importance of skin color to the pre-adolescent Negro, and thus furnishes insights into the operation of child value systems.

Standard sociometric and interview techniques were used to explore the following hypotheses: first, that children in all-Negro grade school classes have incorporated into their value system the color preferences of the adult Negro community;[2] and second, that skin color is operative as a socially differentiating factor at this age level.

A total of 81 children in three all-Negro classes were tested. Two of the classes (X and Y) were combined 3rd and 4th grades, while the third (Class Z) was a combined 5th and 6th grade group, in the same school as Class Y. Table 27–1 contains a breakdown of this sample by sex and

From Melvin Seeman, "Skin Color Values in Three All-Negro School Classes," in *American Sociological Review*, 2 (1946), pp. 315–321.

TABLE 27-1

*Total Sample, by Sex and Color Categories, with Total
Friendship Choices and Reputational Mentions, by School Class*

	Class X	Class Y	Class Z
Pupils by Color Groups			
Very light brown	2	3	0
Light brown	12	2	1
Brown	3	11	12
Dark brown	5	12	10
Very dark brown	1	3	4
Pupils by Sex			
Boys	12	14	11
Girls	11	17	16
Total Pupils	23	31	27
Total Number of Friendship Choices	726	504	561
Total Number of Reputational Mentions	880	503	570

color categories. It reveals a fairly even sex ratio in the three classes; and
a rather close correspondence, within each class, between the number of
friendship choices made and the number of reputational mentions. The
distribution in the color categories reflects a situation similar to that reported by Warner for Chicago; namely, that dark-skinned Negroes are found
in greater proportion in the lower social class groups.[3]

Color ratings were made for each child on the following scale: 1—very
dark brown; 2—dark brown; 3—brown; 4—light brown; and 5—very light
brown.[4] Three independent ratings were made in two of the school classes,
using Negro and white raters in both classes. In Class X, the correlations
among the three raters were +.94, +.91, and +.84; and in Class Z, +.79,
+.78, and +.76. These correlations indicate a very acceptable reliability
in color ratings, with somewhat less satisfactory results obtained in Class
Z.[5]

Expression of Color Values

Four types of evidence regarding lightness or darkness of skin as value
criteria were gathered: first, self-ratings were made by two classes, using
the same color scale as the adult raters; second, motivations for friendship

choice were determined through interviews; third, a "Three Wishes" test was designed to bring out the relative desirability of lightness of skin through 10 such statements as, "I would like to be stronger than I am now," or "I would like to have lighter skin than I have now," etc.; fourth, verbatim responses were recorded to the question, "What skin color do you prefer?"

An inspectional comparison of the self and adult ratings strongly suggests that the children's ratings of themselves are skewed toward the lighter colors, usually one step in the color scale. An analysis for statistical significance of this distortion revealed that the difference in ratings for Class Y was significant at the .05 level of chance; and for Class Z, at the .01 level of chance.[6] Thus, there is a significant tendency on the part of these children to rate themselves lighter than objective adult ratings justify.

Every child in Class X was interviewed to determine whether color preference was expressed as a motivation for friendship choice or rejection. No mention of skin color was made by the investigator until the close of the interview, when a direct question was asked regarding the importance of "looks" in choosing friends. A summary of these data reveals the *almost complete absence of skin color as a verbalized motivation*. Only one child mentioned lightness of skin as a factor in choosing. The bulk of the reasons given centered around compatibility in play, school behavior, and general cooperativeness. The direct question concerning "looks" brought recognition of skin color as a possible factor in choice of friends from three children; but the remainder rejected skin color as a criterion.

The results of the "Three Wishes" test[7] are presented in Table 27–2. Each child was permitted to indicate a first, second, and third choice from among the ten wishes listed; and the frequency of mention for each wish at each level of preference is indicated in Table 27–2. It is clear that these children, faced with ten alternatives given, show relatively little desire for lighter skin and somewhat greater desire for better hair. The greatest desirability, however, attaches to those values (*e.g.* "smarter," and "stronger") which are of more immediate behavioral meaning in the child's world.

Finally, the children in Class X were asked, "What skin color do you prefer?" Space limitations preclude a verbatim report of the answers given, but a large number of the responses were similar to the following: "I'd like to be the color of my uncle, because he's lighter than my family"; or "David's color, because he's light"; and "My own color; it's almost the color I like, not too dark or too light, but smooth." Taken as a whole, these responses indicate a clear pattern of preference for light skin.

TABLE 27-2

Responses to 10 Alternatives in a "Three Wishes" Test, Showing Frequency of First, Second, and Third Choices

School Class	Stronger			Better Liked			Get Along Better with Parent			Smarter			Lighter Skin			Play Games Better			Bigger			More Money			Better Looking Hair			One Very Good Friend		
	1	2	3	1	2	3	1	2	3	1	2	3	1	2	3	1	2	3	1	2	3	1	2	3	1	2	3	1	2	3
X	2	3	3	1	3	0	1	1	1	4	2	4	1	0	2	0	1	6	2	3	1	4	6	2	1	1	3	7	3	1
Y	13	1	0	4	5	3	1	2	1	4	7	0	0	1	0	0	2	1	0	1	3	1	1	3	1	1	6	0	3	7
Z	12	2	3	1	1	0	2	2	0	1	9	1	0	0	2	0	0	0	1	3	5	1	2	3	1	2	0	2	0	7
Sub-total	27	6	6	6	9	3	4	5	2	9	18	5	1	1	4	0	3	7	3	7	9	6	9	8	3	4	9	9	6	15
Totals by wishes	39			18			11			31			6			10			19			23			16			30		

Skin Color and Social Status

Two measures of the operational importance of skin color differences were used, friendship choice and reputation in the group. The former was measured through the Ohio Social Acceptance Scale,[8] which requires each child to rate every other child in his class as follows: 1—"My very, very best friends"; 2—"My other friends"; 3—"Not friends, but okay"; 4—"Don't know them"; 5—"Don't care for them"; and 6—"Dislike them." The choices made through this scale were kept anonymous to the child, but a coding system permitted the investigator to know what ratings were given by each child. A re-test of Class X one week after the initial test produced a correlation of +.90.

The analysis of variance technique was employed to determine whether significant differences in friendship choice status (social acceptance) existed among the several color groups within each of the three classes. For the purpose of this analysis, the null hypothesis was postulated; namely that no significant differences existed among the color groups (*i.e.* that all of the color groups were a homogeneous population with respect to friendship choice). The obtained ratios[9] from this analysis indicated that there were significant differences at the .01 level of chance among the color groups in Class X and Class Y. No significant differences were found in Class Z. The writer tentatively concludes, therefore, that the skin color of the person being rated makes a difference in two of the school classes, while no such difference is evident in Class Z.

For the purpose of further analysis of these differences, mean social acceptance scores were computed for every color group in each class. The results are given in Table 27–3. It should be noted that since the computation of scores was based upon the numbers 1–6 of the Ohio Acceptance Scale (in which 1 is most acceptable and 6 least acceptable), *a low mean social acceptance score is indicative of greater acceptability.*

Table 27–3 reveals at a glance that the "light brown" and "very light brown" color groups, in Classes X and Y, have a higher acceptability than that of the other color groups. The table reveals, also, that there is a rather consistent decline in acceptability as we move from the lighter to the darker groups. This is most evident in Class Y, where there is a steady decline in acceptability, with the slight reversal for the "very dark brown" color group.

These observations are supplemented and sharpened by the results given

TABLE 27-3

Mean Scores in Social Acceptance, by Skin Color, for Three All-Negro School Classes

School Class	Very Light Brown	Light Brown	Brown	Dark Brown	Very Dark Brown
X	2.95	2.53	3.06	3.55	*
Y	2.29	2.33	2.50	3.25	2.97
Z	**	**	2.85	3.02	2.73

*No data since only one child was classified as "very dark brown."
**No data since no children were rated "very light brown," and only one child as "light brown."

in Table 27–4. Fisher's technique for small sample analysis[10] was used to compare each social acceptance mean with every other mean in the same school class to determine the color groups between which statistically significant differences exist.

In Class X, the "light brown"-"dark brown" comparison is the only dif-

TABLE 27-4

Differences in Mean Social Acceptance, Critical Ratios, and Levels of Significance, by Skin Color, Two School Classes

Color Comparison	Class X			Class Y		
	Difference Between Means	Critical Ratio	Significance Level	Difference Between Means	Critical Ratio	Significance Level
Very light brown						
Light brown	.42	1.64	N.S.*	.04	1.43	N.S.
Brown	.11	.36	N.S.	.21	1.08	N.S.
Dark brown	.60	2.19	.05	.96	5.00	.01
Very dark brown	**			.68	2.76	.01
Light brown						
Brown	.53	2.45	.05	.17	.73	N.S.
Dark brown	1.02	6.03	.01	.92	3.98	.01
Very dark brown	**			.64	2.30	.05
Brown						
Dark brown	.49	2.08	.05	.75	6.00	.01
Very dark brown	**			.47	2.37	.05
Dark brown						
Very dark brown	**			.28	1.42	N.S.

*Not significant at the .05 or .01 level of chance.
**No data in the "very dark brown" category since only one child was classified in this category, and was included in the "dark brown" group.

ference which is significant at the .01 level of chance. In Class Y, four color group comparisons are significant: "very light brown"-"dark brown"; "very light brown"-"very dark brown"; "light brown"-"dark brown"; and "brown"-"dark brown." Thus, there are significant differences which consistently point to the greater acceptability of the lighter color groups.

The second measure of the behavioral importance of skin color discriminations was reputation in the group. Reputations were derived through the Ohio Recognition Scale,[11] which asks each child to match members of his group with 18 descriptive paragraphs. Nine of these items are favorable (e.g. "Are there any children in our room who are very, very good in the games we play?"); and nine are unfavorable (e.g. "Are there boys and girls in our room who always think of themselves first?").

To determine whether unfavorable reputations were directed toward the darker skin color groups, a mean skin color rating for each of the 18 reputa-

TABLE 27-5

Mean Skin Color Ratings, Differences, Among Means, and Levels of Significance, for 18 Reputational Items, Two All-Negro School Classes

	Class X				Class Y			
Item No.	Mean Skin Color	Differ- ence*	Critical Ratio	Signifi- cance Level	Mean Skin Color	Differ- ence*	Critical Ratio	Signifi- cance Level
1**	2.87	−.47	3.671	.01	2.70	−.22	1.606	N.S.
2	3.71	+.37	2.984	.01	2.98	+.06	.043	N.S.
3	3.12	−.22	1.642	N.S.	2.54	−.38	2.032	N.S.
4	3.41	+.07	.593	N.S.	3.13	+.21	1.438	N.S.
5	2.82	−.52	3.852	.01	2.12	−.80	3.556	.01
6	3.39	+.05	.382	N.S.	3.40	+.48	1.992	N.S.
7	3.08	−.26	2.149	.05	2.48	−.44	2.683	.05
8	3.49	+.15	1.250	N.S.	3.48	+.56	3.522	.01
9	3.53	+.19	1.557	N.S.	2.32	−.60	3.061	.01
10	3.61	+.27	2.477	.05	3.84	+.92	6.216	.01
11	2.92	−.42	2.979	.01	2.70	−.22	.733	N.S.
12	3.67	+.33	2.481	.05	3.46	+.54	2.888	.01
13	3.42	+.08	.625	N.S.	2.40	−.52	2.708	.05
14	3.71	+.37	3.627	.01	3.08	+.16	1.067	N.S.
15	2.73	−.61	4.729	.01	2.54	−.38	2.197	.05
16	3.66	+.32	2.712	.01	3.57	+.65	2.600	.05
17	2.63	−.71	5.504	.01	2.31	−.61	3.588	.01
18	3.65	+.31	2.870	.01	3.00	+.08	.503	N.S.

*Differences are taken from the grand mean in each school class. For Class X this mean was 3.34; and for Class Y, 2.92.

**Odd-numbered items are undesirable reputations, and even-numbered items are favorable reputations.

tional items was computed, and an analysis of variance made for each of the three classes. Significant differences in skin color rating were found in Class X and Class Y; no significant differences existed in Class Z. It is important to note that these findings parallel the findings in the matter of friendship choice: where no significant differences in friendship were found, no corresponding reputational differences were discovered.

The precise character of the differences in skin color ratings is revealed in Table 27–5. In both school classes, those *favorable* items which show significant skin color difference are being disproportionately directed toward the lighter children (*i.e.* the significant difference is in the direction of a lighter mean skin color rating); and those items which are unfavorable are directed toward the darker children. There is, however, no indiscriminate assignment of favorable or unfavorable reputations by skin color. This is borne out, for example, by the fact that in Class X, six reputational items show no significant differences by skin color. Only two items show significant differences in both school classes. For both school classes, however, there is a consistent rise and fall of skin color rating as we move from favorable to unfavorable items (all even-numbered items being favorable reputations). For Class X, one half of the items show color differences which are significant; while in Class Y, one third show significant differences.

Interpretation

The evidence presented here supports the hypotheses elaborated in a previous section. Third and fourth grade Negro children, in a uniracial group context, reveal clearly their commitment to the superior value of light skin; and skin color differences are associated with differences in friendship and reputational status. No attempt will be made here to summarize this evidence; but several theoretical implications of the data must be explored.

Two aspects of our findings are most striking. First, though favorable friendship choice is significantly associated with lightness of skin, these children do not verbalize skin color preference as a basis for choice. The writer's hypothesis is that color values, like many other social norms, become established quite early as a basic frame of reference for the child; but it is not suggested that the color frame of reference which channelizes choice need be a matter of conscious awareness on the part of the child. Sherif's experiments in the establishment of social norms suggest that these norms may be developed without the subject's awareness of their operation.[12]

Further, it is the writer's suggestion that the skin color frame of reference operates as a "heteronomous" social norm; it is a norm imposed upon the child from without, a norm which is not "interiorized" at this age level.[13] It is, therefore, not verbalized as a motivation because it bears no immediate relation to the pursuits and tasks of the child. Thus, to the grade school Negro child, skin color is less important *per se* than, for example, whether the person chosen is good in games, or refrains from "tattling," etc.; while the adolescent Negro, emerging into a period of competition for occupations and for dates, as well as impending marriage, may exhibit in his choices and rejections a concern more directly related to the important skin color criterion. Our position is that color values may serve as a frame of reference for friendship choice long before these values become associated with the developmental tasks of the child, or with the conscious status striving which involves color. The failure to verbalize color values as a basis for choice may thus be a function, not of inhibition, but of the fact that the values in question are not an integral part of the child's age-level culture.[14]

This theoretical position is based upon several factors: first, the verbatim responses suggest no hesitation on the part of the child in expressing preferences for light skin color. Second, during the interviews, the subjects gave no evidence of inhibition on the score of color. Third, there has been little direct study of child inhibitions of color distinctions, the evidence on this point coming largely from the recall of childhood experience by adults. The inhibitions attendant upon the expression of color distinctions *during these more mature periods* may significantly distort accurate recall.

A second important aspect of our results requires comment; namely, the absence of significant choice differences in Class Z. This class, being in the same school as Class Y, is presumed to have been exposed to roughly the same value patterns. It may be that the difference between the classes is due to the fact that Class Z is composed of older children;[15] but a preliminary analysis of data from another (bi-racial) 5th–6th grade class indicates significant color differences exist at this age level. It is especially to be noted that Class Z exhibited a narrow range of color differences: no child in this group received a color rating of "very light brown," and only one child rated as "light brown." The writer suggests that the absence of significant differences in Class Z is a function of the fact that the frame of reference with respect to color is being constantly recreated in terms of the specific situation in which the individual is involved. Thus, it is held that the children in Class Z choose differently because their color values, being variable under the specific impact of the choice situation, are functionally different. This point of view emphasizes the fact that values must not be viewed as fixed reference points for the individual; but that rather, social norms operate as contextual variables.

This implies that the limitation within which the present study was conceived—i.e. that the classes be all-Negro in composition—bears a fundamental relationship to the results obtained. It further implies that studies of both intraracial and interracial choice must be viewed as presenting choice situations in which the valuational frames of reference created are distinctively different.

NOTES

1. G. Myrdal, *An American Dilemma* (New York, 1944), p. 698. For intensive analyses of the color influence, see especially the volumes prepared under the auspices of the American Youth Commission by Charles S. Johnson, W. Lloyd Warner, E. Franklin Frazier, and Allison Davis and John Dollard.

2. No attempt was made to investigate adult color values. The writer assumed that the adult patterns in the communities studied were comparable to those reported in the works cited in footnote 1. The writer would like to express here his thanks to Dr. Lloyd A. Cook for many helpful suggestions in the conduct of this investigation, and to Dr. Paul Hatt for editorial assistance.

3. Cf. W. Lloyd Warner, et. al., *Color and Human Nature* (Washington, D.C., 1941). No attempt was made to stratify these children rigorously; but data on parental occupations and education were available. Classes Y and Z represent lower class groups in comparison with Class X.

4. For a similar classification arrived at through a numerical scaling technique, of C. H. Parrish, *The Significance of Color in the Negro Community*, unpublished Ph.D. dissertation (University of Chicago, 1944).

5. Class Y was rated by the writer alone. The smaller range of skin color difference in Class Z may account for the less satisfactory correlations.

6. The formula used here is found in G. W. Snedecor and W. G. Cochran, *Statistical Methods* (Ames, Iowa, 1938), p. 53.

7. The items on this test owe much to the "Test of Personality Adjustment," constructed and validated by Carl Rogers. Cf. his *Measuring Personality Adjustment in Children Nine to Thirteen Years of Age* (New York: Teachers College Contributions to Education, #458, 1931).

8. This scale was developed under the guidance of Dr. Louis Raths and has been used in many schools throughout the state of Ohio. The writer is indebted to Dr. Raths for helpful suggestions regarding its use.

9. The analysis of variance technique is essentially a comparison of the variability

within groups with the variability *between* groups to determine whether the between groups' variance may be attributed to chance variation. It is customary to *reject* the null hypothesis if the obtained ratio is significant at the .01 level; to hold the null hypothesis *in doubt* if the ratio is significant between .01 and .05; and to *accept* the null hypothesis if the ratio is above the .05 level of significance. For the purposes of this study, the .01 level of significance is viewed, therefore, as the only level justifying the conclusion that critical differences exist without question. For a similar use of the "F" ratio and its corollary levels of significance, cf. P. O. Johnson and F. Tsao, "Factoral Design and Covariance in the Study of Individual Educational Development," *Psychometrika,* 10 (1945), pp. 133–162.

10. Cf. G. W. Snedecor and W. G. Cochran, *op. cit.*

11. This scale and the Ohio Social Acceptance Scale have been published by the Bureau of Educational Research of the Ohio State University.

12. M. Sherif, *The Psychology of Social Norms* (New York, 1936).

13. For an exposition of the relation of Piaget's concepts of heteronomous and autonomous morality to social norms, cf. M. Sherif, *op. cit.*, pp. 180–181.

14. Cf. C. H. Parrish, *op. cit.* for a view which stresses the importance of inhibitory tendencies.

15. Cf. J. H. Criswell, *A Sociometric Study of Race Cleavage in the Classroom* (Archives of Psychology, #235, 1939).

Index

Abiquiu, New Mexico, 69

Adams, Romanzo, 243

Adloff, Richard, 48

Africa: racial unity and white invasion, 46.
See also South Africa

African culture, survival of, 101–102; in
Bahia, Brazil, *see* Afro-Bahian family

Afro-Bahian family: African cultural survivals in, 103–136; extended family, 121;
extra-legal matings, 120, 125; Gantois
Candomblé, 103, 107, 108, 109–113,
114, 135, 136; polygamy, 120, 126;
Portuguese, influence of, 114–115

Alaska: participation of subordinate indigenous population, 44

Alemanii, 78

Algeria, 47

Algonkin Indians, 56

alienation, 174–181; education and, 179,
180; social isolation distinguished from
estrangement, 176; Srole's anomia scale,
175, 180; types of, 175–176

amásia, 125, 126, 127

American Dilemma, An (Myrdal), 16, 290

American Minority Peoples (Young), 201

American Sociological Review, 14

*Annals of the American Academy of Politi-
cal and Social Science, The*, 17

Armstrong, Louis, 304, 305, 307

Australia: German migration to, 48, 49; indigenous population, 39; Italian migration to, 48, 49; white subordination of
indigenous population, 41

Australoids, 39

Bahia, Brazil, 170, 171; settlement, 103–
104; social organization, 106–107; study

of Negro families in, *see* Afro-Bahian
family

Bainbridge Island, Washington, 247

Baldwin, James: alienation among American Negroes, 180–181

Baltimore Afro-American, 181

Barber, Bernard, 252

Barron, Milton L., 159

Basie, Count, 306

Bay of All Saints, 104

Beiderbecke, Bix, 306–307

Belen, New Mexico, 69

Bell, Wendell, 175, 181

Berne, Switzerland, 78

Beynon, Erdmann D., 201–202

Bigelow, John, 87

Black Muslims, 181

Boers, 42

Bogardus, Emory S., 38

Borrie, W. D., 49

Boston, Massachusetts: and fear of Irish-
Catholic political domination, 48

Brazil: African cultural survivals in, 101,
102, 103–136 (*see also* Afro-Bahian family); interracial behavior in São Paolo,
166–173; Italians in, 172; Japanese in,
172; Lebanese in, 172; Syrians in, 172;
utilization of Negro slaves in, 44, 104

Brickner, Rabbi, 146

British in South Africa, 42

British Guiana: Indian migration to, 44

Brown versus the Board of Education, 164

Bull, Obadiah, 294

Burgess, Ernest Walker, 20

Burgundians, 78

Burlington, Connecticut: Jewish intermarriage in, 147

Burma, John H., 289

DATE DUE

GAYLORD

PRINTED IN U.S.A